Essential Tensions
in Archaeological
Method and Theory

Foundations of Archaeological Inquiry

James M. Skibo, series editor

Essential Tensions in Archaeological Method and Theory

Edited by
Todd L. VanPool and Christine S. VanPool

THE UNIVERSITY OF UTAH PRESS
SALT LAKE CITY

FOUNDATIONS OF ARCHAEOLOGICAL INQUIRY
James M. Skibo, editor

 The Defiance House Man colophon is a registered trademark of the University of Utah Press. It is based upon a four-foot-tall, Ancient Puebloan pictograph (late PIII) near Glen Canyon.

2003   04   04   06   07   08   09
5   4   3   2   1

LIBRARY OF CONGRESS CATALOGING-IN-PUBLICATION DATA

Essential tensions in archaeological method and theory / edited by Todd
L. VanPool and Christine S. VanPool.
      p. cm. — (Foundations of archaeological inquiry)
Includes bibliographical references and index.
     ISBN 0-87480-763-8 (hardcover : alk. paper) — ISBN 0-87480-764-6
(pbk. : alk. paper)
     1. Archaeology—Methodology. 2. Archaeology. I. VanPool, Todd L.,
1968– II. VanPool, Christine S., 1969– III. Series.
     CC75 .E78 2003
     930.1'01—dc21   2003006425

Contents

Figures

Tables

Introduction:
Method, Theory, and the Essential Tension

CHRISTINE S. VANPOOL AND TODD L. VANPOOL

In recent years, archaeological theory appears to have fragmented into "a thousand archaeologies" (Schiffer 1988:479). A variety of perspectives are being applied and refined by archaeologists working on a broader set of empirical issues than ever before. There appears to be no limit to the range of questions asked and phenomena studied by archaeologists. Needless to say, this is an exciting time for archaeology as a discipline.

Because of the current intellectual and epistemological freedom, archaeologists are applying a greater amount of effort than ever before in developing and evaluating theoretical and methodological approaches (e.g., McGuire 1992a; O'Brien and Lyman 2000a; Pruecel and Hodder 1996; Schiffer 1999a; Schiffer and Skibo 1997; Skibo et al. 1995). An important part of this process is recent theoretical discussions that focus on the relationships and similarities between apparently distinct approaches (e.g., Bettinger and Richerson 1996; Boone and Smith 1998; Kosso 1991; Lyman and O'Brien 1998; O'Brien et al. 1998; Schiffer 1996; Spencer 1997; Trigger 1989; VanPool and VanPool 1999; Wylie 1993, 2000). While these discussions do bring important methodological and theoretical issues to light, they frequently amount to attempts to co-op one theoretical perspective by the practitioners of another (e.g., Cullen 1993; Spencer 1997). Such theoretical critiques frequently begin by stressing that the "good" aspects of the victim perspective are

compatible with the critic's own perspective, and then continue by arguing that if the practitioners of the victim perspective would just abandon the portion of their approach that is not compatible, they would have answers to the major theoretical and methodological hurdles facing them.

Underlying many such critiques is the general belief that scientific fields should employ only one theoretical structure, or paradigm, at any one time. This view is certainly evident in the processualist critique of culture history (Binford 1968a; Clark 1993:204–206; Flannery 1967), and the debates between processualists and postprocessualists (Binford 1987; Hodder 1991b) and between processualists and evolutionary archaeologists (Lyman and O'Brien 1998; O'Brien and Wilson 1988; O'Brien et al. 1998; Spencer 1997). For example, Martin's (1971) article in which he talks about his "conversion" to the New Archaeology, and O'Brien and Holland's (1995a:193) statement that evolutionary archaeology is working towards a "complete paradigmatic shift" from other theoretical structures are obvious manifestations of this perspective.

The idea of competing paradigms and the need for an intellectually violent paradigmatic replacement so common in archaeology must be at least partly attributed to the influence of the writings of Thomas Kuhn (1970, originally in 1962). Kuhn's ideas have had so much impact on archaeologists' views

I

on theoretical development that many archaeologists consider his *Structure of Scientific Revolutions* a guidebook for the process of theoretical development (Binford and Sabloff 1982; Clark 1993:203–206; Martin 1971; see also Meltzer 1979). Because of the impact of Kuhn's concept of paradigmatic replacement and theoretical revolutions, we think many archaeologists have the idea that all of the current theoretical structures are battling for supremacy: ONLY ONE MAY REMAIN. They are like gladiators in a coliseum. We can imagine Lewis Binford swinging the broadsword of positivist science, Ian Hodder standing in the background with a net and trident snaring his opponents with their own words, a slightly aged Alfred Kidder using antiquated weapons that are surprisingly effective, and Robert Dunnell relying on natural selection to leave him the last one standing. Most archaeologists are either in the stands as spectators, alternately cheering for one or the other and wishing there was some resolution so that they could get back to the real business of studying the archaeological record, or are simply avoiding the coliseum altogether. We suggest that this perspective of paradigmatic combat is unrealistic for several reasons.

First, archaeology is, or at least potentially could be, the study of past history, economics, sociology, psychology, medicine, art, music, religion, linguistics, engineering, mathematics, astronomy, geography, human biology, botany, philosophy, agricultural science, and anthropology as reflected by material culture. Given that any of these problem domains can potentially and reasonably be addressed in archaeological contexts, it is unrealistic to expect any one theoretical structure to be able to address them all. Archaeologists arguing for theoretical exclusivity are effectively insisting that we develop a "grand unifying theory" for human behavior, a task that few would suggest we can accomplish with modern people, let alone with people we can't even talk to. Given that physicists who are faced with the comparatively simple task of explaining the physical world with all of its laws and regularities and with the benefit of controlled experimentation have been unable to create a unified theory for their subject matter, it is unrealistic to require that archaeologists accomplish such a task in order to have an acceptable theoretical perspective.

As a result, we argue that it is appropriate for archaeologists to use a variety of different theoretical structures to answer different kinds of questions, or if need be, to combine theoretical structures in a logical manner so as to address their research issues (see also Hodder this volume). After all, it is hard to imagine a single theoretical structure that could explain the meaning of symbols on a pot, the function of the symbols within the social/ideological system of a region, and why particular paints and firing techniques were used in the ceramic manufacture. Archaeologists may reasonably ask each of these questions, but they will require very different approaches to answer them.

Second, and perhaps more significant, theoretical plurality can and frequently does lead to greater insight than is possible using a single theoretical perspective by itself. In a book that is less widely read in archaeological circles than his *Structure of Scientific Revolutions* titled *The Essential Tension*, Kuhn (1977) made this point as well. He observes that some of the greatest scientific insights are made possible only through the collaboration of and debate among practitioners of different theoretical perspectives. Without differences in perspectives, incorrect assumptions run rampant and weak premises remain unchallenged. Traditional, established approaches must be challenged by new perspectives, and new perspectives must be evaluated through comparison with those that are more established. Some in archaeology have proffered similar observations (e.g., Hutson 2001; Lyman et al. 1997; McGuire 1992a:xiii; Wylie 2000:232), and we agree wholeheartedly with their conclusions (see also VanPool and VanPool 1999:48). Theoretical plurality does greatly stimulate the careful consideration of explanatory theory by forcing the proponents of the various perspectives to explicitly identify their premises and consider alternate perspectives, if for no other reason than to argue why they are wrong or not applicable in a particular situation (see also Galison 1997: 803). Thus, theoretical plurality can actually help ensure the further development of archaeological method and theory.

In arguing for theoretical and methodological plurality, we do not suggest that "anything goes" as Feyerabend (1975) might argue. Quite to the contrary, the evaluation of archaeological theory is a fundamental task for archaeologists, if they seek to develop rigorous approaches to study their subject matter. Not all theoretical perspectives are equally successful, and some lead to conclusions that are down right wrong. Still, when evaluating alternate methodological and theoretical structures, it is necessary to evaluate them within the context of their use. In other words, we argue that it is not a reasonable critique to argue that a group of researchers are asking the wrong question because it can't be answered using a particular paradigm. Nor is it reasonable to argue that a theoretical/methodological structure should be discarded because it cannot be used to address a particular question. Such criticisms are spurious. Instead, the evaluation process must focus on whether the theoretical structure employed is applicable to and adequate for dealing with the questions being asked.

It is in support of the premise that theoretical plurality is beneficial that we have modified Kuhn's (1977) title for our own purposes as the title of this volume. The contributors have been asked to identify an important theoretical or methodological problem and to present an argument regarding its solution. We have asked for both programmatic statements, that is, statements that address how archaeological research should be structured, and argumentative statements, that is, statements that are intended to convince the reader that the proposed solution is *the* right solution. By presenting possible solutions to unresolved theoretical and methodological questions, the authors pave the way for the conceptual frameworks necessary for a more complete understanding of the archaeological past and present. They also provide a critical evaluation of the current state of archaeological method and theory, illustrating that recurrent issues such as the role of agency within our explanatory frameworks and the importance of social considerations in the formation of archaeological research dominate current archaeological theoretical development. By presenting both the range of important questions and a variety of answers to these questions, this volume contributes to the "essential tension" that will further archaeological theoretical growth.

Many of the papers within this volume are expanded versions of the papers presented during a symposium titled "Method and Theory 2000" organized for the annual meetings of the Society for American Archaeology held in Chicago, Illinois, in 1999. The original participants were Katherine Denning, Ian Hodder, John Kantner, Mark Leone, R. Lee Lyman, Lynn Meskell, Stephanie Moser, Michael J. O'Brien, Colin Renfrew, Dean J. Saitta, Todd L. VanPool, Christine S. VanPool, Patty Jo Watson, and Alison Wylie. Thomas C. Patterson and Robert D. Leonard served as discussants. Many of the symposium participants agreed to contribute their manuscripts to this volume, and the editors solicited the remaining manuscripts from various venues. The key consideration in selecting the papers was that the various manuscripts reflect a wide variety of intellectual perspectives and that each of them advocates a framework that the author(s) believe will benefit archaeology in a general way.

Although obvious, the editors note that the selection of the papers reflect their own diverse interests. This collection does not represent the entire range of theoretical and methodological issues that are important to archaeology; no single volume could possibly hope to do so. Entire methodological and theoretical problem domains such as gender research and feminist approaches to archaeology were not included in the final collection of papers, despite our best efforts. Still, the assembled papers reflect the intellectual diversity in archaeology now and demonstrate ways in which this diversity can be exploited.

Many people have provided invaluable assistance in the completion of this project. We thank Jane Kelley, Thomas C. Patterson, Robert Preucel, and Alison Wylie for their thoughtful comments on various papers and the project as a whole. We also thank Jeff Grathwohl and an anonymous reviewer for the University of Utah Press for their support and time.

Archaeology as a Discontinuous Domain

Ian Hodder

In the last few years, I have increasingly found myself, for various reasons, participating in or attending discussions, seminars, or lectures in other social or humanistic sciences. This experience has reinforced my impression from the literature in these disciplines that a remarkable commonality has emerged across the social, cultural, and humanistic sciences. Sitting in a psychology seminar, it is remarkable how familiar the debates seem. Whether one is in a geography, history, anthropology, sociology, linguistics, philosophy, or archaeology debate, people often refer to the same authors and the same issues. The specific readings and individual questions may vary, but at least the same authors and the same general issues are being addressed.

To some extent I have had the same experience in terms of different regional traditions. Whether one is in Poland, Greece, India, or Britain, very similar issues and debates occupy intellectuals, cultural commentators, and academics.

These are perhaps contentious claims, based on anecdotal evidence. It would be difficult to substantiate an increased degree of intellectual homogeneity across the disciplines and across the globe, and all of us can point to past authors who we might claim achieved widespread currency. However, we at least live today in a world where such homogeneity might be expected to be considerable. Undoubtedly the new information technologies and the new processes of globalization and travel have created closer links between disciplines and regional traditions. A rather different explanation for any claimed homogeneity would be in terms of the singular power of the authors who act as catalysts for the new debates—individuals whose work has such resonance that it crosses disciplinary and regional boundaries—writers such as Foucault, Bourdieu, Douglas, Geertz, Rorty, Habermas, Butler, and so on.

Perhaps it is difficult to make such claims about the disciplines as a whole, and easier to focus on archaeology. Here I feel more confident that this one small discipline has indeed entered into current debate outside its boundaries with some vigor in recent years. Of course, archaeologists have always made efforts to reach across disciplinary boundaries, and some, such as Childe, were extremely successful in this regard. But today the contacts and interactions are widespread. Consider, for example, the *Journal of Material Culture*—this new journal results in subscribers in cultural studies, linguistics, media studies, and so on reading articles by archaeologists on topics such as animal remains in tombs in Neolithic Orkney (Jones 1998).

Archaeology is then, according to this view, involved in a greater commonality of debate across the social and humanistic sciences. At one level, this openness to debate and the integration of wider issues might be welcomed. At least in this way archaeology begins to contribute as an independent discipline to wider intellectual currents. But at another level, this homogeneity and lack of diversity might be seen as dangerous. Personally, I baulk at the sameness if it implies a lack of critique, a lack of debate—if it implies becoming blind to alternative views and if it implies a true "end of history" (Fukuyama 1992).

It is in this context of a fear of homogeneity that I welcome the opposing trend in globalization and in the cultural and social disciplines—that is, towards fragmentation. Many archaeologists in recent years have talked of the fragmentation of their discipline—whether it is Schiffer's (1988:479) "thousand archaeologies," or the pluralistic, multiperspective research heralded by some feminist writers (Conkey and Gero 1997: 430). The divisions and fragmentation are partly doctrinal in character—separating processual, cognitive processual, postprocessual, neo-evolutionary, etc. But they are also regional and methodological—it is undoubtedly the case, for example, that German archaeologists often dig differently from British archaeologists who dig differently from American archaeologists and so on. The differences also concern different types of sites, questions, and periods—so that a Paleolithic excavation focusing on human-environment relations is very different from an excavation of an urban medieval or historical site. Just consider the different ways in which screening and faunal remains are used in these two contexts. Each subarea within the discipline produces its own conferences, journals, books, email lists, etc. We can talk of these subareas as subcultures. The overall diversity of theory and method appears to be increasing as the degree of specialization in the various subfields increases and as diverse groups in post-colonial contexts seek to reach an independent relation with their own pasts.

We can, on the one hand, understand this diversity and fragmentation as a product of the internal development of debate and method within the discipline. Alternatively, we can see it as a general product of wider forces. It is of interest in this latter regard to note similar processes in other disciplines. For example, we can look at physics and the recent description of this discipline by Peter Galison (1997) as a trading zone between different perspectives and specialisms that negotiate, exchange, or trade with each other.

Looking at the diversity of subcultures in archaeology from the outside, say from physics, how can we understand it? Following Galison's analysis of physics I want to suggest three approaches towards understanding diversity in archaeology. First, according to the logical positivists among us, the diversity would stereotypically be seen as worrying because while theoretical diversity is acceptable, experience and data should provide some continuous bedrock that unifies science (Fig. 1.1a). In the logical positivist view, theories might change through time but procedures of observation should stay the same. This notion of a universal acceptance of methods for testing theory against data has been undermined by the methods espoused by the different archaeological subcultures.

Second, according to antipositivists, a "conceptual scheme" underlies both theory and observation. Observations are fully theoretical, theory-laden, and radically diverse. Theory dominates so that through time, breaks in theory will be contemporary with breaks in empirical paradigm (Fig. 1.1b).

In my view, neither the first (logical positivist) nor the second (strict antipositivist) understanding of diversity is correct when applied to archaeology. Rather, the evidence suggests a third view in which there is a degree of disconnection between theory, instruments of measurement, and observational data (Fig.1.1c). One of many examples in archaeology of this third view of diversity is the supposed link between the rise of the New Archaeology theory and the introduction of new instruments such as computers and large-scale data management. In fact, the earliest advances in the use of statistics and computing in archaeology were often made by those such as Doran and Hodson from the late 1950s onwards who rejected links to the theoretical campaign of the New Archaeol-

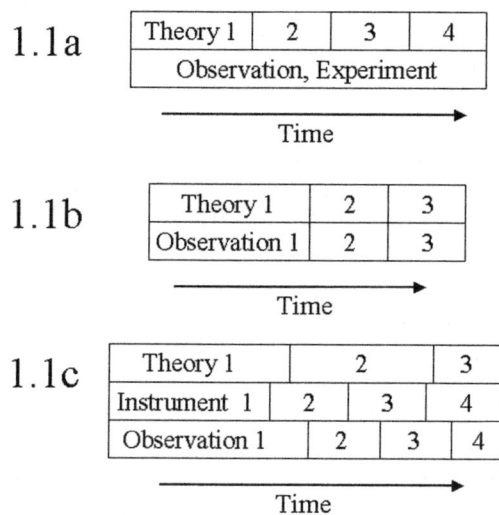

Figure 1.1. Representations of different perspectives on the relationship between theory and observation: (a) represents the processualist perspective in which observation and experimentation underlies theoretical development; (b) represents the antipositivist view that theoretical development and observation are both contingent on an underlying conceptual scheme; (c) represents the proposed view that there is a discontinuity between theory and observation.

ogy. Similarly, while the use of the Harris matrix might be linked in conceptual terms to processual archaeology, its initial use owed much to CRM and the needs for efficiency and standardization in large-scale urban archaeology (Barham 1995; Harris 1989).

Within this third view, archaeology is inhabited by a set of subcultures, each with its own standards of demonstration, its own rhythms of change, its own social networks, assumptions, traditions, etc. These quasi-autonomous traditions are reproduced through (a) pedagogical continuity (who teaches whom), (b) technical continuity (for example, the habitus of excavating in certain ways—in section [profile] or in plan), (c) epistemic continuity (theoretical coherence), and (d) institutional continuity (societies, journals, email lists, etc.).

In arguing for fragmented disciplines in physics and archaeology, I do not want to suggest disorder and chaos. Rather than "anything goes," what we see is a productive use of tensions, diversity, and difference. Change in one subculture often depends on the constraints or continuities offered by other traditions. One such example in archaeology is the use by some feminist archaeologists of postprocessual archaeology while keeping a critical distance; and the similar use by postprocessualist archaeologists of feminist archaeology. Another example is David Clarke's (1968) early use of cultural-historical arguments about Beakers to introduce new technologies in computing—he later used these same new technologies to bolster new processual arguments. A final example is the use by some neoevolutionary writers today of references to postprocessual archaeology as part of the focus on contingency, history, and the individual (Shennan 1993).

So according to this third view (Fig. 1.1c) there is no overall basis for a unified historical development of archaeology. Rather, there are local negotiations between subcultures that manipulate each other strategically. Any apparent unity that is produced is strategic and a matter of perspective. The interactions, differences, and tensions are used productively—the diversity and disconnection are responsible for the strength of the discipline, as one subculture uses another, responds to another, in productive moves.

But perhaps the greatest strength of a diverse discipline is that it is more likely to be able to deal with the multidimensionality of human experience. Far from a relativistic inability to understand anything, the diversity allows different perspectives and scales to be opened up. It allows reality to be pried open. If reality is complex and multidimensional, then multiple perspectives are needed to explore it from different angles and with different tools. We need to recognize, therefore, that an approach that is diverse and multiscalar is better science than a unified science.

This recognition of the need to pry open the complexity of reality from multiple perspectives and from within diverse traditions is the main reason I do not welcome the return in some quarters of archaeology to claims for unified scientific perspectives and "explain-it-all" positions. Rather than these closed worlds, I welcome the diversity in archaeology and other disciplines because it corresponds to and resonates with current diversity in social life and in global communities. The conflicting subculture view recognizes that hierarchical views of science and knowledge are being replaced by horizontal views—that is, by networks of competing interests linked into a diversity of communities. It recognizes that simple utopian solutions do not work, and that real-world problems (from the environmental to the social) are complex and involve multiple interests and negotiations.

So, returning at the end to where I began—that is, with the commonality that we see in current debate across the social, cultural, and humanistic sciences—I believe that one response to fears about this homogeneity is to say that it can, paradoxically, support and engender diversity. Commonality allows diverse traditions to gain access to outside information and to outside legitimization. The horror of internal, self-referential systems of knowledge and authority *can* be subverted by appeal to wider systems of knowledge. The global systems of information flow allow alternative voices to be heard. They allow ideas to run along new paths to new nodes.

I do not underestimate the difficulties here, or the resilience of established modes of thought in resisting new ideas. We see this all around us. Neither do I underestimate the dangers inherent in the new information technologies to create a new hierarchical centralization of knowledge. There is a clear need to be aware of these dangers and to provide alternative channels of communication, particularly for disadvantaged groups. But I do argue that the new networks and the commonalities can be manipulated, and are being actively used by diverse groups to argue for alternative perspectives. We need to be fearful of homogenizing tendencies and to guard against them, but there are also opportunities for the creation and maintenance of diversity

and of diverse subcultures within and across the boundaries of the discipline.

The prime task for archaeology in the twenty-first century will be therefore, in my view, to renegotiate outmoded disciplinary or subcultural boundaries, which are historical products of the nineteenth and twentieth centuries. The four prime boundaries that at present seem most in need of breaking so as to allow debate, interaction, and a fuller understanding of the multiple dimensions of complex human phenomena are as follows.

1. First there is the boundary between archaeology and what has been termed its "fringe" but which must become its center. By fringe I mean popular pasts and personal engagements with the materiality of the past. There is the increasing need to break down disciplinary boundaries and incorporate other voices in heritage, oral tradition, and narratives of identity formation.

2. There is the subcultural boundary between archaeology as a science and as a humanity. This is the archaeological version of the old boundary described by C.P. Snow between the "two cultures" (of science and the arts) dividing intellectual life throughout the nineteenth and twentieth centuries. In archaeology the effect has been the Great Divide between classical (humanistic) and prehistoric (scientific) archaeology, or the divide between historic and prehistoric archaeology. Today this divide is echoed in that between biological and cultural approaches in the discipline. Perhaps one of the major preoccupations of many disciplines in the twenty-first century will be renegotiating the boundaries between biology, culture, and ethics.

3. There are the two subcultural branches of professional archaeology—CRM on the one hand and university-based teaching and research on the other. It seems absolutely clear that renegotiation is needed here because the divide between these two spheres inhibits the flow of ideas and the ability to make sense of archaeological deposits.

4. The fourth boundary that most needs

renegotiating is that which bounds archaeology within the subcultural ghetto of anthropology and the four-field approach. One cannot help but ask today "why only four fields?" and one cannot but wonder whether the anthropological categorization of archaeology has not inhibited openness to other disciplines such as history—but also sociology, psychology, and many others. Paradoxically perhaps, I believe that for archaeology truly to engage in more common and diverse debate, it needs to separate itself intellectually and institutionally from the anthropological label. The challenge of the twenty-first century, from the view I have presented here, is to provide mechanisms for young people to do archaeology within a wide variety of questions and contexts.

In conclusion, to open archaeology up to a commonality of debates from a diversity of subcultural standpoints may involve the four challenges I have listed. If any movements in these directions are to occur they will involve enormous conceptual and institutional change. When else to contemplate the enormity of such tasks than as a millennial moment nears?

2

Archaeology and the Problems of Men

Dean J. Saitta

Eighty-five years ago the American pragmatist philosopher John Dewey urged his contemporaries to turn their attention from the problems of philosophy—those concerned with how we know—to the problems of men—those concerned with how we should live (Dewey 1917). This is good advice for the new millennium.

The problems of knowing are well attended to in current archaeology. Today there even appears to be a widely shared commitment to epistemological realism, the idea that a real world exists which constrains what we can say about it. This consensus includes the postprocessualists who, after an initial fling with relativism, have moved back into the epistemological mainstream with what Hodder (1991c) describes as "qualified objectivism" and Thomas (1996a) describes as "perspectivism." VanPool and VanPool (1999) have recently established that, on philosophical issues, there is more that unites than divides these camps. Thus, I take for granted that in a sense we are all realists now—we all use the "master's tools" (Lorde 1984, cited in Wylie 1995:269–271) of systematic empirical inquiry to deal with experience.

But, this is not to say that we've reached the end of epistemology in archaeology. I believe that the shared commitment to realism is ultimately trivial. There is still room for disagreement on how, and to what purposes, we should use the master's tools. In this regard pragmatism offers an important challenge to the current realist hegemony. Realism applies itself toward knowing, toward "getting things right." Pragmatism applies itself toward living or, in Rorty's (1989) words, toward "making things new." In so doing pragmatism subscribes more fully to the kind of sensibility that equips us for using our craft (sensu Shanks and McGuire 1996) to address the problems of men; that is, human needs.

In the first part of this paper I briefly discuss some key concepts that inform a pragmatist sensibility. In the second, I provide some examples of how a pragmatist archaeology can serve human needs. The most compelling of these is the need to enlarge the community with which archaeology articulates and to which it can contribute; the need to expand the scope of "us." Pragmatism addresses this challenge by directing us to produce knowledges of the past that foreground subaltern groups and concerns, and by offering some alternative criteria for mediating conflicts between groups having different interests in, and understandings of, the past.

A PRAGMATIST SENSIBILITY

There are many understandings of pragmatism. There are also many debates about what the fathers of pragmatism (Charles Pierce, William James, John Dewey) meant, and about the accuracy of various contemporary interpretations (e.g., those of Richard Bernstein and, especially, Richard Rorty).

This diversity and tension is pragmatism's strength. Understood as a "conversation" instead of a thing (Bernstein 1988), pragmatism offers fertile ground for exploring how time-honored—and I think still useful—concepts of truth, experience, and testing can be reformulated in a way sensitive to meeting human need.

The first core pragmatist concept is an antifoundational or fallibilistic notion of truth—the idea that there are no fixed, stable grounds on which knowledge claims can be established. For the pragmatist truth is what is good to believe; truth is belief justified by social need, rather than by the way things are in nature (Posner 1990). Or, put differently, truth is a matter of intersubjective consensus among human beings, not of accurate reflection of something nonhuman (Rorty 1998). One of antifoundationalism's most important implications, for the purposes of this paper, is its warrant for "experimentation" with theory and method in order to arrive at true beliefs. In this sense, pragmatism moves us in directions other than those stipulated by the earliest processualist commentators on archaeology's social relevance. Ford (1973), for example, saw the "indiscriminant publication of unverified hunches" in the discipline as an obstacle to archaeology's ability to serve humanity. Alternatively, I think that liberal production and publication of such hunches—the more the merrier—is critical for moving archaeology toward the sorts of "usable truths" that can serve human need.

The second core concept is the idea that these experimental truths must be evaluated against a broader notion of experience. They must be evaluated in terms of their concrete *consequences* for life today—for how we want to *live* as a pluralistic community. Instead of simply asking whether a claim about the past is empirically sufficient in light of available data, pragmatism asks *what difference the claim makes to how we want to live.* What are the implications of theoretical claims from evolutionary archaeology, interpretive archaeology, Marxist archaeology or, indeed, any other current framework for understanding society and history for how we

think about, and how we might intervene in, human social life? To what extent does a truth-claim expeditiously meet the human needs at stake in reburial or repatriation controversies; i.e., to what extent does it facilitate putting human souls to rest and human minds at ease? "Experience," in this view, is relational, interactive, and creative; it acknowledges our status as social and historical beings; it is genuinely reflexive (Kloppenberg 1996). Defining experience in this way means that we must subsume the usual realist "criterial" rationality for judging truth-claims (i.e., criteria emphasizing logical coherence and correspondence between theory and data) under something much more qualitative and humanistic—what Rorty (1989) has termed "fuzzy" rationality.

A final concept is pragmatism's notion of "testing," specifically as it relates to the evaluation of truth-claims borne of different cultural traditions. Especially germane to archaeology are those truth-claims that divide scientific and traditional knowledges of the past. In contrast to the mainstream scientific view where competing ideas are tested against each other in the light of the empirical record, pragmatism stipulates that we "test" the ideas of other cultures by "weaving" them together with ones we already have (Rorty 1989). Testing is a matter of interweaving and continually reweaving webs of belief so as to increasingly expand and deepen community. It prescribes a "measured relativism" (Appleby et al. 1994) that balances a commitment to evaluation with the parallel belief that cultural pluralism is our best recipe for civil cohesion (Menand 1997:xxviii). Rorty (1989:13) lays the groundwork for such a procedure when he suggests that "the distinction between different cultures differs only in degree from the distinction between theories held by members of a single culture." This strikes me as a useful assumption if the goal is to achieve some sort of commensurability between competing cultural beliefs without essentializing the differences (as tends to happen in postprocessualism) or, worse, essentializing *sameness* (as we are currently seeing, for example, in processualist justifications for scientific study of Kennewick Man—see Preston [1997]—on the grounds that if you go back far enough in time—presumably to humankind's African origins—we all have a common ancestor; i.e., "we're all the same").

The desirable outcome of pragmatism's advocacy of these particular notions of truth, experience, and testing is stronger community—richer and better human activity—rather than some singular, *final* truth about the past or some imagined "more comprehensive" or "more complete" account of history. The loyalty in pragmatism is to other human beings struggling to cope rather than to the realist hope of getting things right; the desire is for *solidarity* rather than objectivity.

PRAGMATIST PRACTICE

Archaeology is currently faced with the challenge of better integrating the various constituencies that have a stake in its operations, and better engaging a public that is often utterly indifferent to whether it operates or not. How, then, can a pragmatist archaeology concretely serve the enlargement of community?

One obvious way is through the production of knowledge that takes stock of neglected peoples and histories, and that focuses on questions other than the kinds of "origins questions" (about the evolution of humanity, agriculture, civilization) traditionally addressed by our discipline's most important popularizers (e.g., Lewis Binford, Brian Fagan). Of interest are questions about everyday life—its conditions, variations, rhythms, and disjunctions—with answers developed in such a way that they are accessible to those living peoples having a stake in the interpretations. As Wylie (1995) points out, this ambition is only realizable if those whose lives are affected are directly involved in the research enterprise as partners and collaborators, instead of just subjects or informants.

Archaeology is making good progress in this area. Many alternative or "counter-narrative" understandings of the past are now developing, including those produced by the gender archaeologies, the various subaltern archaeologies that address such things as

slave life, and the anti-colonialist archaeologies that focus on indigenous peoples and their histories (Schmidt and Patterson 1995). Our own efforts to develop a "working class" archaeology can be added to this list (e.g., Duke and Saitta 1998; Ludlow Collective 2001; McGuire and Walker 1999). We are currently using the master's tools to produce a "critical" history of the lives of early twentieth-century coal miners in southern Colorado that can stand with the more "official" (sensu Bodnar 1992) histories of the West. Official history—especially in the American West—is patriotic, progressive, and triumphal, emphasizing social unity and the continuity of the social order. Critical histories deal with context, transformation, and rupture, addressing both the historical process *and* different narratives about that process (Trouillot 1995). Our archaeological work in the Colorado coalfield includes a program of excavation at the Ludlow Tent Colony, a National Historic Register site where, on April 20, 1914, striking coal miners, women, and children were killed by a strikebreaking force of Colorado militiamen and coal company guards. In this work we are having to engage people—including organized labor, our primary clients—who have never had much use for archaeology, realist or otherwise, and who embrace "vernacular" (again, see Bodnar 1992) histories of coalfield events. Vernacular histories are local, "kitchen table" histories, derived from the first-hand, everyday experience of those people who were directly involved with history's events. Negotiating between these different peoples and histories has not been easy. The gulf between academic and working-class cultures is palpable in our research area (Duke and Saitta 1998). As one miner put it to me at a 1997 union local meeting, where I went seeking permission to excavate at Ludlow (with just a bit of hostility in his voice), "I can tell you everything you need to know about Ludlow in three words—they got fucked."

In our case, a key to narrowing this gulf has been to appreciate that Ludlow and other coalfield sites are part of a living history and long commemorative tradition, and considered sacred ground by the descendants of miners who lived and died on them. This appreciation has earned us a place on the speaker's platform at the annual Ludlow Memorial Service, where we update the local community (including direct descendants of the Ludlow miners as well as a wider interested public) about our work. In conjunction with the fieldwork we also offer Summer Teacher Institutes dedicated to building a labor history curriculum for Colorado middle and high schools. The Institutes compare, contrast, and explore the synergies between official, vernacular, and critical histories of southern coal field events. A pragmatist sensibility is thus helping us satisfy the different interests that come together in the Colorado coalfields, and promises to help raise archaeology's stock as a socially relevant discipline.

Much less progress is being made in coping with the bigger conflicts in archaeological interpretation, such as surround NAGPRA compliance. These conflicts, especially, beg for pragmatic interventions more attuned to "living" than "knowing." By law, NAGPRA compliance is governed by a realist, criterial rationality. The success of a claim for cultural affiliation depends on whether it is supported by *most* of the available biological, linguistic, archaeological, and documentary evidence. Happily, in this scheme native oral traditions are assigned an evidentiary status equal to the other kinds of evidence (see Anyon et al. 1997; Echo-Hawk 2000; cf. Mason 2000). However, NAGPRA's "preponderance of evidence" criterion remains deeply problematic, both because of the elastic nature of evidence in archaeology (resulting from the particular quality of archaeological data combined with the fact that such data only become "evidence" in light of theory), and because of the often deep contentiousness of tribal oral traditions.

Given this situation, a realist, criterial rationality may not be the most appropriate or productive. Instead, we might follow the lead of those pragmatist philosophers *and* Native Americans who suggest that a more important and relevant criterion is the consequences of knowledge—claims for everyday life: for how we want to live, and for the building of a genuinely pluralist community characterized by mutual understanding and respect. At some recent NAGPRA consultations in Durango several Pueblo tribal representatives implicitly endorsed pragmatist evaluative criteria where they argued, in so many words, that history is less important than survival and the maintenance of harmonious relationships among the tribes (Duke 1999). Survival is understood broadly as political, economic, *and* cultural. Naranjo (1996:249) takes a similar stand where she asserts that, in her view, the Pueblo Indian's primary concern is with "the larger issues of breathing and dying," rather than with the specific details of knowing that focus scientific world views. This concern for the present as well as the past—for living as well as knowing—represents a significant convergence between pragmatist and tribal epistemologies that is worth exploiting for its unifying potential. But, this unity can only be established if we're willing to rethink the usual scientific criteria, i.e., empirical and logical sufficiency, for judging and integrating knowledge claims.

Other convergences are apparent in the realm of methodology. Speaking at a conference dedicated to the topic of "Indigenous People and Archaeology," Lomaomvaya and Ferguson (1999) note that:

> In Hopi culture, what stands the test of time is substantive information about the past. Collection and analysis of data requires theory, but for Hopi it is the Hopi past itself that is most important, not what we think this past means for the world beyond Hopi.

This primary interest in archaeological "thick description" of a *particular* past converges with the pragmatist belief that human solidarity is best achieved not by those disciplines—theology, science, philosophy—charged with "penetrating behind the many private appearances to the one general common reality," but rather by those which sensitize humans to the experience of diverse "others" through exploration of the private and idiosyncratic (Rorty 1989:94). Rorty (1989:94) notes that "novels and ethnographies" are especially well suited to building this kind of solidarity. It seems to me that archaeological narratives attuned to human cultural variability across space and time can be just as useful.

Despite its critique of criterial rationality and preference for thick description over nomothetics, the pragmatist alternative need not be antiscience. Indeed, in the pragmatist view, and all things being equal, science is an excellent model of human community and solidarity (Rorty 1989:15). But, all things are rarely equal. Where compromises are required it is science that must lead the way, since it has for too long (and as a consequence of unequal power relationships) dominated other ways of knowing. In his *Federalist No. 10* James Madison noted the threat to community presented by "majority factions" (Madison et al. 1987). For Madison, the best corrective to the majoritarian threat was enlarging the scope of community; i.e., the number of interests represented at the table of democracy. To the extent that mainstream, realist science is a majority faction in American archaeology it poses the greatest threat to the project of reconciling competing knowledges and expanding community. For those archaeologists and native peoples alike who cringe at *any* call for compromise in the service of reconciliation and stronger community, perhaps Rorty (1998:52) provides some comfort when he reminds us that, in democratic societies, "you often get things done by compromising principles in order to form alliances with groups about whom you have grave doubts."

SUMMARY AND CONCLUSION

I have argued in this paper for archaeology to turn from realism to pragmatism as a governing sensibility. Pragmatism emphasizes ways of living instead of rules for knowing, the "weaving together" of knowledges instead of their "validation against" experience, and the social utility of narratives instead of the objectivity of laws and theories. Pragmatism subsumes Enlightenment criterial rationality and nomothetics to more humanistic, albeit fuzzier, regulative ideals. In so doing, it converges with some key subaltern priorities and concerns about the wider social context and consequences of knowledge claims. At the same time it departs from *both* the analytical and continental philosophical traditions that so many have found wanting as underpinnings for, respectively, processual and postprocessual archaeology.

Even though pragmatism is only just emerging as a framework for archaeological inquiry, different understandings of its project are already afoot. Reid and Whittlesey (1999) have recently discussed pragmatism's utility as a philosophical toolkit for Southwestern archaeology. These authors approvingly view pragmatism's antifoundationalism not as a stand against philosophical truth but rather as a stand against academic authority. They take the pragmatist concern for experience to be exemplified in archaeology by pursuits such as ethnoarchaeology and experimental archaeology. Finally, they cast pragmatist method as turning on the unbiased collection of *all* available data, and pragmatist theory as requiring equal parts common sense, intuition, and appeals to "human nature." Although seen by the authors as preferable to processualism, this version of pragmatism bears little resemblance to mine. Rather than leading beyond processualism, Reid and Whittlesey's pragmatism seems to recall an unreflective, disengaged empiricism where knowing rather than living rules the day. It will be very interesting to see where the conversation about pragmatism's regulative ideals, and relevance for archaeology, goes from here.

ACKNOWLEDGMENTS

Archaeological work in the southern Colorado coalfield is supported by the United Mine Workers of America, and by grants from the Colorado Historical Society–State Historical Fund.

3

The Origins of Questions in Historical Archaeology

MARK P. LEONE

This is an essay that attempts to inject some passion about scientific discoveries into historical archaeology. If it manages to do the same for prehistoric archaeology in the United States, that is desirable too. I do not limit my appraisal of historical archaeology to the United States. I argue that it needs reconceptualizing on a worldwide basis so that its conclusions make general discoveries.

If one looks at recent books on historical archaeology, one sees flashes of excitement and accomplishment in return for the effort that has gone into the work. The work itself often comes from emergency excavations, CRM reporting, or from sampling a small piece of an enormous ruin or abandoned landscape. The World Archaeological Congress has produced several volumes (Hodder 1989; Layton 1989) containing essays on worldwide historical archaeology. Britain has come alive with several efforts (Johnson 1996; Tarlow and West 1999). Matthew Johnson (1996) has written generally on the transition to capitalism from the Middle Ages in Britain. Kate Giles (Tarlow and West 1999:87–102) and Tom Williamson (Tarlow and West 1999:19–34) write on Britain in the early modern and modern periods. Pedro Funari has emerged in the English-speaking world as an historical archaeologist writing on slavery and class from Brazil.

My own choices for examples of work that contain important efforts are Carmel Schrire's *Digging Through Darkness* and Christopher Tilley's *Metaphor and Material Culture*. Neither of these books fits into the mainstream definition of historical archaeology, but both are important efforts to bring the field into the world of modern intellectual life. It is the process of moving historical archaeology into the intellectual life of anthropology that is missing from the institutional apparatus of historical archaeology. A method for this movement needs to be enunciated as well as exemplified as I attempt to do here using Schrire and Tilley.

Carmel Schrire and Christopher Tilley have written quite different books. Schrire's won a prize from the Society for American Archaeology for the best book making archaeology accessible to the public. The book has drawn no attention to itself within historical archaeology and was dismissed privately as not being historical archaeology. The dismissal came in a private conversation with the accusation that it was not how to write historical archaeology, therefore, it wasn't worth discussing as a model for how to proceed in the field.

Digging Through Darkness is about racial hatred in South Africa. Schrire moves from present to periods in the past in South Africa to show who lived in South Africa when the Dutch arrived. She shows who the Dutch were and how terribly they behaved. She shows the destruction of the environment and the values that form the face of colonial capitalism. The book virtually turns its pages for a reader; it is a fast read. Schrire's book is an ideal combination of first-rate understanding, emotional engagement, and personal quest. But the leaders of the field of historical archaeology deny any part of it: it isn't historical archaeology. It took years to write, but it is not right for them. But the status quo is.

Metaphor and Material Culture attempts to explain why material remains of the past are significant. Tilley takes on a huge question, one invisible in archaeology. How do "things" take on and aid meaning? If Schrire takes on the origins of hatred in South Africa, Tilley takes on why things matter.

Tilley argues that things can convey more meaning, longer than language, because of their permanence. Things matter because they are matter, not like spoken words which are gone, once said. The solidity of things gives their meanings relative permanence. Things serve to communicate because through their form, color, texture, weight, and like qualities, they create a nonverbal image in the mind. The images are linked to the experiences in which the objects are used. These, obviously, can be quite varied and thus, so can the meanings of the objects. This is the reason objects can have different meanings, or can contain ambiguity. When the object/image is subject to linguistic experience, such as naming or description, the impression of the object, plus a name, can create a new understanding of the world. "This is work of the metaphorical mind in which one thing is conceived in terms of another and is most likely to be activated in ritual and learning contexts where what is taken for granted needs to be explicated or represented" (Tilley 1999:270). Something new can achieve this because it is a thing named, or described, or seen in a novel way. More research is needed on this serious question, because behind it is the relationship behind the existence of monuments, museums, memorabilia on one hand, and the significance many new and threatened groups' place in and on heritage, on the other. Tilley's idea may also explain the popular veneration of the material archaeologists are responsible for.

These are significant questions and are of a recognizably general kind. But because neither author nor question is recognized as important to historical archaeology, it is important to introduce them to the field. The questions are important even though these authors do not make it clear how each got to the question in a way that others can use as a model. All this discussion exemplifies the need to have a model for historical archaeology which unifies general questions with the methods for discovering their answers. My aim here is to create for historical archaeology nothing more than the condition within prehistoric archaeology where many of the basic, general questions and methods for finding answers are taught as common knowledge.

The origin of the two general questions I have outlined extend beyond Schrire's wanting to know why natives came to hate European colonials, and beyond Tilley's asking why things matter. They gain their validity because we are all curious about their answers; the questions exist within a modern context. It is the immediate recognition of their importance that is central.

How does one start to find questions like these? From one's own daily life. Schrire grew up in South Africa, saw apartheid face-to-face, and knows the racial hatred engendered by colonialism. Tilley has walked henge monuments for years and has been concerned with Bronze Age archaeology for decades. Then, he visited a modern site in Melanesia and saw stone monuments in modern use in a nation-building context that was used to create tourism and enhance local identity. He wondered how the monument worked. These are conventional places to begin. The problem is that one hardly notices such early steps: you begin with your own experiences and shape them so that a question comes forward that has an empirical answer. How can a method be made from this for practicing historical archaeologists? In order to begin to provide an answer, I would like to combine several insights from Quetzil Castañeda's *In the Museum of Maya Culture* with some descriptions from Benedict Anderson's *Imag-*

ined Communities to create the first step in a method.

Just as the origin of the main questions in prehistoric archaeology comes from the nineteenth-century attempt to decenter the Bible and to enhance Europe's claims to have civilized the rest of the world, so the origin of questions in historical archaeology should begin with the descendants of colonization and nationalism. These descendants are the people who are absent when America's origins are proclaimed to be English, when it is proclaimed that Africans lost their culture in the Diaspora, that people in Appalachia have a little bit of Britain left in them, that the Irish were denatured by their own diaspora in the Famine, and that Creole culture is chunks but not a whole and is without the kind of integrity the rest of us have. We can create a historical archaeology that is directed toward communities affected by our own intrusions. We can deal with the integrity of their cultures.

There are two vast problems that all graduate students in archaeology are trained to see. One is that it is very difficult to make a link between past and present. Such an assumption builds a chasm that is hard to cross between then and now which would, if bridged, answer the question of how we got to be here today looking like we do. The second problem is how to create a picture of the whole culture that we assume once existed. We use the unifying concept of culture, yet face the daunting problem of adding together the fragments excavated to make a whole.

Quetzil Castañeda's *In the Museum of Maya Culture* can be crafted into a productive plan for archaeology that aids the effort to resolve the dilemma. Castañeda's immediate interest is in how Chichén Itzá was made into a tourist zone by using the concept of Maya culture. His work is concerned with why tourism exists today, and with the role of archaeology and anthropology in creating an environment that is fit for tourists. Castañeda depends on Benedict Anderson's description of archaeology's role in the creation of ancient monuments around the world. In *Imagined Communities* Anderson describes the use of great archaeological zones to celebrate the noble origins of current elites, but also as proof of just how far now-colonized locals have fallen from their former great culture. Castañeda is most at home with Anderson's last point, namely how little culture there is in the towns, villages, and homesteads where the descendants of those who once were great now live. His particular concern is with Pisté, the Mexican town near Chichén Itzá where many of the museum's workers live. Robert Redfield described this as a town without culture, meaning that the people were neither traditional Maya, nor fully modern Mexicans. These were people for whom no noble Maya past could be claimed, nor were they Mexican enough to have a modern national future.

Castañeda sees Redfield's dilemma as coming from the concept of culture itself. In the course of attempting to discover culture, anthropologists often doubt the fit between what they see and the concept, or find the culture incomplete. Castañeda insists that anthropologists are responsible for finding culture incomplete, mixed, partial, or spurious. This is particularly true when we deal with the remnants of an ancient culture still present, as among the living Maya. Ethnographers and archaeologists have long treated ethnographic peoples as holding some clue that might help understand the material remains from the past. The incompleteness of both the archaeological artifacts and the practices from the past seen among the living, has often been a source of regret or sadness for anthropologists because it left an incomplete understanding of either past or present, and worse, of how the past becomes the present.

It is easy enough to see, following Anderson's lead, how this dilemma is part of the colonial practice of finding the culture of peasants peripheral to a new national or imperial economy, because the peasants were not national, and therefore had only an incomplete version of the real culture they would eventually absorb. They therefore had less integrity than their urban or nationalistic compatriots. The other reason peasants could not have a fully integrated culture was due to their being a shadow of what was there, the formerly great. Castañeda argues that such partiality or incompleteness marks peoples as creoles, remnants, vestiges, living survivors, last primitives, or even descendant communities.

All these people are those often studied by anthropologists because they were thought to retain some integrity left from not being touched by or integrated into modern life. These peoples were not Westernized, or not fully Westernized. This characteristic is why anthropologists sought them out for understanding in the first place. Because the concept of culture lacks an effective definition of class, and in Britain and the United States was almost untouched by Marxist theory, peasants or villages that were on the margins of national elites or newly formed nationalizing states, were seen as avoiding or as unintegrated into progress. They were no longer primitive. They were no longer members of a dead kingdom or empire. And they were not modern either. As a result, it was hard for anthropologists to find their culture. All this constitutes Castañeda's argument.

Castañeda also points out, generalizing from his reading of Robert Redfield and the Maya of Yucatan, that places where we as ethnographers and archaeologists cannot find norms and traditions and thus little culture, are also places where war, pillage, exploitation, peonage, tenancy, slavery, and the violent struggles associated with the imposition of wage labor have all happened. Such people do not want progress because they have experienced its results directly. Anthropologists have denied them culture because such people are neither old nor fully new. Our concept of culture has not allowed for anything else. Historical archaeologists have the material remains of these people's immediate pasts, calling it our data, often digging through it for earlier, greater periods. We should stop at the top for the impact of modernization and the formation of class.

Given that anthropologists have consistently found communities without fully developed national cultures and therefore lacking integration, and, further, that archaeologists by scientific caution always hold back their strongest inferences as tentative, then our own concepts and methods are responsible for denying wholeness to some peoples. I argue that this dilemma should be called a site of struggle. This is where historical archaeology should exist. The goal of a historical archaeologist is to find a whole or worthwhile culture, where others do not see one. Normally, the obligation historical archaeologists take on is that of recovering the history of those left without a voice, record, tale, or trace. The goal is based on the assumption that everybody left something in the ground, despite illiteracy, anonymity, or destruction. Thus, the forgotten can be remembered.

Archaeologists played a direct and celebrated role in building Chichén Itzá, Colonial Williamsburg, restored Annapolis, the restored Texas and California missions, Plimoth Plantation, Tikal, Guatemala, Machu Pichu, and the Old City of Jerusalem. Archaeology was actively used in all these attractions and in virtually every other site that has become an ancient monument since the eighteenth century. Since our role is fairly clear, we can also understand that the many local people, who cannot see themselves in these monuments, but who live nearby and who have dug for us, and who sell trinkets to tourists, and who also are the incomplete modern descendants of the noble peoples who are now lost, have an archaeology too. It is at the top of the ground. It is the proper locus of historical archaeology.

I propose that historical archaeologists, who already save everything from the top down, reverse their values and use the material at the top in order to accept Castañeda's invitation to complete culture. Such a move would be a method for achieving one of the universally agreed on goals of historical archaeology: giving voice to the descended people of the world. The top layer contains the evidence for Indian removal at Maya sites, black dispersal during American urban renewal, the destruction of Palestinian villages in Israel, the eradication of all those funky lower middle class families from Williamsburg since the 1920s, and the Americanization of the California missions. Those who were removed are the people who had no culture, or not enough.

The best illustration of how our own creation in anthropology traps us within the colonialist and nationalist dilemma is how our field has tried to characterize the African aspects of African-American culture. The enslavement process that accompanied the African Diaspora entailed the massive loss of African culture, including languages, according to Frazier (1965). That claim has lead to the question of whether anything was left from African culture among African Americans. There is a long list of African elements relatively recently discovered in U.S. culture that are said to be survivals from Africa. These include the round dance, call and response music, shot-gun houses, conjuration or Hoodoo and its wide range of practices in rooms, grave sites, and yard art. Does this make up a culture? The normal answers are that African-American culture contains some elements surviving from Africa, or alternatively that it is a creole culture, a mix of items blended together into a new culture adapting to the needs of those brutalized in New World slavery and racism. Only in the last sense of culture is there room for integrity or wholeness, including the formation of classes and racially designated groups.

People of subordinate status are often found by anthropologists in the immediate past to have an incomplete culture. What do we as historical archaeologists do about that? We often have the opportunity to excavate the places that prove the conclusion to be untrue. The place to dig is in the very monumental zones where archaeologists worked a century and more ago and where the erasures of peasant life happened that resulted in disfranchising the then newly discovered and incomplete peoples. Someone could dig at the town of Pisté, outside of Chichén Itzá, to see how long it has been there and how its material culture was made and where it came from. How was the town tied to Mexican and worldwide markets? The fauna and ceramics will tell that in two or three archaeological seasons. The slave cabins at Williamsburg and those in the surrounding plantations show African culture, but it is the removal of these cabins in the 1930s through the 1950s that shows how the monument was built and how African-American culture was denied a past and thus made incomplete. Such removal is how the black community in Williamsburg today appears to be so groundless. It is in the area's tenant farmsteads that integrity lies, as well as in the former cabins of slaves and free African Americans.

The top of the monumental zones contains the archaeological evidence for how museums are created and what was removed in order to create them. But it is in the struggles within museum settings and the surrounding towns and districts where we will find the questions about who people really are and where we will be provided with the need to re-dig those zones in order to find out who the other owners were and are. Such re-excavation may find the absence of culture that will complete the partial picture of the creolized, marginalized, and unassimilated who now work in the ruin and are the lower class members who are comparatively underrepresented.

For historical archaeologists, more than for prehistorians, words and things are the objects of study, not social relations, to which they are an index. Because of the much closer tie between prehistorians and the rest of anthropology, prehistoric archaeologists tend not to forget that culture is in social relations and that things are only an entre to them. Objects may also help to create social relations, but that is a much more recent insight. For some reason, bottles, tin cans, nails, dishes, architecture, and the printed word have taken on a reality as proper subject matter among historical archaeologists that they do not deserve.

Historical archaeology's true subject matter is racism, class formation, national identity, the construction of the modern notion of self, the ideology of homogeneity and of equal opportunity, and the notion that we can learn from the past. In order to achieve some knowledge of these colonial and nationalistic practices, we need to combine our knowledge of ceramics with the questions provided by those who are subordinate.

When my colleagues and I did this in Annapolis with some African Americans, we discovered just how far nporth in the United States Hoodoo existed; just how pervasive West African religion was in Annapolis households; and how much more varied its sacred pharmacopoeia was than anyone had ever said (Leone and Fry 1999; Leone et al. 2001). We also found a relatively unknown variant of Christianity. To make this discovery, we dug in the parts of the monumental zone of the historic district of Annapolis, a zone created in part by our own actions, and took the top layers, not the early ones. We did this because others told us that their history was in them. They were correct, and we discovered Hoodoo. But the truth of our mutual discovery is not that Hoodoo is a missing part, or another chunk to the creole mixture, but is a religion intended to be all pervasive and a major alternative to European Christianity. That is not a minor fact, nor an incomplete, partial, surviving, mixed, or lost piece of culture. It is a serious achievement and it is whole, with a history, and is worthwhile.

Is defining a variant of Christianity, one forged in slavery and racism, a general matter, or is it a historical pursuit? My effort in this essay is to provide a reason for historical archaeology to work, a reason that both satisfies those expelled from the mainstream —which is one of the main goals of the field—and one that attempts to understand the modern and early modern worlds. This is the world of European expansion, of nascent and developed capitalism and the worldwide triumph of colonialism. Are these categories general? Yes. Do we need to compare our subject groups to tribes, bands, chiefdoms, or with Mesopotamia to be scientific? No. But if not, then what is general? It is not general to write only about South Africa, but it is general to understand how racial hatred occurs. The form of rhetoric is not important. It is not general to write about a stone monument in Melanesia, but it is general to be able to distinguish how things are given meaning and how that is different from spoken words.

Because Christianity is so large and so active in the world, it is quite varied. While a history of Hoodoo might be historical, seeing Hoodoo as a slave religion is to have to be engaged in a generalizing effort to characterize it as having none of the passive piety of Catholicism, or the predetermined salvation of an optimistic Calvinism, but as having the capacity to demand action of God needed by those who are oppressed. To be general, one asks: is it a religion of the oppressed, or of the marginalized, or of a class of people marginalized but desiring to be mainstream? The general answer is yes, but the saving details that offer historical redemption and validation to the living are particular. As historical archaeologists we can have both as long as we stay in the modern world of descendent communities and current anthropological theory.

4

Rethinking Style in Archaeology

Jerimy J. Cunningham

CHILDE'S PARADOX

[Ideas] are given in experience and derived from the external world. [They] must therefore somehow correspond to that world—Childe 1956:55

The ideal reproduction of the external world in society's heads is not, and in fact never can be, an exact reflection of that world...—Childe 1956:58

Most people would recognize that the problem with these two statements is that they are both true, and yet they are contradictory. Despite research that identifies carrying capacities and adaptive necessities, it is undeniable that we interact with the world only through our ideas about it. And regardless of how much current theoretical fashions invoke hermeneutic models or point to the underdetermination of theory by data, it is also true that our ideas about the world must conform somehow to that world if we continue to survive. Trigger (1998) has recently made this very point, and the problem remains the same today as it did when Childe wrote in the middle part of the twentieth century (Childe 1956, see also 1949): we exist suspended in a tumultuous web of knowledge based partially in realities we create and partially in the constraints imposed by the world. Culture, no matter how defined, is thus always a body of knowledge derived from the hybrid influences of our culture's history and our ecological setting. Unfortunately, knowing this

truth does not make the task of social scientists any easier and "Childe's Paradox" remains one of the most enduring problems in modern social science.

Not surprisingly, archaeology has found itself dealing with this very issue. While much of the processual-postprocessual debate has focused on positivist versus idealist epistemology (Trigger 1998), the debate can also be seen as a dispute over materialist and idealist ontologies of culture. Materialist outlooks like Binford's (e.g., 1962) and Schiffer's (e.g., 1976) emphasize Childe's first statement and take behavior to be the result of rational individuals who attempt to deal with material circumstances in the real world. These patterns can be explained by relating them to the constraints and opportunities in the environment. Hodder's (1985) idealist perspective draws from Childe's second statement to assert that environmental constraints play an insignificant role because our view of the world is always defined by ideas drawn from a unique history. "Constraints" are social conventions defined according to cultural rather than environmental contexts, and behavior is explained by its relationship to particular culture histories and cognitive structures. However, it would be a mistake to assume that these positions each represent pure forms of materialism and idealism. Even within the polemics of the debate, researchers have navigated both truisms in Childe's Paradox and integrate elements of both materialist and idealist ontologies. Binford's (1962) earliest model, which firmly rejected the idealism of culture-history, allowed normative elements in the form of "style." Hodder (1982a) recognizes the need to examine adaptive processes but, as counterpoints to Binford's norms, these remain a secondary or residual part of his thinking. Archaeologists on both sides of the processual-postprocessual debate have thus found themselves negotiating the hybrid nature of culture.

In the following discussion, I examine how archaeologists have envisioned relationships between human ecology and culture-history. I accomplish this by making plain what I perceive to be two implicit conceptual relationships operating in the archaeological literature. Because archaeology only observes behavior through the material record, the relationship between ecology and culture-history can be identified in the way archaeologists explain "cultural patterns" (as opposed to the "noncultural" or taphonomic patterns) in the archaeological record. Cultural patterns are generally assumed to take one of two forms: they are either "stylistic" or "functional." Contrary to many conventional definitions that treat style and function as cultural "givens," I suggest here that "style" and "function" are statuses archaeologists assign to these patterns. Moreover, these statuses relate directly to broader idealist and materialist ontologies of culture. If a pattern is stylistic, it is thought to be caused by historical processes such as the formation of group or individual identity, the constitution of the self, or the explicit attempt to transmit symbolic information. If a pattern is functional, then it is thought to be explained by processes related to constraints or opportunities posed by an environment. Admittedly, the influence of postmodernism means that discussions of "function" are now rarely found in the style literature, partly because it has too many inconsistent meanings (see Miller 1985). Ironically, this criticism of function is rivaled by the ambiguity surrounding "style," which Conkey and Hastorf

(1990:1) have correctly described as a "black box" (also see Schiffer and Skibo 1997; Wobst 1999). I hope to exercise the ambiguity found in both terms by explicitly tying them to broader premises about the nature of culture, and thus to the paradox so cogently identified by V. Gordon Childe. This perspective provides a framework with which I revisit some current style models, demonstrating that many of the unresolved questions about style, such as "where in formal variation does style reside?" or "what does style do?", result from the way archaeologists have addressed the hybrid character of culture. I conclude by suggesting we should avoid broader ontological commitments and instead adopt a pluralistic approach to the explanation of artifact variability.

MATERIALISM AND IDEALISM

Before moving into the style literature, it is important to outline some tenets of materialist and idealist ontologies of culture. This will make clear the connection I draw below between "function" and the brand of ecological materialism found in archaeology and between "style" and normative or historically based idealism. In their most pristine form, materialism and idealism hearken back to the rationalistic thought of the Enlightenment and the nonrationalistic reaction of the Romantic period. Differences between empiricist and hermeneutic epistemologies, nominalist and realist cultural ontologies, and utilitarianist and normative theories of action all originate in this opposition. Nineteenth-century thinkers such as Hegel, Marx, Comte, Nietzsche, and John Stuart Mill drew from these poles to create their own works, occasionally mixing elements found in both the Enlightenment and in Romanticism (Saiedi 1993). In the modern era, the tendency to reduce complex systems like that of Marx to simple catch-all terms of materialism or idealism has resulted in substantial confusion as to what sorts of analysis should qualify under the materialist or idealist rubric. In framing my own discussion, I have attempted to stay true to the broadest convictions of rationalism and nonrationalism succinctly captured in Childe's Paradox, while at the same time focusing on those elements directly relevant to the issue at hand. Below I reproduce Pfaffenberger's (1992:494–495) useful caricature of a materialist perspective of technology and then develop my own parody based on his subsequent idealist orientation. It should be stressed that caricatures are rhetorical ploys often used to transform complex theoretical positions into indefensible "strawpersons" that can be easily refuted. Indeed, Pfaffenberger uses his caricature of materialism in exactly this way. This is not my intent. I introduce them only to focus our attention on those elements of materialism and idealism that are relevant to style and function. Note that Pfaffenberger explicitly uses the masculine pronoun to reinforce what he describes as the "gendered ideology" of materialism.

Materialism
Necessity is the mother of invention. As Man has been faced with severe survival challenges, certain extraordinary individuals have seen, often in a brilliant flash of inspiration, how to address the challenge of Need by applying the forces, potentialities and affordances of Nature to the fabrication of tools and material artifacts. The power of nature is there, waiting to be harnessed, to the extent that the inventor can clear away the cobwebs of culture to see the world from a purely utilitarian standpoint…

Form follows function. To be sure, Man decorates his tools and artifacts, but artifacts are adopted to the extent that their form shows a clear and rational relationship to the artifacts' intended function—that is, its ability to satisfy the need that was the raison d'être of the artifact's creation. Thus, a society's material culture becomes a physical record of its characteristic survival adaptation; material culture is the primary means by which society effects its reproduction. The meaning of human artifacts is a surface matter of style…

By viewing the material record of

Man's technological achievements, one can directly perceive the challenges Man faced in the past, and how he met those challenges. This record shows a unilinear progression over time, because technology is cumulative. Each new level of penetration into Nature's secrets builds on the previous one, producing even more powerful inventions… (Pfaffenberger 1992:494–495, emphasis in original).

Idealism
There are no universal human needs, and thus there are no "ideal artifacts." Needs are defined by a particular history and not by nature, and they may be met by any one of a number of different options. When adaptation happens, if this can be assessed at all, it occurs mainly because of social relationships and cultural knowledge and only marginally because of artifacts.

It is irrelevant, then, whether a given activity or artifact "works" in a utilitarian sense. The function of an artifact is the part that is most ephemeral, contingent and subject to cultural definition. Style is thus an object's function and understanding technology is a matter of knowing the conceptual framework in which it is embedded and the social determinates of its use.

Power taints all things, and all behavior is a manifestation of the structures of knowledge that are reified and symbolically reflected in social and economic life. In new situations, actors recycle old structures of meaning in new ways. People in positions of power draw upon hegemonies and mobilize labor to advance their own ends. At the same time, people resist. Through these actions—domination and resistance—meanings of the past are transformed. Material culture, as a material symbol, has its purpose in the creation and recreation of power and meaning.

As the caricatures show, these particular brands of idealism and materialism are opposite perspectives on social life (see Table 4.1).

Table 4.1. Simple Oppositions between Materialism and Idealism

Materialism	Idealism
Direct empirical access to the world	Ideas determine empirical observations
Ecological processes	Cultural-historical processes
Environmental determinism	Cultural determinism
External explanation of change	Internal explanation of change

Yet, by themselves they are painfully incomplete. While each illuminates an important facet of culture, in isolation they fail to capture the scope and complexity of observed human activity. As a result, archaeologists—like the nineteenth-century philosophers before them—have found it necessary to combine elements of both in their theory. While such combinations can be found in broad-level theorizing about culture, it is through mid-range notions like style and function that we get our clearest sense of how archaeologists have creatively integrated these elements. Cultural models tend to be highly optimistic and often remain insulated from the messiness of "on the ground" research. As Watson and others (1984) have suggested, archaeological theorizing tends to be dominated by "shotgun" approaches where mid-level theories are applied to the record without ever being explicitly framed by broad-range concepts. This does not mean that mid-level theory is completely divorced from axioms regarding culture, or that broad-range tenets are never modified by archaeological data. Indeed, my purpose here is to explore exactly these sorts of relationships. Rather, mid-level theories have gained a degree of freedom from overarching premises because they are more frequently adjusted to account for the vagaries in empirical data. Therefore, style and function reflect not just how archaeologists have thought about Childe's Paradox, but also how they have grappled with it in everyday practice.

Overall, style and function have been integrated by making one side of the paradox more essential to the explanation of culture. "Strong forms" of essentialism, like those outlined by the above caricatures, go as far as to consider one side of the dichotomy emergent or epiphenomenal in relation to the other. "Soft forms" of essentialism take a more sophisticated approach because they see both ecology and culture-history as influencing cultural patterns. In this latter case, culture may be partitioned into distinct stylistic (cultural-historical) and functional (ecological) spheres. These spheres are distinguished from each other two different ways. First, style and function may refer to discrete and mutually exclusive patterns in variation. The belief that pottery decoration refers only to style and ceramic morphology only to function is a typical example. By making this sort of distinction, ecological and cultural-historical processes remain effectively insulated from each other. Second, style and function may be thought to operate in separate temporal levels similar to the *durées* posited by Annales historians (after Braudel 1976; e.g., Blintliff 1991; Knapp 1992). Functions may be associated with a durable, adaptive structure while style will only be found in daily practice. Essentialism, albeit in a softer form than we see in the caricatures, is often present in these models as well because they marginalize ecological or cultural-historical processes. For example, style has been defined negatively as variation that does not have an obvious functional explanation—a definition that leaves it peripheral to function in explanation. Style has also been defined as variation that operates within the constraints imposed by a structure of functional requirements, which similarly gives it a reduced role in the explanation of this variability.

As we will see below, essentialist approaches to style have many problems. Harder forms of essentialism remain consistent with the axioms of materialist and idealist philosophies, but do so by ignoring a large portion of human behavior. Softer forms of essentialism seem more realistic, but have had trouble applying partitioned models to empirical data. Bluntly stated, they have yet to find where style ends and function begins. More importantly, the essentialism found in all these models limits a priori what sorts of patterns are given a stylistic or a functional status. This effectively restricts the explanations that can be given for these patterns. Most style models thus overlook what I take to be the key insight behind Childe's Paradox: *cultural patterns are always the result of both cultural-historical and ecological processes.* And although it is unlikely that these influences are always equal, we should be able to examine both "style" and "function" in most, if not all, dimensions of artifact variability. As I hope to show in the following section, "stylistic analyses" that rely on essentialism inherently limit our ability to accomplish this very task.

ESSENTIALISM AND PARTITIONING IN STYLE AND FUNCTION

> Stylistic analysis has become a boring routine which rests on shaky foundations—Wobst 1977:317

In three seminal essays, Binford outlined a perspective of culture that was to define the bulk of style research for the next 40 years (Binford 1962, 1963, 1965). Following Leslie White (1959), Binford defined culture as "man's extrasomatic means of adaptation" (Binford 1965:205). Adaptation occurs through the interrelationship of three separate cultural subsystems (1962). The technological system articulates society with the environment and, in many ways, is a direct adaptive response to an environmental niche. The sociological subsystem articulates with the technological subsystem and represents the social structure of the society. Built upon the social subsystem rests the ideological subsystem which "provides the symbolic milieu in which individuals are acculturated [and is] a necessity if [people] are to take their place as functional participants in the social system" (1962:219–220). As a result, the technological, social, and ideological subsystems, which are represented archaeologically by technomic, sociotechnic, and ideotechnic artifacts, are determined by the environment. Binford's model thus emphasizes an ecologically centered materialist ontology of culture (see Wylie 1989b).

In contrast to this perspective, Binford also posited that archaeological materials may demonstrate stylistic variability. Style was defined as variation that crosscuts but cannot be attributed to any one of these three functional subsystems. This variation provides "a symbolically diverse yet pervasive artifactual environment promoting group solidarity and serving as a basis for group awareness and identity" (Binford 1962:220). In a later paper, he redefined style as "secondary functional variation" that was a byproduct of the social context of manufacture and use, and contrasted this with "primary functional variation," which related to the intended use of an object (1965:206–207). As Conkey (1990) has noted, both definitions make style a normative component of his overtly materialist model.

Despite the overt materialism in Binford's view of culture, the model he outlines adopts a "soft form" of essentialism. Both types of partitioning are used to integrate the influences of ecology and culture-history. First, style and function are attributed to entirely different elements of variation, with style defined negatively as that which is not functional (Wobst 1977). At several places, Binford states this quite clearly. He argued that historical traditions are "seen in secondary functional variability only…the tradition is seen in continuity in those formal attributes which vary with the social context of manufacture *exclusive* of the variability related to the use of the item. This is termed stylistic variability" (1965:208, emphasis added). Style and function are thus relegated to distinct patterns of variation, with normative influences operating in a secondary and residual capacity. His second approach to partitioning is far more complex. In his discussion of "Red Ocher Caches" from Michigan (1963), he introduced the concept of "functional equivalents." Functional equivalents represent alternate ways of addressing the same functional ends. Providing functional requirements are met, variation may "drift" in response to historical factors that affect cultural transmission. Drift is kept within manageable limits by selective pressures that act on the adaptive system lying behind daily experience:

> It should be pointed out that...[stylistic drift] would be operative only within the individual's cultural idiolect or the shared behavioral aspects of culture. Cultural systems as such and the normative structures of the system would not be subject to the processes of drift, being modified only through processes of readaption or evolutionary change. Culture content alone would be subject to such a process. (Binford 1963:92)

The patterns Binford describes as "functionally equivalent" thus result from the combined influence of both ecological and cultural-historical processes. This integration is accomplished by positioning them in discrete structural levels or scales of time (cf. Blintliff 1991; Braudel 1976; Knapp 1992; see especially Smith 1992). Long-term selective processes affect the adaptive structure that lies behind experience, with the short-term historical processes that create stylistic drift only present in daily practice. Furthermore, while stylistic drift is actively constrained by long-term ecological processes like selection, historical processes have no comparable impact on the adaptive structure. The adaptive structure is therefore the primary explanation for functionally equivalent variation. As with Binford's partitioning of style and function into discrete areas of variation, the structural partitioning found in functional equivalents maintains the essential position of materialism.

The partitioning associated with "functional equivalents" comes with a very interesting problem. How do we deal with variation that results from both ecological and cultural-historical processes? This issue has been most directly addressed by James Sackett, and was the center of his debate with Polly Wiessner. Sackett has consistently

maintained a soft materialist position that draws heavily on Binford's original thinking (compare Sackett 1973, 1977, 1982, 1985a, 1985b, 1986a, 1986b, 1990). Like Binford, Sackett argues that there is a purely stylistic element in variation. This "iconic style" can be actively manipulated by human agents because it is found in variation completely divorced from (or "adjunct" to) functional constraints. Style thus remains a negative category of function, with purely cultural-historical explanations only allowed for attributes like decoration that are clearly "nonfunctional." He also draws on Binford's functional equivalents to assert that style is present in all variability, including that which is patently functional (Sackett 1977; see 1973 for a nascent version). "Isochrestic style" reflects the fact that there are many ways that artifacts can achieve the same functional ends. From one generation to the next, this type of style is *passively* transmitted, indicating shared norms of manufacture within the adaptive framework. This is an important point and, as with Binford, it is the key to Sackett's integration of ecological and cultural-historical influences in variability. Isochrestic style *must* remain entirely passive because this variation is primarily produced by ecological processes operating on the adaptive structure. If isochrestic variation were ever anything more than passive (i.e., required the sort of purely cultural-historical explanation generally given for iconic style), it would challenge the essential position of the adaptative structure and the materialist underpinnings of the entire model. Moreover, if the essential position of this adaptive structure is undermined, it becomes incredibly difficult to identify whether "functionally equivalent" variation requires ecological or cultural-historical explanations.

Indeed, it is exactly this problem that arises in the debate between Sackett and Wiessner (Sackett 1985a, 1986a, 1990; Wiessner 1983, 1985, 1990). In the late 1970s, Wiessner conducted an ethnoarchaeological study among Kalahari San groups to identify how different groups invested specific attributes with social information. Following Wobst (1977; but also see Wobst 1999), she argued that style was "formal variation in material culture that transmits information about personal and social identity" and conveys an adaptive advantage (Wiessner 1983:256). Two types of style are assumed to exist. "Emblemic Style" is formal variation that transmits messages about group identity, while "Assertive Style" is taken to reflect individual expressions of identity. Wiessner hypothesizes that assertive style should display a larger degree of randomness than emblemic style, which should show a discrete distribution. She also predicts that those artifacts possessing style would be actively used by the society longer, would require more energy or "transformational stages" for their production (following Wilmsen and Roberts 1978), would possess more decoration, and finally would vary in relation to known social boundaries (1983:260). Given these expectations, her findings were quite startling (Wiessner 1983:260, emphasis added):

> Attributes that contain emblemic style and assertive style vary from those that are detached from function and technology and are used largely to shape a point, such as shape of sides and barbs, to others that play an important role in the functional performance of an arrow—size, tip shape, and thickness. These results support the proposal of Stiles (1979) that *in choosing stylistic attributes, one should omit only attributes whose variation can be proven by experiment to be exclusively caused by function.* Until such variables are established by experiment, the method proposed by Close (1979) is effective if carried out conservatively. That is, *items and attributes on these items which vary over space are selected as potential carriers of social information, and then functional hypotheses that might explain this variation are systematically excluded.*

We see Wiessner balancing two different positions. Her assertion that style should be entirely removed from function echoes the partitioning present in Binford's and Sackett's models. By also making style a negative component of function, she defines her allegiance to a materialist approach. However, her data lead her to refute one of materialism's central tenets: the attributes she identifies as "actively stylistic" (size, tip shape, and thickness) are clearly "functional equivalents" that should remain "passively stylistic." By finding that these attributes are actively used to communicate information about identity, and are not adjunct to functional constraints, she undercuts her own materialist position. Predictably, Sackett's (1985a) critique points this out and states that what she identifies as emblemic style is in fact isochrestic variation. These attributes were never invested with messages, but were simply a part of the unconscious way San people met functional requirements. Her reply further downplays the importance of adaptive constraints: "Style can lapse into isochrestic variation if an artifact's symbolic role wanes and the stylistic comparison no longer incites social comparison. Likewise, if social meaning becomes attached to different isochrestic forms, isochrestic variation can be activated into style" (Wiessner 1985:163).

By looking at style and function as statuses related to idealism and materialism, we see that what is at stake is far more than the accurate interpretation of a few iron points. Wiessner's findings challenge the materialism at the heart of Binford's and Sackett's model. Indeed, her later revision of isochrestism actually pushes the balance in the opposite direction, effectively disconnecting functional equivalents from adaptive constraints and making style and cultural-historical processes the primary determinant of "functionally equivalent" variation. Ironically, Sackett alone recognizes this point (1990), with Wiessner and other commentators viewing the dispute as a question over whether style is generally "active" or "passive." The issue is more accurately whether patterns that play an ecological role can be actively manipulated for cultural-historical ends. For Binford and later Sackett, the relative positions of function and style make this a priori impossible.[1] In contrast, Wiessner's findings suggest that "functional equivalents" result from a far more complex interaction of ecological and cultural-historical processes. The exchange brings into sharp focus the broader paradox of how archaeologists should address the overlapping influences of culture-history and ecology in their explanations of formal variability.

Despite problems with functional equivalent forms of partitioning, other researchers continued to separate function and style with structural levels. This is clearly seen in evolutionary approaches to style (Braun 1995; Dunnell 1978a; Hill 1985; O'Brien and Holland 1990; also see Conkey 1978). David Braun (1995), for example, perceives different causal processes to operate at different scales of time. Like Binford, he argues that long-term selective pressures are essential to culture. The short-term activities of human agents create "blind" sources of variation acted upon by cultural and then by natural selection. Cultural selection filters variation by biasing what practices will be selected for transmission to subsequent generations, and natural selection acts upon those practices perpetuated across many generations. For Braun, style becomes important when it has transgenerational social effects:

> Stylistic practices *can* have social effects. These effects arise because, whether intentionally or not, people can and do use appearances to help them assess the social identity of an object's artisan or owner, or assess social similarities or differences between themselves and others... Nothing dictates that stylistic variation *must* have such social effects. However, when alternative stylistic practices *do* have different social effects, they necessarily will fall subject to cultural and natural selection. (Braun 1995:134; emphasis in original)

The selective processes that result in broad transgenerational patterns are the only cultural phenomenon that Braun believes can be explained (1995:137). As a result, short-term stylistic processes like drift or information exchange are epiphenomenal. Structural levels are thus key to his separation of style and function. Patterns are stylistic until they have social effects and evolutionary consequences, at which time then they have a functional

(ecological) role. Apparently, a pattern's temporal durability would indicate that it played such a functional role because, for a pattern to survive across generations, it must have an adaptive significance. However, this ignores the fact that historical processes can themselves form durable structures. Indeed, I take this to be the importance of Boyd and Richerson's (1985) "cultural selection," which argues behavioral patterns can exist for long periods without encountering natural selection,[2] and the Annales concept of *mentalités,* which suggests ideological processes may operate at the *longue durée.* To use Annales's terminology further, I see no reason to believe that selective processes alone affect the *longue durée* and it seems far more likely that many processes, both ecological and cultural-historical, operate across different temporal levels (see Cunningham n.d.; Hexter 1972:533, n.114).

In fact, postprocessual approaches to style actually invert the partitioning used by Braun and argue that cultural-historical processes alone form long-term structures. Ecological processes, while present, only operate in daily practice. Hodder's work on spatial analysis (Hodder and Orton 1976) and his subsequent ethnoarchaeological studies (Hodder 1982a) greatly challenged the dominance of the materialist model by showing how material culture could be actively manipulated in different situations to emphasize or hide social similarities and differences. Instead of a passive reflection of society, all aspects of material culture, including those conventionally thought to be functional, suddenly became a medium through which social life was actively created (Conkey 1990). Drawing on practice theorists like Bourdieu (1977) and Giddens (1979), Hodder (1982a, 1982b, 1985) argued that a cognitive framework structures daily practice, which in turn, reconstitutes the structure. The framework is made up of binary oppositions similar to those advocated by Lévi-Strauss (1968).[3] Among the Nuba, for example, Hodder (1982a:215) identifies oppositions such as "clean/dirty, male/female and life/death" and argues that these form a unique cognitive framework of meaning that directs the "social and ecological strategies" found in daily practice. The meaning found in this structure is key to Hodder's understanding of cultural behavior:

Cultural patterning is...both the *framework within which action and adaptation have meaning*, and it is also reproduced in those actions and in the adaptive responses that are made. There is no dichotomy between an interest in culture and meaning and a concern with adaptive variability. Indeed, interpretation of the past must integrate both research aims. (Hodder 1982a:214, emphasis added)

When compared to the processual models of Binford, Sackett, and even Wiessner, the postprocessual approach to style is quite conservative. Except evolutionary approaches, processual models all posited a separate area of variation shaped exclusively by cultural-historical processes (e.g., iconic style). Despite their materialism, they were thus able to address some elements of normative behavior. In contrast, postprocessual archaeology places ecological influences in daily practice that is itself dictated by the cognitive framework. While ecological processes may influence variation, they only do so within the limits imposed by the cognitive framework. This reorientation universalizes an inverted version of Binford's "functional equivalents," with ecological processes holding the same epiphenomenal position under postprocessualism that stylistic drift did for processual approaches (see Hodder, especially 1986 Chapter 2). As Hodder tells us, "style comes to have a central place in archaeological discourse because it refers to the historical particularity of culture and can be observed in all spheres of life, since all spheres are meaningful. Thus the economy is as much stylistic as the decoration on a potsherd" (Hodder 1985: 10; also see Hodder 1982b, 1986, 1990a). Shanks and Tilley make a similar point by arguing that, if a pot's "adaptive role" is as a container, all it needs are four walls and a bottom (1987:86–95; 1992:140–145). Everything else is style (also see Miller 1985, Chapter 4).

It is worth briefly digressing to note that postprocessual studies of style are able to sustain such a position because they stay clear of variation that would require some consideration of ecological process. Instead, they focus on patterns that would be "stylistic" even by processual standards, like decorative elements and rock art (Braithwaite 1982; Conkey 1982; Hodder 1982a; Shanks and Tilley 1992, Chapter 8; Wiessner 1989; Yates 1989), burial practices (Hodder 1984, 1990b; Shanks and Tilley 1982), and the organization of domestic space and architecture (Hodder 1982a; Moore 1982; see also Morris 1995; Neitzel 1995). In doing so, postprocessualist researchers have paralleled processualists who have long focused on "adjunct" dimensions of variability like decoration (e.g., the "learning/interactionist" approaches of Deetz 1965; Hill 1970; Longacre 1964, 1970; Whallon 1968; see Hegmon 1992 and Plog 1976, 1978, 1983 for reviews and critiques). In dealing with the same subject matter (stylistic variation in the most conventional sense), both processualists and postprocessualists have found a common bond, despite ongoing conflicts over epistemology. Later reviewers have even come to see Hodder's version of style simply as a more "active" or "dialectical" approach in a general field of stylistic studies (Braun 1995; Carr and Neitzel 1995a; Hegmon 1992; Vos and Younge 1995; Wiessner 1990). As a result, Sackett's and Wiessner's brief but informative exchange remains the last time that anyone has considered the partitioning underlying the distinction between style and function.

The models I have just reviewed all follow softer forms of essentialism because they hold that culture-history and ecology both influence human behavior. Integration is possible because these models separate both sets of processes into distinct areas of culture. Two other approaches avoid the difficulties of partitioning and instead argue that either ecological or cultural-historical processes influence the entire range of variation. To do this, they adopt more extreme forms of essentialism than we have seen above. In the first case, proponents of behavioral archaeology have argued that "style" and "function" are vacuous terms lacking explanatory power (Schiffer 1999b; Schiffer and Skibo 1987, 1997). Instead, Schiffer and Skibo develop a materialist-centered model that they claim "incorporates all causes of variability and establishes standards for specific explanation" (1997:28). The model they propose draws heavily on technology studies (e.g. Lechtman 1977, 1984; Lemonnier 1986, 1989) and focuses on the interactions that occur along different stages of a "behavioral chain." For example, procurement, design, manufacture and use would represent different stages in the chain, with each stage including patterned interactions between people, or between people and their environment. These patterned interactions are *any kind of matter-energy transaction*—mechanical, chemical, thermal, electrical, electromagnetic, visual, acoustic, etc." (Schiffer and Skibo 1997:29, emphasis in original). The technical choices made in the behavioral chain result in an object having specific formal properties (such as thermal shock resistance) that affect its overall performance in the cultural milieu. Thus, the influences of the local environment do not condition a distinct "functional" area of culture, but permeate every aspect of variation. For example, their brief but informative discussion of "visual performance characteristics" suggests that even archaeological patterns conventionally assigned a stylistic status (like elaborate decorations on tableware) may be subject to a series of technological constraints (Schiffer and Skibo 1997:37–43). These constraints are not negligible, but can exert a substantial influence on patterns that would be given a stylistic status by other models.

At times, the materialist focus of Schiffer and Skibo's model demonstrates the pitfalls of adopting such an extreme position. In order to stick closely to behavioralist tenets, cultural patterns must be explained without any reference to ideas. At times, extensive maneuvering is required to sustain this position, especially in Schiffer's attempt to develop a theory of communication that does not refer at all to symbols, interpretations, or

even memory (Schiffer 1999b:204). Instead he uses neologisms like "correlon" to fulfill the role "ideas" would play in a less dogmatic model (1999b:204–205). Interestingly, the proponents have briefly suggested that other bodies of theory may be needed to investigate historical questions focused on the social context (Schiffer and Skibo 1997:44), but it awaits to be seen how the authors will articulate them with their own framework. We may yet see more moderate perspectives emerge within behavioral archaeology.

The antithesis of behavioral archaeology's materialism is found among the various poststructural and interpretive archaeologies (e.g., Bapty and Yates 1990a; Boast 1997; Thomas 1996b; Tilley 1990, 1999). It is difficult to do justice to poststructuralist archaeology because of the diversity of positions held (Bapty and Yates 1990b), but as the name implies poststructuralists tend to reject a "structural" backdrop to human behavior. Thus, social, economic, or cognitive structures do not exist, but are created anew during social praxis. This nominalism tends toward an idealist cultural ontology that emphasizes the interpretive and idiosyncratic standpoint of each person's experience. These idiosyncrasies form a loosely shared *structure of intelligibility*" (Thomas 1996b:65) through which we are made aware of the world. Thus, our knowledge is not based on a dissociated appraisal of empirical phenomena, but on our socialization within a world built of indexical meaning. Artifacts are thus remnants of the way people created their subjective realities in the past. Furthermore, there is no neutral medium for the investigation of these artifacts in the present, because they only become understandable to us through our own structures of intelligibility. The implication is that a "correct" interpretation (i.e., correspondence with the world as it exists) cannot be generated because archaeologists—just like the people archaeologists study—are unable to transcend their structures of intelligibility to access anything fully independent (see Karlsson 1998; Thomas 1996b:235). Poststructuralist researchers thus embrace a strong form of relativism.

Instead of studying cultural systems, they investigate issues like "temporality" (Thomas 1996b), metaphor (Tilley 1999), material landscapes (Barrett 1994), and the way that artifacts themselves take on agentive qualities (Boast 1997 after Latour 1987; also see Ashmore et al. 1994). Style as a concept has little use because it assumes that "the significance of the form and decoration of material items is relatively fixed and bounded, and remains stable through time. However, it is increasingly clear that different aspects of an artifact's style and form may be drawn upon and foregrounded from moment to moment in social discourse..." (Thomas 1996b:209). While we might be skeptical of the cultural dependency poststructuralists assign to the physical world, their analyses do underscore the importance of conceptual schemes in orienting daily practice. Not only is human existence constituted through religion and ideology, but even our most banal and ecologically driven activities are shaped by how we conceptualize the world and see our place within it. In terms of the present analysis, such an orientation reminds us that cultural-historical processes affect dimensions of variability far beyond those to which we conventionally assigned to style.

These two last examples demonstrate two things. First, more essentialist forms of materialism and idealism reject terms like style and function. This is expected. As I suggested earlier, these statuses have been introduced to address the complex influences of ecology and culture-history. Because strongly essentialist approaches tend to focus on only one set of processes, they have little need for such distinctions. Second, these approaches suggest, I think correctly, that ecological and historical influences extend beyond the boundaries conventionally established by partitioning. Despite a half-century of research, archaeologists have yet to agree on how style and function should be separated (through mutually exclusive patterns or by structural partitions) or whether the separation should favor a materialist or idealist ontology of culture. Regardless of which model we would support, what seems ab-

solutely clear is that these frameworks limit the sort of analysis that can be undertaken. The Binfordian model's partitioning makes it very difficult to analyze how the cultural-historical processes affect "function" or how ecological processes affect "style"; postprocessual and evolutionary archaeology's reliance on structural partitioning effectively limits the importance of ecological or cultural-historical processes respectively; and behavioral and poststructural archaeology's focus on just one set of processes precludes on a priori grounds which processes may be investigated. When it comes to issues of style, it seems that archaeologists are not in an enviable position. If anything, the paradox that opened this discussion—and formed the core of the Sackett-Wiessner debate—is again of fundamental importance: How do we begin to explain archaeological patterns when we know human behavior results from the simultaneous influence of cultural-historical and ecological process?

DISCUSSION: DISUNIFYING STYLE AND FUNCTION

The above discussion constitutes an attempt to situate style and function within broader discourses in the social sciences—to tie "on the ground" terminology to metanarrative. Nowhere is this more needed than in the style literature. Many of the current style discussions effectively "talk past one another" because these terms have rarely been placed in their broader theoretical context. One result has been the tendency to treat "style" and "function" as cultural givens; as properties of cultural systems rather than as tools in our own analysis. In such an environment, it becomes easy to believe that "style" is a thing—an attribute to be found or an essence to be uncovered (after McIntosh 1992). Earlier, two unresolved questions regarding style were introduced: "What does style do?" and "Where in formal variation does style reside?" It should now be clear that both questions reflect the idea that style is a special area of variation where historical processes are concentrated and ecological processes are absent; it is through "style" that we should see social and cognitive life in the past. In contrast, the above analysis is meant to show that "style" in archaeology is an artifact of our analyses. It is a product of the way we have sought to explain the patterns we uncover.

But to complete the hermeneutic we need to cycle back to metanarrative. I have been suggesting that the problem we have with style and function originates in our own attempts to integrate the broad-range concepts of materialism and idealism. Similar difficulties have been encountered by other social sciences with which we share this element of our disciplinary history. Ecological anthropology, to give one example, exhibits a similar tendency to essentialize and partition the influence of ecology and culture-history. The most recent theoretical school to arrive on the scene, termed the "New Ecology" (with all the flair of the "New Archaeology" in its heyday), is an idealist reaction to the vulgar materialism of 1960s and 1970s (e.g., Harris 1974; see Biersack 1999; Ellen 1982; and Escobar 1999 for overviews). Occasionally, proponents of the New Ecology go as far as to deny the existence of nature as anything other than an ideational construct (e.g., Escobar 1999). Such "antiessentialism," which should be seen as an equally essentialist form of antimaterialism, closely reflects the positions held by postprocessualism and poststructuralism, because ecological constraints are taken to be nonexplanatory (see Stonich 1999). Minnegal (1996) has even suggested that researchers need to identify spheres of behavior that relate directly to ecology and culture-history. She introduces the partitioning theme by arguing that instead of simply choosing between different explanations of behavior, "we need to explore the articulation between the two" (Minnegal 1996:141). In this case, Minnegal identifies specific areas where these explanations apply: ecological explanations are used to describe the effects production has on patterns of consumption, while social explanations are found in the way consumption activities feed back into production. Despite her comparatively balanced separation of these two spheres, it

seems unlikely that this model will bear fruit when we reflect upon our own problems with style and function. Undoubtedly, social and ecological explanations can be generated for the full spectrum of the production-consumption cycle. More importantly, the parallel uses of essentialism and partitioning in ecological anthropology and in archaeology indicates that these may be common strategies to account for the dichotomy imposed by materialist and idealist readings of culture.

For this reason, I suspect it is far easier to make low-cost statements to the effect that we need to move past the materialist-dichotomy and develop a new synthesis than it is to put such a wish into practice. Even Marxism, long recognized as the most ambitious attempt to synthesize the materialist-idealist chasm into a single model of culture, has since dissipated into a series of more "sectarian" interests (to use Trigger's [1993] vocabulary). Rather than integration, the major—but by no means distinct—streams of structural and critical Marxism in archaeology respectively emphasize either Marx's later materialism or follow the Frankfurt School in stressing his early Hegelian and more idealistic tendencies (see McGuire 1993; Trigger 1993). While the analysis remains to be done, I suspect a familiar pattern of essentialism and partitioning may lurk here as well; although, it is probably far more visible in Marxism's "on the ground" applications than in theoretical posturing. Proponents of the models outlined above would also be quick to remind us that their frameworks aim to create just such a synthetic view of culture. With the possible exception of behavioral archaeology and poststructuralism, all of the models so far discussed make very real attempts to integrate materialist and idealist perspectives in a single explanation of archaeological variability. And all of them seem to believe that their solutions resolve Childe's Paradox. Yet, the analysis above shows that, despite their complexity and sophistication, each model continues to treat culture as if it made up of two sets of alternative "givens"—of distinct, immutable truths that can only be integrated by keeping them entirely separate.

If partitioning and essentialism are inevitable outcomes of a synthetic solution to materialism and idealism, then I would recommend we move away from artificial attempts at syntheses and adopt a robust form of pluralism. At the very least, this would allow us to recognize that style and function are perspectives on variation rather than properties of cultural systems. Pluralism would also let us bypass the artificial limits that were placed on analysis by the preceding models by enabling us to conduct "stylistic" and "functional" investigations of all cultural patterns. But, to adopt pluralism, it is necessary to make two important conceptual adjustments. First, we need to remain theoretically agnostic toward the competing *cultural ontologies* of materialism and idealism.[4] The truisms in Childe's Paradox each capture an important facet of culture—in that they reflect real processes that affect human behavior—yet they do not represent essential and mutually exclusive divisions in culture. Instead, they should be seen as useful heuristics: as different perspectives on a very complex phenomenon. Second, rather than investigating "style" and "function," we should focus more explicitly on the underlying processes encapsulated by each term. This adjustment opens up two complementary axes of research that allow us to get a better understanding of archaeological variability. First, we can ask how a single process affects formal variability in different contexts. Second, we can begin to examine how different processes combine to create specific patterns in the archaeological record. I should be clear that by emphasizing patterns, I am not advocating a narrow form of classificationism. Archaeologists of all persuasions find themselves explaining patterns in material culture, whether their focus is contextual and interpretive or more processual. An emphasis on patterns may also seem contrary to Conkey's (1999:137–138) suggestion that we focus less on patterning and more on people, but I suspect that our goals are the same. We find people through archaeological patterns, and to focus on people we need to know how they relate to the patterns we can observe. Focusing on people in the past is thus not a matter of ignoring variability, but of recognizing the complex array of processes that cause variability.

By seeking to answer how specific cultural processes affect variability, we encounter a methodological issue that previous models of style and function appeared to solve. Archaeological sites contain an astounding amount of variability. Even in a single medium like pottery we find many cross-cutting morphological, decorative, and composition patterns, each with unique distributions across space and through time. The partitioning found in the preceding models limited us to specific start points for different types of research. An investigation of ethnicity should begin by looking at decorative variability rather than temper; while patterns in temper were thought to tell us about ecological processes in a way that decoration could not. Carr and Neitzel's approach (1995a, 1995b; see especially Carr 1995a, 1995b) is perhaps the most detailed attempt to develop such relationships. The authors painstakingly design an entire framework of cross-cultural causal processes and aim to demonstrate how each relates to patterns of variability. Unfortunately, their methodological shortcuts ultimately rest on the sort of partitioning I have outlined above. If we adopt a pluralistic solution to Childe's Paradox, then we need to begin by questioning exactly these kinds of theoretical proxies. General relationships between processes and patterns may eventually support methodological shortcuts, and many shortcuts we currently enjoy may even be found reliable, but these need to be built up empirically. For now, I would suggest that we expand our research to look at areas that have been ignored. For example, how do ecological processes affect decoration? Or are there patterns in morphology or even temper that reflect an explicit attempt to symbolize group identity? These are questions that were difficult to ask under conventional programs of research, and it is here that we should begin new analysis.

In suggesting that we move our focus from style and function to the specific processes that affect archaeological patterns, I am not advocating that style and function be completely exercised from archaeological theory. In archaeology, style and function epitomize the original "middle-range problem"—a problem that should be addressed through further ethnoarchaeological work and more innovative methodologies. Yet, the real predicament has not between middle-range theories and the data, but results from the disassociation of these middle-range theories from the high-level propositions that give them life. If we simply replace style and function with "processes," and investigate processes as if they, too, were somehow completely independent from broad-range theory, then we risk recreating rather than transcending the essentialism and partitioning that define existing approaches to artifact variability. Recognized as statuses, however, style and function can act as provisional frames of reference —as benign, middle-range reminders that the opposition between idealism and materialism is an active constituent in our programs of research.

A pluralistic approach has already been recognized as the most promising method to investigate the way that different processes combine in a particular archaeological pattern (Conkey 1999; Sackett 1990). Unfortunately, nowhere has a pluralistic approach to variability been developed in detail, and to do so here would be to digress far beyond the bounds of the present discussion (see Longino 2002, Chapter 8 for a succinct overview of pluralism). To my own mind, John Dupré's (1993) form of pluralism—provocatively titled "promiscuous realism"—is perhaps the best available model for an analysis of artifact variability.[5] Briefly, Dupré's pluralism rejects the essentialism we see with materialism and idealism and instead begins from the position that the world is a complex place. Complexity is an inherent (i.e., ontological) component of the world, with multiple processes operating across many scales of order. Scientists bring into focus different parts of this complexity depending on the purposes they use to frame their analysis. It is thus possible to perceive the world from several theoretical standpoints, many or all of which may be scientifically valid. In Dupré's program, this pluralism is combined with categorical empiricism. While the purposes behind a body of research will bring part of the world into focus, the empirical patterns that emerge constrain which interpretations appear plausible. For example, biological species have been defined differently according to which properties of the individual organisms are considered important for the taxonomy (Dupré 1993; also see Ereshefsky 1995, 1998): cladistic taxonomies will focus on DNA patterns, morphological taxonomies will examine patterns in gross attributes; and taxonomy based on sexual compatibility will look at the ability of organisms to interbreed. These different approaches can result in the same individual organism being ascribed to different species. However, this does not preclude that these groupings continue to reflect an empirical reality—the patterns uncovered by each approach are discernable breaks in the order of the world. They thus actively constrain interpretation. By combining explicit purposes and empiricism, Dupré is able to propose a form of pluralism that does not rest in relativism:

> Certainly I can see no possible reason why commitment to many overlapping kinds of things should threaten the reality of any of them. A certain entity might be a real whale, a real mammal, [or] a real top predator...Many, perhaps all, of these designations might be the appropriate characterization of that object for some legitimately scientific purpose. (Dupré 1993:262)

The obvious concern with such a framework is knowing when our interpretations are more and less plausible. Seemingly, a pluralistic approach would cast us free in a sea of theory, with no firm bottom on which to drop an anchor. Indeed, previous approaches to style were able to assess their interpretations according to their conformity with certain theoretical "givens." Sackett's rejection of Wiessner's ethnographic study is a prime example of exactly this sort of evaluation. However, while a pluralistic approach does reduce the importance of these axioms in the appraisal of interpretations, it does not leave us adrift. Instead, these premises move from venerated truths to purposeful standpoints that themselves must be critically evaluated and justified. To this end, Dupré argues that interpretations need to be assessed according to epistemic virtues[6] like "sensitivity to empirical fact, plausible background assumptions, coherence with other things we know, [and] exposure to criticism from the widest variety of sources" (Dupré 1993:243; also see Wylie 2000). These criteria are not new to archaeologists. VanPool and VanPool (1999) have demonstrated that processual and postprocessual archaeology already employ a body of common epistemic norms nearly identical to those put forward by Dupré. Thus, moving away from essentialism does not require a substantial shift in research practice. On the other hand, a pluralistic approach could allow us to make better interpretations. As Wylie has shown several times (1992, 1999, 2000), archaeologists use the pluralism created by gender research, the use of historical sources and the disunities in scientific practice to create increasingly secure interpretations. If research based in independent premises triangulates on the same interpretation, then it is likely correct because it would be miraculous for the biases in each approach to all end in the same false conclusion (see especially Wylie 1999, 2000). This epistemic virtue, which is described elsewhere as robustness (e.g., Wimsatt 1994:210–211), becomes a technique we can use more explicitly if we adopt a pluralistic approach to variability. Therefore, over time an epistemology based on robust pluralism may be more solidly grounded and productive than the one it would replace.

Competing investigations of process, including those framed in terms of "style" or "function," may provide a series of checks and balances against the erroneous interpretation of archaeological patterns. We must await future research to see exactly how such an approach will form, but my own analysis

of early Late Woodland pottery hints at its potential. My project examined the stylistic processes that influenced decorative variation from the Van Bree site, a small eleventh-century occupation located on a border between Western Basin and Iroquoian peoples in southwestern Ontario (Cunningham 1999, 2001). The site consists of 45 ceramic vessels, a small circular house, and a number of pit features running along a sandy ridge above a tributary of the Ausable River. Pottery from the site contained a mixture of attributes from both Western Basin and Ontario Iroquoian traditions. I hypothesized that the site's occupants were a group of people who lived in a "borderland" between Iroquoian and Western Basin groups. The variation in their assemblage thus symbolized their hybrid and ambiguous social identity. I began the analysis by seeking finer temporal control over the site so I could assess the amount of decorative variation that was typical for a single occupation. Following Timmins (1997), I used a ceramic crossmend analysis to identify roughly contemporaneous pit features on the site. By mapping overlaps, I was able to find two distinct clusters of features. Unexpectedly, this procedure resulted in one cluster containing all the "typical" Western Basin tradition pottery while the other cluster only contained vessels with Iroquoian characteristics. Instead of hybridization, it appeared that the site was sequentially occupied by distinct groups of Western Basin and Iroquoian people. Moreover, when I considered the spatial distribution of the features and received the results of two radiocarbon dates, it seemed that these occupations may have occurred within the same generation. If this was the case, then the Van Bree site showed that distinct decorative tendencies were maintained right up to each group's territorial boundary. My hypothesis was therefore adjusted to examine whether or not these distinct styles reflect the explicit attempt by both groups to symbolize their ethnic identities.

To assess the new hypotheses, I initiated two lines of investigation. The first line of analysis assessed the assemblage using a standard "stylistic" approach: I attempted to identify attributes that were relatively homogeneous within each assemblage but that varied between the two clusters. My goal was to thus identify those attributes that may have been "emblematic" of ethnic identity (after Wiessner 1983). The ensuing attribute analysis did uncover a number of attributes whose patterning was consistent with this expectation (see Cunningham 1999:52–58, 2001 for details). The second line of investigation focused in more detail on variation within each cluster of features. The goal was to look at whether individual potters could be identified on the basis of habitual mechanical tendencies and/or the use of the same decorative tool. The ensuing information could then be used to assess the degree that individual potters were conforming to a template of "emblemic" variation. The outcome of this analysis was that it demonstrated a series of relationships between production and ceramic variation. Despite the fact that one or two potters probably produced most of the pots from the Western Basin component (see Murphy and Ferris 1990), no individual potters could be identified in this cluster. Instead, the assemblage is characterized by a high amount of variability. This variability appears to result from the combined influence of small-scale and infrequent manufacture and the use of expedient potting tools. Except for those few general tendencies outlined by the attribute analysis, vessels appear to have been decorated differently each time they were made. Vessels from the Iroquoian cluster likewise suggested the use of expedient decorative tools, however there is evidence of one potter with a distinct mechanical tendency; in two cases the same tool was used on two different vessels. A higher rate of ceramic production is the most likely explanation for this pattern and also accounts for greater degree of homogeneity observable in the Iroquoian assemblage. Notably, the vessels that shared decorative tools also tended to share some decorative motifs, suggesting that these were repeated during production.

When combined, these two lines of analysis hint at the complexity behind decorative variation. While each cluster does appear to relate to distinct ethnic entities that followed different decorative programs, symbolizing ethnicity does not appear to have been the main process affecting ceramic decoration. If it were, the decorative patterns should have shown more resistance to the effects of production. Instead, the scale and frequency of production seems to have had a direct effect on ceramic variation. These findings are relatively unexpected given the conventional lore—drawn from the style-function distinction—about which causal processes should determine decorative patterning.

CONCLUSION

As we have seen, many of the problems with style and function originate in our attempt to integrate materialist and idealist assumptions about culture into a single approach to artifact variability. To do this, it has been necessary to essentialize one set of processes at the expense of the other and/or to partition culture into discrete ecological and cultural-historical spheres. The effect of this strategy has been the a priori marginalization of certain questions, despite the fact that—as Childe's Paradox underscores—ecological and cultural-historical processes impact the entire range of human behavior. Culture is far more complex than either idealist or materialist ontologies of culture have so far presupposed. To account for this complexity, an agnostic position must be adopted that treats materialist and idealist cultural ontologies as useful heuristics within a pluralistic environment. From this position, we can begin to investigate how processes combine in the production of archaeological patterns.

Two larger lessons can be gleaned from the style-function problem. First, style and function have always been on-the-ground notions fundamental to "getting on" with the task of interpreting the archaeological record. That these "practical concepts" are inextricably linked to the sort of broad-range theory generally left in the custody of "theorists" should perhaps suggest that we need to rethink the way our labors are allocated. Not only does broad-range theory directly affect the way we perform archaeology's most mundane tasks, such as sorting "styles" in the lab, but the results of those sorts may in turn give us the ability to reassess those broad-range principles. Research programs that move up and down the latticework of theory may therefore be more productive than those that focus primarily on either "theoretical" or "applied" topics. In a similar vein, it is important to underscore that the essentialism found in the different style models systematically limits research in some areas. This problem echoes many other critical analyses that look at how colonial, gendered, or racial biases create "silences" or "blind spots" in scientific research (contributions to Schmidt and Patterson 1995; Trigger 1980; Trouillot 1995; Wylie 1992, 1999). In terms of style, it is not the imposition of societal biases that results in "silences" (although we could undoubtedly make such connections and trace the evolution of style models through postwar scientism to postmodernism), but the tendency to focus on certain questions that render others inaccessible. We need to be aware that, even while pursuing lines of research that appear "politically innocent," we unavoidably create blind spots that may have unforeseen consequences (Cunningham n.d.). We need to enact research that allows us to minimize—or at least recognize—where blind spots of this sort occur. A pluralistic approach is an important step toward this goal. It will not stop omissions (given the complexity of our subject, this is unavoidable) but it should reduce the systematic exclusion that has so far typified dominant models of artifact variability.

ACKNOWLEDGMENTS

I would like to thank Todd and Chris Van-Pool for inviting me to contribute this paper to their edited volume despite not being present at the original SAA conference session. My investigation of style in archaeology began with my M.A. thesis in the Department of Anthropology at the University of Western Ontario. I would like to thank my supervisors at UWO, Mike Spence and Alison Wylie, for their advice and support. I would like to thank Neal Ferris, who introduced me to the Van Bree site, and for our many discussions about ceramic variation in southwestern Ontario. My original argument was substantially revised and expanded while I was a doctoral candidate in the Department of Anthropology at McGill University. I would like to thank my supervisor at McGill, Bruce Trigger, for his always insightful readings of the many versions of this essay. Aubrey Cannon, Neal Ferris, Scott MacEachern, Robert Preucel, Jerome Rousseau, Mike Spence, Todd and Chris VanPool, and three anonymous reviewers have offered comments on different drafts of the manuscript, and although I have not been able to address all of their remarks, their suggestions helped me greatly clarify the argument. An abstracted version of this paper was given in the session "Style and Theory" at the 33rd Annual Chacmool Conference in Calgary entitled "Art for Archaeology's Sake: Material Culture and Style across the Disciplines." Any errors or omissions are my responsibility.

Notes

1. It is worth pointing out that Binford has not recognized Sackett as a supporter of his materialist goals. Binford (1989:64) charges that Sackett holds a "commitment to traditional ideas of cultural variability" because he links ethnicity with functionally equivalent variation.

2. While I agree that cultures fall under selective pressures, I see no reason to claim that *all* cultural behaviors need to be explained in reference to these selective pressures. The attempt to reduce behaviors to some materialist cause, such as Boyd and Richerson's (1985:204–205) assertion that kamikazes' beliefs are not explained through their relation to samurai military code but must be seen in terms of the evolutionary consequences of altruism, seem to me entirely unrealistic.

3. In taking this position, Hodder draws from theoreticians such as Bourdieu and Giddens who, because of their emphasis on the reproduction of structures through practice, are often described as poststructuralist rather than structuralist. Indeed, much of Hodder's theoretical work could be described as a form of poststructuralism, but his actual interpretations of style seem to rely on a more structuralist approach (see Hodder 1982a, 1990a, 1990b).

4. There is a difference between treating materialist and idealist *ontologies of culture* as heuristics and the statement that *idealism* and

materialism are equally valid ontological positions that should be treated heuristically. I find Trigger's (1998; following Boyd and Richerson 1985) argument for a materialist ontology based on an evolutionary perspective entirely persuasive. As his discussion outlines, idealist ontologies are largely untenable. Culture—as a historically based system of learned behavior—has provided, and continues to provide, an evolutionary advantage to human populations. Hence, what we generally consider to be "idealism" can be subsumed within a materialist understanding of how culture helped humans evolve. As several commentators on earlier versions of this paper have pointed out, in the light of evolutionary theory there is no general paradox to what I identify as "Childe's Paradox." However, if the integration of idealism within evolutionary theory explains why "ideas" are an important part of human evolution, it provides little guidance for those who wish to explain specific behaviors, under-

stand cultural regularities, or account for patterns in the archaeological record. At the level of *cultural ontology* (the foundational propositions about the structure/nature/purpose of "Culture"), then, the paradox between idealism and materialism remains unresolved; and it is here, in our ontologies of culture, that I would suggest we consider the tenets of idealism and materialism to be heuristic.

5. What follows is a very limited overview of Dupré's philosophy that does not capture the complexity or extent of his arguments against essentialism (which are disputed in some cases; see Davies 1996; Ereshefsky 1995). I have also not mentioned his treatment of reductionism and determinism, both of which are fundamental to his argument for "promiscuous realism." Readers are directed to Dupré's original text and to numerous reviews and critiques.

6. Kuhn (1986) and Bohman (1991) have outlined comparable criteria.

5

Materiality and the Immaterial in Historical–Processual Archaeology

Timothy R. Pauketat

After years of archaeological debate over the epistemological underpinnings of culture-historical, processual, and postprocessual archaeology, VanPool and VanPool (1999) have asked, are not all archaeologists, including postprocessualists, doing "scientific archaeology" (see also Preucel 1995)? Their affirmative answer to that question seemingly dissolves years of contentious debate and denies postprocessualism the status of "paradigm," in the sense of Kuhn (1970). Or does it? While VanPool and VanPool are doubtless correct, the question posed and answered—are not most archaeologists scientific?—is not the question that defines what I have elsewhere called an emerging paradigm in archaeology (Pauketat 2001a, 2001b, 2003). The crucial paradigmatic question, in fact, is not epistemological at all, but ontological and processual: how did people produce and reproduce culture?

Anthropologists and their forerunners have asked this question repeatedly and in different ways. For example, Thomas Hobbes (1985) pondered how the multitudes united to create "common-wealths." Emile Durkheim (1964) saw collective consciousness as the basis for society, while Karl Marx extended the logic to political-cultural domination via "ideologies" (Marx and Engels 1989). More recently, Pierre Bourdieu (1977) identified "orthodoxies" as the politicized or unified "doxas" of everyday life, while Michel-

Rolph Trouillot (1995) helps explain how this may be understood as a history-making process. Even archaeological considerations of everything from styles to civilizations are ultimately studies of how "peoples" become "a people" (e.g., Conkey 1990; Jones 1997; Renfrew 1987; Wheatley 1975). So how did people create cultures?

My answer draws on many contemporary varieties of archaeology—postprocessual, processual, culture-historical, feminist, cognitive-processual, neo-Darwinian, and historical-materialist—and it points to a real paradigmatic shift only partially realized by the postprocessual debate. This shift, what I have elsewhere labeled "historical processualism" (Pauketat 2001b), entails an alteration in how we conceive of culture and process, and it involves a change in how we explain the past. These modifications rest on the principles of "materiality" and "spatiality" (see Joyce and Hendon 2000; Thomas 1996b; Tilley 1994). For present purposes, I focus on materiality in order to explicate the impending change in how we explain the past.

A thorough review of this emerging paradigm is beyond the scope of this paper, and may prove premature. That is, historical processualism does not yet exist fully formed as a paradigm even though many different practicing archaeologists would fall within its still-vague bounds at present, including many people who are not sure what to call themselves. Whatever it is or becomes, historical processualism is more than the theoretical reconciliation of various sorts of archaeologies. It is a new common sense that cultures are not static, shared, systemic, or integrated wholes. They are "better seen as a series of processes that construct, reconstruct, and dismantle cultural materials" (Wolf 1982: 387). These processes occur through space and material media. That is, they have a spatiality and a materiality, which gives archaeology considerable explanatory opportunity unrealized in other "paradigms."

I will return to the processes of how people make cultures—cultural construction—following a brief introduction to historical processualism and a review of three well-known archaeological cases. The cases are used to illustrate the significance of understanding the materiality of cultural construction. The upshot of this consideration of materiality, cultural construction, and historical processualism is the promise that archaeological theory is reemerging in a "holistic" sense out of the ashes of thirty years of debate (Schiffer 1999a; Trigger 1991).

HISTORICAL PROCESSUALISM

VanPool and VanPool (1999:48) conclude by advising postprocessualists not to "adopt a new name indicating their scientific status, or change their behavior or research to ensure that they remain scientific." I would agree only to the extent that postprocessualists ever existed as a group. However, I would also argue that the approach emerging out of recent theoretical debates is neither postprocessual, as commonly understood, nor processual. In fact, it shares certain attributes with both traditional culture-history and a straightforward historical archaeology, in addition to the array of contemporary approaches mentioned earlier (see Pauketat 2001b). Given this, there is sufficient reason to call for a new label that crosscuts the old ones: historical processualism.

The primary point of overlap of the various historical-processual approaches is the concern for understanding *how* cultures changed. "How" here is a historical question, unlike "why" questions that appeal to law-like universal statements about human behavior. As opposed to those ultimate why questions, answering how demands understanding the "genealogies" of production, the "biographies" of artifacts, the histories of "negotiations," the "sequences of technical operations" or "technological styles," and even the "phenomenology" of landscapes (Dietler and Herbich 1989, 1998; Dobres 1999; Dobres and Hoffman 1994; Joyce 2000; Joyce and Hendon 2000; Kopytoff 1986; Lechtman 1977; Pauketat 2000b; Shennan 1993; Thomas 1996b; Tilley 1994; van der Leeuw 1993, 1994). Answering how, that is, means improving and expanding our cultural histories, paying particular attention to data-rich arrays of what Shennan (1993) and others have called "micro-scale" evidence in order to comprehend the significance of macroscale patterns. This said, it is crucial to note two significant differences between historical processualism and various other approaches. The differences center on the uses and abuses of behavior and structure as conceptual devices.

The Problem of Behavior

Behavior can be a relatively benign term if it is used as a synonym for action. Certainly, many archaeologists use it without intending to insinuate that action is repetitive, redundant, and uniform. Unfortunately, despite intentions (or lack thereof), the idea of behavior does promote just such a sense of intergroup regularity, often rooted in the belief that action is motivated by a universal rationality that is hard-wired into the human animal. For instance, "Behavioral Archaeology" could be seen to reinforce a sense that all people discarded objects in the same way in accordance with least-effort principles (Schiffer 1995). Likewise, optimization and risk avoidance models posit that all people, under certain abstract economic conditions, behave alike. When taken to a logical extreme, behaviors are construed as phenotypes: internally homogeneous, static, and subject to "selection" (O'Brien and Holland 1990:35).

Change, from this selectionist perspective, is a shift in proportions of behaviors through time, since the phenotypes themselves do not change save through "mutations" (i.e., innovations; see O'Brien et al. 1994:294).

What is wrong with such a notion of behavior? For starters, it makes the practices of people, which vary from time to time and place to place (contingent on cultural histories), seem as if they are uniform qualities of populations. If one assumes such a behavioral position, even inadvertently, one need not pay attention to the seemingly mundane variation of everyday living. Behaviorists generalize about households, communities, or societies without worrying about the broader implications of the continuous context-contingent alterations in human actions and representations. Cooking in a grit-tempered pot, such behaviorists might say, was a behavior that would change only when an external or technological pressure altered the cooking or the temper choice, irrespective of where and with (or for) whom that cooking or temper selection occurred.

Opposed to this invariate, phenotypic view of behavior is the increasingly popular notion of practice (e.g., Dobres 2000; Dobres and Hoffman 1994; Hendon 1996; Lightfoot et al. 1998; Pauketat 1994, 2000b). Practices are the actions, embodiments, or representations of people: cooking, hunting, manufacturing, singing, transporting, abandoning, building, etc. Importantly, practices are context contingent. How people practice is *always* contingent on the social context: the circumstances and relationships of the experience matter. Practices, no matter how mundane, are situated in culturally charged fields of relations that continually change *through the practices* themselves, even if they *seem* to remain unchanged at some scales of analysis. Thus, even the most mundane act is actually a "negotiation" of meaning, power, tradition, gender, and the like (see Pauketat 2001a, 2001b).[1] Contexts change; associations change; the balance of power changes. Intentionally or not, practices create change, sometimes profound, sometimes not. They do not "reflect" macroscale entities: polity, identity, landscape, culture, etc. They continuously construct those entities.

The Problem of Structure

The second problematic concept that hinders a historical-processual understanding of the past is a series of macroscale concepts that I will lump together here under the rubric of "structure." The idea that structures, those suprasituational phenomena that exist outside of the activity of people, delimit or cause human behavior is deeply ingrained within the psyche of many archaeologists. This is particularly true of the material conditions that are thought to either determine or constrain what people think or do. I would hazard a guess that nine-tenths of the readers of this paper would be hard pressed to disagree with the common-sense separation of structures from practices (or of material conditions from human behavior). This would even include some who advocate an "agency" approach to the past (see papers in Dobres and Robb 2000b).

However, structures have been criticized as obscuring variability (e.g., Lyman and O'Brien 1998; Lyman et al. 1997; Shennan 1993; Yoffee 1993). The danger, they say, is that we reify social abstractions as if they were real things and then give those things causal power to change human cultures. In their vociferous criticisms of artificial "essentialist" constructs, the neo-Darwinists are correct.[2] Archaeologists of all stripes reify abstractions; topping the hit parade are function, role, strategy, institution, organization, ideology, sacred landscape, society, exchange system, identity, and culture. They treat these things as if they emerged, had a life span, and then were transformed into some*thing* else. These *things* are the structures or the material conditions that archaeologists have long sought to reconstruct, with the transitions between the various states of their existence being the processes of change.

However, such things never existed outside their continuous reproduction through practice. It does not matter that people in the past might have been cognizant of some structures, say of their own identity, class affiliation, cosmology, or environmental circumstance. This is because cognizance would have varied widely across space and time, from person to person within and between groups. Certainly, any "cognized model" would have constrained practice (cf. Rappaport 1979), but a cognized model (i.e., an ideology)—or a function, role, strategy, institution, organization, sacred landscape, society, exchange system, identity, or culture—is not a static thing that affected everyone the same or that everyone understood the same. These things, by themselves, did not constrain practices; people acting as if these things mattered is what constrained practices. In a sense, that is, structures are never things, but are always in a state of becoming, as per Giddens's (1979) use of "structuration."

When we envision any structure as a real thing, then an explanation entails identifying the causal link between things. Archaeology is replete with these sorts of linear transformations that masquerade as explanations. Here are four common ones, with the "structures" in bold face and the "processes" in italics for emphasis: (1) a collector **strategy** *evolved* into a sedentary food-producing **strategy** when the cost-benefit ratio of storing food surpassed that of collecting it; (2) the intergroup inequalities of a tribal **society** were *institutionalized* as a **chiefdom**; (3) the **artwork** of specialists *legitimized* the **state**; and (4) new pottery vessel **forms** were *selected* over old vessel **types** owing to their mechanical properties.

As summaries, such descriptive scenarios might be accurate enough. However, note that, as processes, *all of these hypothetical evolutions, institutionalizations, legitimizations, or selections are invoked to explain a change in structures but are seldom themselves explained*. In part, this may be attributed to the fact that these processes or mechanisms of change are almost always *immaterial*. The structures are presumed to be real, and often material in form, but the processes invoked to explain the movements from one state to the next do not possess a material form. They are only inferred (see

Wylie 1993). What archaeologist ever claimed to have found an evolution, an institutionalization, a legitimization, or a selection? Instead, archaeology—particularly the older "processualist" archaeology—has sought the "material correlates," expressions, signatures, or materializations of structures ranging from kinds of behaviors to types of societies (see Binford 1983a; Raab and Goodyear 1984; Schiffer 1995).

Materiality, Spatiality, and Cultural Construction

The popular perception is that "postprocessual" archaeology, not "processual" archaeology, is concerned with "unseen" structures (VanPool and VanPool 1999:43). However, as explained above, an older "processual" archaeology, based on materialist principles, also strongly advocates *cultural processes as unseen, immaterial phenomena*! A nonarchaeologist might conclude that, with all of these unseen structures or processes, archaeological arguments seem a bit speculative. What about all the hard evidence that archaeologists find? Is it really necessary to infer the unseen "dynamics" from the "static" archaeological remains by invoking immaterial processes?

As opposed to the postprocessual inferences about mental structures or the standard materialist reliance on immaterial processes, a historical-processual argument elevates the material to the level of process. It rejects the existence of "unseen" processes that transform structures. Most importantly, it understands that structures—the meanings, ethnicities, governments, traditions, styles, and the like—are not self-perpetuating things. That is, to exist, to be *perceived* as things, they must be realized in practice. Structures exist only as "moments" of cultural construction and those moments are the practices themselves (Robb 1998:337ff.). Structures may seem like static things, especially when we discuss and compare them. However, in reality they are always in the process of becoming (e.g., Appadurai 1986; Giddens 1979, 1984; Sztompka 1991). This goes for the manufacture of meaning-laden objects, the construction of sacred landscapes, the cooking and eating of traditional foods, and the singing of songs, dancing of dances, or speaking of languages (Shennan 1993). The objects, landscapes, foods, songs, dances, and languages do not exist outside the manufacture, construction, cooking, eating, singing, dancing, and speaking of them.

How meanings were produced is a historical-processual issue, akin to how ethnicities were created, how governments were legitimized, how traditions were reproduced, how styles changed through time, or even how species evolved. It is also, necessarily, a process with a material or spatial dimension.[3] DeMarrais and others (1996:16) would call this "materialization," emphasizing "the ongoing process of creation.... [I]deas and norms are encapsulated as much in their practice and in the conditions of daily life as in individuals' minds." Note that extant ideologies or traditions are not "materialized" through the actions of people. Materialization for them is simultaneously the construction of ideologies. Thus, their materialization is identical to Giddens's (1979) "structuration" albeit in tangible form.

Picking up a point well-worn by Hodder (1986:6, emphasis original), "[m]aterial culture...does not passively *reflect* society— rather, it creates society through the actions of individuals." I would modify Hodder's statement to emphasize that culture is produced, and it is this production that comprises the process that anthropologists must explain (see Marcus and Fischer 1986:85; Wolf 1982:387–391). Note that culture—as a set of meanings—is not, and cannot, be explained as a thing that was transformed from one state to another. Therefore, archaeologists will continue to have a very difficult time isolating a set of meanings from the past and then interpreting those meanings. Indeed, in contrast to Hodder's (1986) original program of structural and symbolic archaeology, there is no reason to believe that archaeologists should interpret cultural meanings as a primary research goal. I say this because of the earlier noted cognizance problem and because what some *thing* meant is entirely contingent on *how* it meant it (see also Cowgill 1993; Kohl 1993; Shennan 1993).

Practices, as creative, meaningful moments are contingent on the contexts of people relating to one another, transmitting, communicating, socializing, making, doing, embodying, representing, etc. How could we isolate the diverse meanings of so many moments through time and across space? Would not it be better to seek to understand how meanings were created regardless of knowing what actor X thought something meant at some specific place and point in time? Meanings are ambiguous, multivocal, inherently unstable, and context contingent; add the shifting and often contradictory senses of the people involved and meanings must necessarily be recognized as difficult to locate in time and space. Then again, if meanings are difficult to see, how meanings are produced is not so invisible. That is, cultural construction invariably possesses matter or occupies space and, ideally, can be measured and explained by archaeologists.

That cultural construction is a material and a spatial process is the gist of recent emphases on material-symbolic production (see also Clark and Parry 1990; Costin and Wright 1998; Helms 1994a; Robb 1999). It is the point behind recent applications of *chaînes opératoires,* technological styles, and tradition building (e.g., Dietler and Herbich 1998; Dobres 1999, 2000; Dobres and Hoffman 1994; Pauketat 2001c; Stark 1998). Traditions, as material process, include embodied practices: tattoos, body paints, hairdos, clothing, ornaments, gestures, or dances (Farnell 1999; Joyce 1996, 2000; Loren 2001). Likewise, the building, viewing, and experiencing of spaces, physically modified by people or not, are creative moments of practice that generate history (Anschuetz et al. 2001; Knapp and Ashmore 1999; e.g., Bradley 1996; Johnson 1996; Pauketat 2000b; Tilley 1994; Thomas 1996b). Merely eating lunch is an ethnicized, engendered and, sometimes, politicized cultural practice (Hendon

1996; e.g., Hastorf 1991; Scott 2002; Stein 1999).

All of these dimensions of practice, call them technologies, traditions, embodiments, or experiences, have a material form or occupy space. Given their capacity to generate change, they are processes. Unlike explanatory scenarios that feature the unseen links between structures, these processes of cultural construction are not immaterial transformations. Rather, they are always material and spatial; structures are illusory. Archaeologists will not find the material correlates of structures. Archaeologists will find the materiality and spatiality of the processes themselves, if we look. Looking, in this sense, means adopting a historical-processual perspective.

NORTH AMERICA'S PRECOCIOUS CULTURAL CONSTRUCTIONS

Let us briefly consider materiality by reviewing three well-known archaeological complexes. These include what have been said to be North America's most prominent, most precocious, and most problematic phenomena: Poverty Point, Chaco Canyon, and Cahokia. A few characteristics of each will be mentioned here sufficient to make the point that the ontological and processual question before us—how were cultures continuously made by people?— is the crux of a paradigmatic shift in American archaeology.

The Poverty Point site and a series of other mounded centers in or adjacent to northeastern Louisiana are said to have been associated with a distinctive "exchange system" between about 1600 and 1300 B.C. (Gibson 2000, fig. 5.9). Various researchers at one time or another thought that Poverty Point and its sister complexes constituted an anomalous chiefdom-level phenomenon, while others saw it as an exceptionally successful hunter-gatherer adaptation to a lush environment (Earle 1994; Gibson 1974; Jackson 1991; Kidder 1991). Besides its earthen tumuli, a defining feature of the principal Poverty Point sites in and around Louisiana is the array of exotic novaculite, quartz crystal, chert, quartzite, galena, copper, hematite,

slate, steatite, and greenstone artifacts, along with those made from locally derived materials (Ford and Webb 1956; Gibson 1986, 1994a, 1994b, 1996, 2000; Jeter and Jackson 1990; Walthall et al. 1982; Webb 1968). These materials, originating from as far away as the lower Ohio Valley, the Ouachita Mountains in Arkansas, and the south Appalachians in Alabama and Georgia, were made into zoomorphs, beads, plummets, pendants, and abstract forms at the Poverty Point site and its outliers. A microlith technology is testimony to pervasive lapidary practices in the making of these stone ornaments and fetishes (Ford and Webb 1956; Johnson 1993; Webb and Gibson 1981).

Yet, while there is ample evidence of the consumption of exotic raw materials at and around Poverty Point, evidence that finished Poverty Point products were widely redistributed is not apparent (Gibson 1996:302, 2000). Many elements of "Poverty Point culture" identified as far north as southern Illinois and Indiana are typically only the mundane baked-clay or chipped-stone copies of Poverty Point items (Perino 1973; Webb 1968). There is little evidence that these objects, made by local Poverty Point people, were not also retained by or circulated within these same Poverty Point communities (Johnson 1994:111; Sassaman 1995:192). In fact, the spatial layouts, mound constructions, and artifact assemblages of each Poverty Point complex—including Poverty Point proper, Jaketown, Slate, and Teoc Creek—exhibit "remarkable differences" from the others (Johnson 1993:59; see Ford et al. 1955; Lehmann 1982).

Centered in northwestern New Mexico, Chaco Canyon is a unique "Puebloan" cultural complex dating to about A.D. 900 to 1130 (see Lekson 1999; Lekson et al. 1988; Plog 1997). To the extent that Chaco Canyon's elaborate "Great Houses" and "Great Kivas," with their elaborate masonry walls, are at the center of an expansive web of "outliers" connected by roads and signal stations, the Chacoan phenomenon might be seen as an analogous albeit exaggerated version of Poverty Point culture. This expansiveness itself is problematic, some seeing Chaco Canyon at the center of Puebloan development, others seeing Chaco Canyon as only one local expression of a pan-regional Puebloan "adaptation" to a Southwestern environment (see Lekson 1999). Like Poverty Point, investigators typically begin explanations of the Chacoan phenomenon by seeking to know the functions of various sites and artifacts. Presumably, it is reasoned, knowing the functional diversity or homogeneity of such things will allow an assessment of the Chacoan system's level of integration, in turn pointing to why such a macroscale phenomenon might have evolved in the first place.

Importantly, like Poverty Point, outlier Great Houses and settlements betray remarkable differences. The complete array of Chacoan-style architectural traits is found in Chaco Canyon and, to lesser extent, at outliers which, while identifiable as "Chacoan," are often said to be different in plan, composition, construction history, or function (Cameron 1998). Elaborately crafted objects made from exotic raw materials or, as commonly, the exotic materials and animals themselves (e.g., turquoise, macaws) are found most commonly amidst the Great Houses, Great Kivas, and walled mounds of Chaco Canyon proper, some with seemingly high-status burials (Toll 1991). This has led Sebastian (1991) to infer that a prestige-goods economy might have been the means whereby a few individuals in Chaco Canyon were able to mobilize labor for the periodic Great House or Great Kiva constructions. Indeed, among construction debris in the mounds is evidence of large-scale rituals, pointing to episodes of substantial labor coordination in the canyon (Stein and Lekson 1992).

Turning our attention to the third case at the northern fringe of the Southeast, the giant of all North American monumental centers appeared at about A.D. 1050. The biggest earthen platforms, the largest plazas, and the most people—this was Cahokia (Pauketat 1998; Pauketat and Emerson 1997). For two centuries, these earliest "Mississippians" were hosting giant festivals and making distinctly Cahokian objects from local and exotic raw materials (see also Emerson and Hughes 2000; Pauketat et al. 2002). Large pools of coordinated labor enlarged platform mounds, raised huge cypress marker posts, and rebuilt pole-and-thatch buildings atop the mounds at regular intervals (Pauketat 1993, 1996, 1997a, 2000b). A Mississippian wall-trench house style was adopted by Cahokians, a technology less frequently or in hybridized form practiced at outlying settlements (Alt 2001).

Once thought by some to be at the center of pan-Mississippi River commerce or a vast prestige-goods exchange network, Cahokia now appears to have been an intensive but localized political-cultural phenomenon (Emerson 1997; Emerson and Hughes 2000; Milner 1998; Pauketat 1994, 1998). The best information now available from Cahokia suggests a scenario where extensive local "interaction," the possible influx of "foreign" potters from outside the regional communal network, and the likely welding of new community identities around prominent families or clans led up to a dramatic flashpoint at A.D. 1050. At that point, the regional demographic landscape was rearranged, with some settlements abandoned, some founded in new locations, and large numbers of people relocating to Cahokia proper (Pauketat 2003). New material symbols and spaces were created, articulated via giant public rituals in Cahokia's main 19-hectare plaza (see Pauketat 1998). The archaeological evidence of craft production, in the form of temporally and spatially segregated signatures of sub-communities manufacturing items from exotic raw material or in esoteric forms, suggests relatively large pools of craft producers. Comparable to Poverty Point, the manufactured shell beads, redstone figurines, ground stone ax heads, and pots were primarily circulated within a restricted area of the central Mississippi Valley that we now recognize as Greater Cahokia (Pauketat 1998). As common are local minerals, pigments, and crystals associated with domestic and public contexts. Production debris from the manufacture of the fancy goods and ornaments found in high-status mortuaries litter residential areas and ritual residues at Cahokia proper (Pauketat 1997a, 1997b, 1998). The process here was not an immaterial mechanism that caused a new political structure. The process was embodied in private and public ritual, mound construction, house building, craft production, and abandonment and relocation practices themselves (see Pauketat 2001a).

DISCUSSION

In the recent past, all three precocious archaeological complexes—Poverty Point, Chaco Canyon, and Cahokia—have been explained as macroscale "systems" or "culture areas" that, once evolved, constrained the behaviors of populations. For instance, the standardized styles of architecture or artifacts associated with Poverty Point, Chacoan, and Cahokian type sites are thought by some to have resulted from the evolution of integrated production and exchange systems. Likewise, the monumental construction and evidence of labor coordination at type sites have been explained as an expression or legitimization of political authority. All three archaeological complexes, in other words, have been understood as structures that resulted from transformations—unseen processes ranging from the formation of exchange networks to the centralization of political power.

Because of their expansive size and early florescence,[4] however, each complex has been difficult to fit within the generally accepted (materialist) summaries of their respective areas. To varying degrees, each seems hierarchical, on one hand, and nonhierarchical, on the other. The widely scattered exchange objects or styles of Poverty Point, Chaco, and Cahokia are thought to be either the material correlates of a prestige-driven integrative strategy or the innocuous backdrop behind a gradual, cultural adaptation (cf. Jackson 1991; Jefferies 1996; Johnson 1994; Lekson 1999; Milner 1998; Pauketat 1994; Plog 1997). Finally, the exotic raw materials and craft goods that characterize each seem to point to the importance of material-goods production and exchange (à la Earle 1994),

and yet few centrally made products seem to have been traded out into the hinterlands.

The difficulty in fitting the data into one or another model is not a problem of sampling error. The difficulty with interpretation, I propose, is rooted in the causal logic that assumes preexisting behavioral and structural entities and then invokes unseen mechanisms that transform those entities. So-called explanations asserting that Poverty Point, Chaco Canyon, and Cahokia were structures (polities, exchange systems, cultures, etc.) that resulted from changes in behavior (adaptive food-producing strategies, prestige-aggrandizement, population growth, or environmentally induced shifts) never address the question: "how were these cultures being constructed by people living there at the time?" Explanation in behavioral or structural terms is little more than a sleight of hand where a "process" is invoked to move the scenario from one structural state to another.

Such a behaviorist or structuralist logic forces researchers into an explanatory dead end. For instance, Milner (1998:168), possibly sensing the explanatory dilemma with regard to Cahokia, states that the historical "circumstances that started Cahokia on the path to regional dominance will *never* be known" (emphasis added). His solution, and that of many archaeologists who have attempted to explain North America's precocious cultural constructions, is twofold: (1) an assertion is made that the case at hand is not significantly different from other cases of its kind; and (2) an appeal is made to general behavioral principles—for instance to the evolutionary consequences of risk-management and political-behavioral strategies—in order to explain "why" a particular polity, exchange system, or culture emerged. As I have noted elsewhere (Pauketat 2001a, 2001b), answers to these "why" questions tend "to leapfrog over historical data, making them reductionist to the point of being trivial or easily debunked..."

Of such arguments, we must ask ourselves a question that goes unasked in many studies: *how* were risk-management or political strategies (or any number of behaviors) uniformly instilled in all people in some times and places? Would automaton-like people in particular places and at particular times spontaneously adopt some behavior? Would people, particularly the masses who might not directly benefit from some political strategy, accommodate the strategy nonetheless? There are good historical and anthropological reasons to doubt that they would, and there are reasons to suspect that the masses of people did not behave in accordance with the strategies of the few (e.g., Lears 1985; Miller et al. 1989; Paynter and McGuire 1991; Scott 1990). So perhaps we should not continue to rely on explanations that attempt to generalize about the dynamics of types of societies, behaviors, or structures while glossing over the agency of the masses. Certainly, the scale, dating, and content of the three precocious archaeological complexes reviewed here cannot be adequately explained using standard models that employ the problematic concepts of behavior and structure. To the contrary, researchers have commented that explaining the Southeast and the Southwest would be easier if Poverty Point, Chaco Canyon, and Cahokia had never existed (Gibson 1996; Knight 1997; Lekson 1999; Sebastian 1992).

However, this explanatory quandary is unnecessary once we assume a historical-processual position. That position rests on the axiom that the practices of people, which are always manifest in space and matter, *are* the processes of cultural construction. In terms of our precocious North American cases, explanations of the processes of cultural construction entail viewing the construction or production and "use" of buildings, mounds, or portable objects as integral processes of creation. As processes enmeshed within elaborate and large-scale collective ritual cycles, physical construction and manufacture can hardly be separated from many other facets of cultural construction (Pauketat et al. 2002; Stein and Lekson 1992). Architecturally speaking, each event, experience, or practice in that location, as noted earlier, would have been an act of cultural construction that necessarily altered the asso-

ciations, referents, and "functions" of the space.[5] Determining the function of space, at least in a final sense, would be difficult. Indeed, determining function is the wrong approach altogether, as it reifies structures and assumes behavioral uniformity rather than practical diversity. That is, from a historical-processual perspective, function is nothing more than the cumulative experiences of a place. For instance, designating space as private, domestic, or communal collapses a diachronic experience (that might well have involved some public, ritualized, and even politicized practices) into a category that is necessarily opposed to public, sacred, or political space. Consider, however, that the conflation of the two—public with private, domestic with ritual, or communal with political—could have been a fundamental part of the process that gave rise to places like Poverty Point, Chaco Canyon, and Greater Cahokia (e.g., Hastorf 1991; Kus and Raharijaona 1990; Pauketat and Emerson 1999). The spaces never merely functioned for some*thing;* their histories, however, were part of the continuous creation of cultural meanings and identities (Thomas 1996b:83; Tilley 1994:27).

Likewise, the material-goods production of Poverty Point, Chaco Canyon, and Cahokia may be seen as a dimension of a process of cultural construction. Toward that end, the acquisition, possession, manipulation, and production of symbols from raw symbols rather than the circulation of the actual finished things themselves is a particularly prominent component of the North American cases. The finishing of these things, not their functions or meanings of the things, is a *chaîne opératoire* of cultural construction that helps explain the process whereby these places came about and, by extension, how supposed cultural orders were created.

It might be helpful to think of cultural construction in this sense as the work of social movements, community coalitions, cults, or social "formations" of sorts (Kertzer 1988; Williams 1977). Such social-historical phenomena are common enough throughout human history. Yet, movements, coalitions, cults, or formations are not the equivalent of organizations, institutions, behaviors, or other such structures that constrain people's practices. Instead, movements consist of people from diverse backgrounds mobilized around a central idea, principle, or cultural theme promoted by some people and accommodated by others (see Toch 1965; cf. Brumfiel's [1994] "factions"). Most importantly, in various well-known cases of social movements, the processes of change themselves are observable at a microscale. There are performances or displays that *involve* followers in spaces or through material media. In some religious revitalizations, "traditional acts" (i.e., microscale practices) clearly generated social change at a macro-scale (e.g., messianic movements, religious "revolutions," or cults). Histories of entire peoples have been altered.

My point is that the precocious complexes discussed here are, in the sense of social movements, *themselves* the processes of cultural construction. They are not merely the outcomes of a process. The many chipped-stone, baked-clay, and lapidary practices of Louisianans three millennia ago, the use of exotic minerals, pots, and feathers at Chaco Canyon, and the crafting of stone, clay, and shell into Cahokian goods was, in an important sense, the creation of Poverty Point, Chaco Canyon, and Cahokia. They are the material dimensions of cultural construction, not the end products of some unseen process. Thus, the cultural construction of places (such as Poverty Point, Chaco Canyon, and Cahokia) "caused" the macroscale patterns that contributed to what we know today as the Southeast and the Southwest (for other approaches to similar problems, see Lomnitz-Adler 1991 and Wheatley 1975). The end product of these cultural constructions was history.

Now, the cautious skeptic, when contemplating any number of seemingly unique cultural centers, might say "Yes, but why there?" or "Why then?" My response would be that the good historical processualist would of course have to consider the specific contingencies and "constraints" of the case in question (see Pauketat 2001a:5). Where and when matter greatly, and nine-tenths of an archaeologist's job is necessarily measuring and evaluating such constraints. But the good historical processualist would also recognize that the constraints are always "mediated," which is to say culturally constructed, by the ongoing practices of people (e.g., Comaroff 1982). For the three precocious cases at hand, answers to the questions "why there?" and "why then?" are being sought by regional archaeologists even as you read this. However, the answers to such questions are not only complex, but they change with every generation of new archaeologists, each of whom has their own set of biases that they bring to the table of knowledge production. I think that the historical-processual answers, those explaining *how* (rather than *why*) change came about through spatiality and materiality, are less susceptible to the biases of unseen inferences and, thus, are not quite so reflexively problematic.[6]

Perhaps this is precisely what is demonstrated by the uncomfortable sense that Poverty Point, Chaco, and Cahokia do not seem to fit the standard explanatory constructs commonly invoked. We now know enough about *how*, that is, to doubt the old *why* scenarios. In important ways, Poverty Point, Chaco, and Cahokia seem to appear in the archaeological record and to then have historical effects on what follows, rather than being easily derived from forerunners in a gradual evolutionary trajectory. The grounds and material goods of each seem to be novel creations that draw on esoteric referents and exotic raw materials and that are produced locally (at a microscale) if not also for local effect. The local effects of each place appear not to have been simply transferred between peer polities or surrounding regions. Rather, they were reinterpreted in other localities (i.e., localized), producing in appearance a "remarkable" heterogeneity even within the cultural regions of concern.

CONCLUSIONS

I contend that the problems of explanation are in large measure due to our theoretical constructs. Commonly used kinds of cause-

and-effect scenarios assert that the places in question were the consequences of mechanisms that transformed uniform behaviors or structures. They further suggest that the precise set of historical circumstances that gave rise to such places are irrelevant. Yet such scenarios fail to explain the so-called mechanisms that supposedly account for structural transformations. In fact, these mechanisms cannot be directly observed by archaeologists and are not subject to verification. Moreover, they do not tell us *how* change occurred, but instead provide us with ready-made explanations that discourage attempts to discover the historical circumstances that led up to cultural changes. Under these explanatory conditions, there may not be much epistemological basis to distinguishing processual from postprocessual archaeologies (VanPool and VanPool 1999).

However, the ontological issue at the heart of a historical-processual paradigm—how did people create cultures—is as important as any epistemological argument over whether various kinds of archaeology are or are not scientific. The reason is that the ontological question engenders an appreciation of culture as a process rather than as a structure. Culture is participatory. What people do and how they live takes material form and occupies space. Given that archaeologists recover materials in space, we are well situated to observe the process of cultural construction. The archaeological remains of Poverty Point, Chaco, and Cahokia, then, are not just the products (i.e., structures) of culture making, they are in some sense the materiality and the spatiality of the processes themselves. These processes were inscribed on landscapes as the central grounds and manufactured objects of the precocious cultural complexes in question. In so doing, they produced distinctive cultural histories and impinged upon the cultural histories of other people across vast portions of the North American continent.

Understanding archaeological remains in this way is fundamentally different from materialist and structuralist modes of explanation. Typically, we have viewed societies, cultures, political structures, strategies, etc., as

the products of processes that go largely unseen and unverified. We have called the invocation of such unseen processes "theories." However, a historical-processual logic reverses the significance of material culture and space in explanation. Instead of the usual explanatory formula, where structures are real and processes unseen, it substitutes a historical-processual logic: processes are concrete, structures are illusory. Instead of seeing material remains and space as mere reflections of structures, materials and spaces are recognized to have embodied human agency. Instead of explaining structures, we explain history (as a process of cultural construction). Artifacts and spaces are more directly related to processes than generally supposed. History and theory become quite difficult to dissociate (see also Joyce and Hendon 2000).

Thus, the question of whether Poverty Point, for instance, was a chiefdom or not is rather moot. We would need to know this only if a set of unseen processes must be invoked to explain its rise, cycling, and fall. But the real question is: How did craft producers there and nearby generate places and identities by converting raw material from distant realms into local symbols that were then adapted or localized by distant people? The political economy of places, in fact, is arguably inseparable from this cultural dynamic, as I have elsewhere argued for Cahokia (Pauketat 1997a). The same goes for everything from the social relations and boundary formation of hunter-gatherers to the missionization and creolization of colonial peoples (e.g., Comaroff and Comaroff 1991; Sassaman 1998). How and under what conditions did people construct collectivities, regardless of whether we describe their societies as bands, chiefdoms, states, etc.

Given such a shift in research focus, our attention is turned toward dissecting the practices of those who constructed monuments, performed ritual acts, embodied beliefs, or resisted ideas in order to develop theories of the construction of culture of relevance to understanding all of world history. Such dissection of course entails methodological alterations for archaeology. A historical-processual paradigm demands that we be better cultural historians and better processual archaeologists. It demands that we focus on retrieving genealogies of practices, biographies of artifacts, and histories of construction and occupation across space and through time. It will be insufficient to excavate small samples from one or two sites and generalize about the behaviors, institutions, political systems, and economies of whole time periods, regions, or types of societies. Heterogeneity within and between settlements, regions, and continents is to be expected, and the degree of cultural heterogeneity is an important consideration in explaining how peoples were producing cultures. Cultural homogeneity, if identified, would thus demand an explanation. Indeed, how would such cultural orthodoxies, commonwealths, or collectivities have been conceived, accommodated, negotiated, or resisted?

In asking such questions in this manner, we are repositioning archaeology squarely in the realm of the emerging historical-processual paradigm. Historical-processual archaeology has paradigmatic qualities because, for starters, it makes us ask different questions of our data (how did the materiality of cultural practices shape history, rather than how did history shape material culture?). Then, it forces us to gather data differently (emphasizing greater chronological and spatial controls over "production" and "construction" than on types and functional inferences). How did people, shaping artifacts and landscapes, construct society, rather than how was society expressed in artifacts and landscapes?[7] There are already significant numbers of researchers thinking along these lines (Pauketat 2001b; e.g., Dietler and Herbich 1998; Dobres 2000; Ferguson 1992; Joyce 2000; Joyce and Hendon 2000; Lightfoot et al. 1998; Shennan 1993; Thomas 1996b). I predict many more as archaeology is repositioned to address the globalizing world of the twenty-first century.

Repositioned thus, archaeologists of various sorts—prehistoric and historical, evolutionary and behavioral, processual and post-processual, idealist and materialist—are asking (or should be asking) similar questions of diverse data sets. Great theoretical distinctions between us will cease to exist, imparting a new holism to the field. This new holism, or historical-processualism, will not violate the "scientific" standards as discussed by Van-Pool and VanPool (1999). Rather it will make the deeply ingrained but highly problematic notions of behavior and structure truly immaterial.

ACKNOWLEDGMENTS

The Cahokia research summarized here was supported by the National Science Foundation (BNS-9305404 and SBR 99-96169), the National Geographic Society (6319-98), the Cahokia Mounds Museum Society, the Illinois Department of Natural Resources, the Illinois Department of Transportation, the Illinois Transportation Archaeological Research Program, and the Department of Anthropology at the University of Illinois at Urbana–Champaign. This paper has benefitted from the comments and advice of Thomas Emerson, Robert Preucel, Chris VanPool, Todd VanPool, and Charles Varela. I doubt that any of them would agree with everything here, so that I'm forced to claim responsibility for it.

Notes

1. This is not to suggest that practices are necessarily conscious, goal-oriented acts, but are just as likely to be spontaneous and done without conscious reflection.

2. This, and their insistence on historical processes, may be the only part of the spate of programmatic puffery that is correct. While theoretical bright spots exist (I've called these the "transmissionists" elsewhere), the "selectionist" program is wholly flawed (Pauketat 2001b). It cannot overcome its dedication to the de-historicizing concept of behavior, nor the belief that technological efficiency is an absolute arbiter of social change.

3. Note that even speech is an act (sometimes a public act), and as such occupies space (even sometimes analyzed by archaeologists as the acoustical and experiential features of the built environment).

4. Relative to prolonged "mound-building," Puebloan, or Mississippian periods.

5. Even if there was a "construction phase" that gave way to a "use phase" (which is doubtful).

6. Perhaps this is why Shennan (1993) has emphasized the place of "reportage" in archaeology.

7. With reference to the earlier-mentioned common linear transformations that masquerade as processes, we could rephrase them as follows: When do hunter-gatherer practices become strategies, and do the intentional and unintentional actions and representations of other people play a part in the forming of them (e.g., Sassaman 1995, 1998)? How might social negotiations have been inscribed in spaces and materials to generate a collective sense of institutionality (e.g., Joyce 1996; Pauketat 2000b; Stein and Lekson 1992)? How were states created through art or theater (e.g., Clark 1997; DeMarrais et al. 1996; Joyce 1996)? Who made, who accommodated, and who promoted new pottery vessels, and under what conditions (e.g., Dietler and Herbich 1998; Hastorf 1991; Hendon 1996; Stark 1998)?

6

Back to Basics: The Middle-Range Program as Pragmatic Archaeology

Philip J. Arnold III

Like many of you, I approach most discussions of archaeological theory with trepidation. The language can be ponderous, the points esoteric, and you may need a scorecard to know which philosopher is the current darling-of-the-month. "Is any of this relevant to my particular archaeological project, collections, and/or deadlines?," I have wondered. In my more petulant moods I even question why I should heed someone who may have never directed an archaeological excavation or conducted ethnoarchaeological fieldwork. Theory just doesn't have the same panache when you are mapping a tricky feature late Friday afternoon in the rain.

So I appreciate the strong temptation to respond to yet another theoretical paper with an exasperated eye roll and a dismissive "What*ever*!" After all, aren't some of these exchanges just tit-for-tat posturing? Well, yes, they certainly can be, but the sour taste of bombast is not the most serious problem. A larger concern stems from far more pragmatic realities. Most archaeologists are looking for ideas and insights to improve their research activities. If those insights are rendered incomprehensible by tortured language or appeals to obscure thinkers, we are tempted to close the book and simply keep digging.

The Middle-Range Program (MRP) originally proposed by Binford (1977, 1978, 1981) suffers from such a reaction. The MRP includes Middle-Range Research (MRR) and Middle-Range Theory (MRT), two distinct activities united within a single strategy to aid archaeological explanation. The MRP was developed to identify causal relationships in the present and use that knowledge as a frame of reference with respect to the archaeological record. The MRP advocated tactics familiar to archaeology (i.e., radiocarbon dating, use-wear analysis) and sought to identify additional cause-and-effect relationships and extend them to new archaeological domains.

But somewhere along the way the MRP was blown off-course. After a promising maiden voyage, it was becalmed within the Latitudes of Ethnoarchaeology, where all actualistic research was commandeered under the same Jolly Roger (see discussions in Kent 1987:33–39). Later, huffs of humanism fouled its riggings and challenged its structural integrity (e.g., Hodder 1982a, 1986, 1991a; Shanks and Tilley 1987). Could the MRP weather the antiprocessual maelstrom? Most recently, theory-wielding shipwrights recommissioned the MRP, refitting its deep-cutting bow of science with a flat-bottom, shallow hull of relativism (Kosso 1991; Tschauner 1996; VanPool and VanPool 1999:46).

Obviously, I believe that the MRP has been poorly served over the last twenty-five years. My goal, therefore, is to redirect attention toward the original purpose of MRR and MRT;

namely, to establish more secure methods to transform a mute material record into independently verifiable statements about past human behavior. But this discussion will not review all attempts to use the middle-range moniker (e.g., Raab and Goodyear 1984; Schiffer 1988; see Tschauner 1996 for an overview). Rather, in the spirit of going back to basics, I concentrate on the MRP as originally outlined by Binford (1977, 1981). My goal is to serve up a more digestible discussion than the entrées now available, one flavored with more method and less theory than the usual fare (e.g., Carr 1995b).

The following presentation falls into three parts. Accepting that those who ignore the past are condemned to repeat it, I briefly retrace how the MRP came into existence. This section recounts the New Archaeology's early emphasis on a research program whereby hypotheses about the past were tested against the archaeological record. It also notes that such attempts were doomed to failure. Most contemporary archaeologists already know this, as it was the lack of results stemming from this misplaced application of science that prompted antiprocessual movements during the early 1980s (e.g., Dunnell 1986; Hodder 1982a, 1985). Many archaeologists may not realize, however, that this same dissatisfaction prompted initial calls for the MRP.

The theme of the second section is "If it ain't broke, don't fix it." This discussion addresses recent misrepresentations of the MRP; it specifically concerns those statements that equate the MRP with the hermeneutic circle of contextualism (e.g., Kosso 1991; Tschauner 1996). The conflation of these two strategies is serious, as it unnecessarily agitates and muddies the methodological waters of archaeological research. In this section I discuss the dual criteria of coherence and correspondence on the one hand and the confusion over ethnographic analogy and ethnoarchaeology on the other. I suggest that, despite superficial similarities, the likeness between the MRP and hermeneutics is considerably more apparent than real.

The final section explores how the MRP is supposed to work. Like a datum point used to map an archaeological site, the MRP provides a fixed point of reference to frame behavioral variation. Without reference to a secure standard, identifying and explaining variation becomes increasingly problematic. I suggest that much of what currently passes for basic, business-as-usual archaeology makes use of MRP principles. By way of example I discuss my own foray into middle-range research.

BACKGROUND TO THE
MIDDLE-RANGE PROGRAM

Most historical treatments of the New Archaeology agree—its proponents opposed the notion that archaeological interpretations should be evaluated through appeals to a scholar's personal credentials. This reaction prompted a search for a more "scientific" approach—in this case an inordinate fondness for deductively derived hypotheses. These hypotheses, in turn, were to be tested against the archaeological record. Hypothesis testing became the battle cry of the New Archaeology.

Unfortunately, despite its mantra-like invocation, there was a general failure to specify what was meant by testing and how it should proceed. Consequently, researchers sympathetic to the cause adopted the most familiar testing protocols; namely hypothesis testing modeled after controlled laboratory experiments (e.g., Fritz and Plog 1970). Thus, by the early 1970s one finds references to the archaeological record as a "laboratory" in which scientific research and testing are carried out (e.g., Bayard 1969:337; Plog 1974:35; Watson et al. 1971:24).

Proper testing includes two distinct stages (e.g., Binford and Sabloff 1982:137). The first is the acquisition of data with respect to a specified hypothesis. The second is the evaluation of that hypothesis in terms of the acquired data. Many archaeologists began to fixate on the former goal, apparently believing that controlled data collection necessarily led to scientifically sound results. Thus, controlled data collection became a proxy for hypothesis evaluation. In other words, the two distinct stages were conflated.

Consistent with this attitude, discussions of data collection dominated the methodological literature of the 1970s. Sampling was a particularly common topic. Excavation and survey as a controlled experiment became the way to operationalize a scientific archaeology (e.g., Ingersoll et al. 1977). Considerations of the appropriate methods for hypothesis evaluation, however, remained few and far between.

The now-obvious reality is that this testing program is simply untenable. Archaeological fieldwork will never be a controlled experiment of the "white lab-coat" variety. The conditions that brought about the material patterns cannot be directly observed. Thus, results that appear to support a hypothesis may instead move us toward the fallacy of affirming the consequent. In other words, in the absence of necessary causal connections, logic does not allow us to argue that a specified effect was the product of a hypothesized cause.

As an example, suppose that we want to know if it has rained in the last few hours. We have observed rainstorms on numerous occasions and we are satisfied that, where sidewalks occur, rain invariably results in a wet sidewalk. So we look outside our window, observe a wet sidewalk, and conclude that it has recently rained.

Is this conclusion logically valid? No. And why not? Because rain is but one of many possible reasons why a sidewalk may become wet. Our neighbors may have just turned on their lawn sprinklers, the street cleaner may have recently passed, or a nearby fire hydrant may be leaking. These various possibilities are know as antecedent conditions, and are often subsumed under the term equifinality. Thus, rain is *sufficient* to make the sidewalk wet, but it is not the only antecedent condition—that is, it is not *necessary* to bring about a wet sidewalk. According to the logic of inferential arguments we cannot validly reason "backwards" from a deduced result

to its cause if the links between the two do not include a necessary causal connection.

For archaeologists the conclusion is inescapable. Without an understanding of necessary causal relationships, we cannot use the archaeological record (as the consequent) to substantiate statements about past behavior (as the antecedent) in a logically reasoned manner. Furthermore, we cannot derive these causal principles from the archaeological record itself, since that register offers only the results of some unknown behavior. This scenario contributes to the "interpretive dilemma" discussed by Wylie (1989a). This same dilemma led directly to Binford's (1977, 1981, 1982, 1983a:12–15) call for a middle-range program of investigation.

Thus, the MRP proposed by Binford is really quite simple, perhaps deceptively so. In a nutshell, the MRP seeks to establish necessary causal relationships in the present and apply them to the past. The MRP is actualistic because it involves those contexts in which both cause and effect can be monitored. These necessary causal relationships are used to support the uniformitarian assumptions that *must be made* when explaining the archaeological record (Wylie 1985). If we cannot support a claim that in some way the past was like the present, then the past becomes inaccessible to any but the most imaginative and fictitious enterprise.

MIDDLE-RANGE CONFUSION

Seen from this perspective, a middle-range program of research should be an indispensable part of archaeological practice. Recent discussions, however, characterize the MRP as little more than a ratchet in the postmodern toolbox (e.g., Kosso 1991; Tschuner 1996). Swinging a mallet of relativism, such (re)do-it-yourselfers incessantly hammer home the contextual nature of the discipline (see Kaplan 1964:28–29, on the Law of the Instrument). Perhaps deafened by their own pounding, they seem unaware that most of the discipline abandoned hyper-objectivity long ago (e.g., Arnold and Wilkens 2001). Other critics insist on "Dealer's Choice" and bid the faulty assumption that the MRP creates the past in terms of cultural universals. Their trump is the anthropological wild card that cultural behavior is different across space and through time. Clearly, such gamesmanship says more about the players themselves than it does about the MRP.

While these misrepresentations can be easily dismissed, other charges are potentially more damning and merit closer inspection. Two claims are among the most prominent. The first suggests that appeals to the hermeneutic twin criteria of coherence and correspondence also regulate the MRP, therefore hermeneutics and the MRP are essentially identical. The second suggests that any observations made in the present day serve a middle-range end. These charges are wrong on both counts and are discussed below.

Coherence and Correspondence

One of the current strategies used to equate hermeneutics and the MRP is to call upon the hero twins of coherence and correspondence (Kosso 1991; Tschauner 1996). Coherence in this case refers to the internal logic of the argument; asking if the argument "makes sense" such that the derived conclusions are consonant with the original premise (e.g., Hodder 1991a:100). Correspondence, its brother in arms, asks to what degree the available facts mesh with the argument's expectations. Both a hermeneutic approach and the MRP profit from appeals to consistency and reference to noncontradictory data. Thus, "doing archaeology" under the banner of either program has been presented as essentially the same procedure (Kosso 1991: 626; also see David and Kramer 2001:37; Tschauner 1996:28; VanPool and VanPool 1999:46).

Despite such claims, the similarity between hermeneutics and the MRP is more apparent than real. Let us first consider coherence. Assertions that coherence provides a significant defining criterion are merely platitudes; it would be remarkable to take seriously a statement that was internally *inconsistent*. In other words, given a rational thought process, it is amusing to imagine a situation in which a premise is supported because a contradictory conclusion was reached! I doubt most readers would find such argumentation compelling.

But does this concession mean that hermeneutics and the MRP constitute identical forms of archaeological practice? Certainly not. It simply means that, on a very general level, both strategies make use of inferential arguments. And, as such, their structures are specified by definition: "There is an important characteristic of all inferential arguments, simply that *we can never reason in a valid manner from premises to a conclusion that contradicts the premises with which we start*" (Binford 1981:29, original emphasis). Kosso (1991) is certainly correct when he notes this superficial similarity between hermeneutics and the MRP. Nonetheless, the fact that both deal with inferences in no way corroborates his conclusion that the MRP and hermeneutics are "fundamentally the same method" (Kosso 1991:626).

The real issue, of course, is how one goes about *evaluating* such inferential statements. In other words, what testing procedures are employed and/or considered appropriate? The desire to evaluate competing ideas is the cue for correspondence to make an entrance. Correspondence provides an assessment of validity by comparing our expectations to the facts as understood. But correspondence is more than a bit player with the single line "Is there a good fit between expectations and the available data?" Correspondence also manages the backdrop of accountability by asking "How was that fit achieved?"

The hermeneutic circle advocated by postprocessualists achieves correspondence by fitting expectations to the data. Hodder (1991a:187) describes it as moving "backwards and forwards between theory and data, trying to fit or accommodate one to the other." The strategy is to build up a scenario based on one's understanding of the archaeological information. This approach "attaches meaning to a particular piece of data by embedding it more and more fully in the surrounding data, searching for a theory that makes all the data 'fit' and makes sense of the whole in terms of the parts and the parts in terms of the whole" (Tschauner 1996:18). As you can readily appreciate, such "hypothesis fitting" invariably promotes a closer correspondence between expectations and data.

The fact that expectations are fit to the data may satisfy some archaeologists, but it does not constitute a scientific evaluation of those expectations. This lack of accountability could prove to be a real show-stopper if ideas are confronted with unexpected data. But not to worry; at this point in the script the *deus ex machina* of accommodative argument descends from above, arriving in the nick of time to preserve the premise in the face of contradictory evidence. Fans of the hermeneutic passion play loudly applaud this cameo since, as Hodder (1991a:100) affirms, "Archaeology uses accommodative arguments; it has no other viable options."

Across the aisle, however, proponents of the MRP jeer the overly contrived finale, noting that correspondence is not tantamount to evaluation. In fact, this very situation provided a foil for critiques of traditional archaeological practice:

> The only source of statements on dynamics at that time rested with our imaginations...Of course we were generally smart enough to imagine conditions that would accommodate the statics as known. We were literally locked into a very weak form of argument, the post hoc accommodative argument. The only test is the "goodness of fit" between our imagined past and the empirical archaeological present. This is the very form of argument that I and others had argued was inadequate, where the important step of "testing" had not been performed. (Binford 1983b:67)

Viewed from the processual seats, the correspondence offered by the hermeneutic circle is not the "kind of testing" that Kosso (1991: 624) claims. Instead, it more closely resembles plausibility, an understudy who stands on shaky knees and delivers lines fed from the wings.

Unfortunately, several recent discussants have uncritically perpetuated this conflation

of hypothesis testing with hypothesis fitting (e.g., Kuznar 1995:167; VanPool and VanPool 1999:46). An inability to distinguish the two is explicit in Tschauner's (1996:24) characterization of contextual archaeology: "Hodder's contextual analysis clearly is a hypothesis-testing or -fitting procedure." In fact, these two procedures are not synonymous and hermeneutics falls squarely in the latter camp rather than the former.

Perhaps a quick illustration will nail down the distinction. A wonderful example of the difference achieved by the two programs is provided by Dart's early hominid research in South Africa. Dart (1957) proposed the well-known "osteodontokeratic" culture, based on the presence of animal skeletal remains associated with hominid fossils. In the absence of evidence for stone tools, certain animal remains were interpreted as tools and weapons used by australopithecine hunters.

In terms of coherence, Dart's model provides an internally consistent scenario. After all, no stone tools were recovered, and, given the assumption of tool use, the bones, teeth, and horn made for excellent technological substitutes. Dart's reconstruction, created by working "backwards and forwards between theory and data" (e.g., Hodder 1991a:187), was internally consistent.

And what of correspondence? Well, since the model was fitted to the evidence, expectations and data correspond closely. But what about unanticipated patterns? For example, how was Dart to account for the consistent, unexpected absence of certain animal parts from the assemblage, such as the tail sections (caudal vertebrae) of bovids? He responded with an elegant accommodative argument, noting the tails are imbued with religious and symbolic meaning within hunter-gatherers and complex society alike:

> To "tail" anything still signifies to "track it down"...Tails spontaneously form flexible whips or flagella for beating thickets and grass-lands after game. The flagellum was one of the badges of the Pharaoh!...Horse-tails used to be emblems of rank formerly in Turkey... Every South African witch-doctor carries

an animal's brush preferably that of a wildebeest as every European witch carried a broom. It seems likely from the significance attached to tails universally by mankind in myth and history that their disappearance from the Makapansgat breccia is significant; they were all probably in great demand as signals and whips in organized group-hunting outside the cavern. (Dart 1957:167–168; cited in Ascher 1961:320–321)

Although rarely presented as such, Dart's (1957) interpretation is an excellent example of the hermeneutic circle in operation, established with the criterion of coherence and supported via the criterion of correspondence.

Of course, the reader is well aware that the osteodontokeratic model is no longer considered viable. And why not? Not because the hermeneutic circle is self-correcting. Rather, a number of scholars sought to resolve these and other unexpected faunal patterns in terms of the MRP (e.g., Behrensmeyer and Hill 1980; Binford 1981; Brain 1969). This research determined that the association of Dart's hominids and animal skeletal remains was a function of mostly nonhominid agents. Based on actualistic studies that securely linked the formation and character of faunal assemblages with the activities of natural predators and scavengers, investigators gained insight into how bone deposits come into existence under different circumstances. Thus, the MRP was used to discount the role of early hominids in accumulating the faunal assemblage at Makapansgat, a scenario that otherwise appeared imminently reasonable according to the coherence and correspondence criteria of the hermeneutic circle.

Ethnographic Analogy and Ethnoarchaeology

A second tactic used by those who equate hermeneutics and the MRP confuses the methods that link the present to the past. Because the MRP is informed by contemporary behavior, the assumption appears to be that any argument from ethnographic analogy or the citation of ethnoarchaeological findings constitutes a middle-range argument. In point of fact, MRR occupies a very small and specific subset of what currently passes for ethnoarchaeology. Thus, while all MRR and MRT derive from analogical reasoning and are ethnoarchaeological in a general sense, very little use of ethnographic analogy and ethnoarchaeology can be reasonably considered as part of the MRP.

Perhaps this confusion is understandable, as rarely has there been an explicit accounting of similarities and differences. Many of Binford's (1977, 1978, 1982) initial statements regarding the MRP are relatively ambiguous on this account, as they were mostly concerned with justifying the need for both MRR and MRT. Apart from acknowledging the actualistic character of the research, discussions that set out the specific modus operandi were practically non-existent (but see Binford 1981:289–297). As long as the discussion focused on the MRP's theoretical underpinning as opposed to its pragmatic applications, the MRP was destined to suffer from misreadings at the hands of critics and revisionists alike.

Kosso's (1991) conclusion that the MRP and hermeneutics are essentially the same methods provides a case in point. As an example of "middle-range theories in action," he argues that the distribution of potsherds in areas of Greece can serve as the basis for a reconstruction of ancient Greek farming practices:

The light scatter of sherds can be taken as evidence of cultivation in light of middle-range theories that describe a pattern of rural Greeks discarding old pots near their houses where the broken bits get inadvertently mixed into the manure of farm animals kept at the place of residence...Where manuring has been done, the link between off-site sherds and cultivation can be exploited as a middle-range theory. (Kosso 1991:623)

Apparently, Kosso (1991) believes that a description of ethnographic behavior provides the sole basis for middle-range theory-building and its simple application to a pre-historic context presents an example of MRT "in action."

Unfortunately, Kosso's (1991) vignette is not MRT, or even MRR; it is unadulterated ethnographic analogy, pure and simple. "Contemporary rural Greek farmers exhibit a certain behavior with respect to potsherds and fertilization," goes the reasoning, "thus, when we find ancient Greek potsherds 'off-site' we are justified in concluding that the same behavior occurred in the past." This statement is a simple assertion that ancient Greek farmers acted like contemporary Greek farmers.

As noted above, a basic requirement of any MRP is the identification of necessary causal relationships between the behavior observed and the resultant material pattern (e.g., Binford 1981:26). So a reasonable question is "Are there other means by which potsherds might be introduced into areas surrounding residential occupation?" Kosso (1991:623) cites studies by Wilkinson (1982) and Blintiff and Snodgrass (1988) to support his analogy. Ironically, a quick perusal of both works shows that these authors would respond to the above question with a resounding affirmative. Wilkinson (1982:331–332) specifically mentions nomad encampments and plowing ancient burial mounds as possibilities, while Blintiff and Snodgrass (1988:507–508) refer to nonagricultural off-site activities in general. Given this array of possible antecedent conditions, where are the necessary causal connections between manuring and sherd distributions? Put another way, where are the signatures of sherds deposited specifically as a by-product of fertilization? Kosso (1991:623) offers none because none have been established—his example of "middle-range theories in action" is just a thinly veiled instance of direct historical analogy (e.g., Ascher 1961; Wylie 1985).

Kosso (1991) is not alone in the failure to differentiate ethnographic analogy from the MRP, although his discussion enjoys frequent citation in the literature (e.g., David and Kramer 2001:37; Kuznar 1995:167; Saitta 1992:888; VanPool and VanPool 1999:46). Tschauner's (1996) recent treatment of the MRP and postempiricist philosophy of science offers a similar confusion. He presents Braithwaite's (1984) investigation of ritual and social differences in ancient Wessex as being "essentially identical to processualist, MRT-based procedures" (Tschauner 1996: 12). On what evidence is this conclusion reached? According to Tschauner (1996:10), Braithwaite's "entire inferential edifice is in fact built on a number of generalizations" culled from ethnographic analogies:

> The source of her generalizations is typically ethnographic analogy... MRT-like, cross cultural generalizations (cf. Binford 1987, p. 401) and analogical reasoning form the backbone of Braithwaite's reconstruction. (Tschauner 1996:12)

Like Kosso (1991), Tschauner (1996) erroneously equates the MRP with simple ethnographic analogy and cross-cultural generalizations.

How do we account for such fundamental misunderstanding? After all, Binford (1983a) is fairly explicit that his reservations with simple analogical arguments prompted his dissatisfaction with the traditional methods of archaeological reasoning.

> If argument from analogy was the method used by archaeologists to warrant their interpretations of the past, the implication was clear: *Archaeologists lacked appropriate methods for making accurate statements about the past based on archaeological observations.* (Binford 1983a:8, original emphasis)

As noted earlier, it was the search for more appropriate methods that led to the original suggestion of the MRP as a vehicle for archaeological investigation (Binford 1977, 1981).

Thus, some attempts to equate the MRP with hermeneutics stem from an inability to distinguish ethnographic analogy, ethnoarchaeology, and the MRP. We have already noted that most ethnographic analogy is not to be confused with the MRP. What about ethnoarchaeology? Where does it fit in?

Both ethnoarchaeology and the MRP belong within the category of actualistic research by virtue of the fact that they monitor present-day activities. Moreover, it is fair to say that ethnoarchaeology, like the MRP, developed out of a desire to improve assumptions about the archaeological record (e.g., Gould 1978b; Kramer 1979). And of course, Binford's (e.g., Binford and Binford 1968) emphasis on ethnoarchaeology was an important part of the New Archaeology as initially formulated

But that's about the extent of any similarities. By the mid 1980s, at the same time that antiprocessual movements were gaining steam, ethnoarchaeology began to back off from its commitment to link the present and the past.

The Gould and Watson (1982) dialogue on ethnoarchaeology signaled the gathering storm. Neither participant suggested that ethnoarchaeology could serve to anchor the past to the present. Instead, Gould (1978a; Gould and Watson 1982:375–376) argued that actualistic research should be used to highlight seemingly anomalous situations. In contrast, Watson (Gould and Watson 1982: 363) stayed the course of the early New Archaeology and suggested that ethnoarchaeology should provide hypotheses that are tested against the archaeological record. Neither approach to ethnoarchaeology was consistent with the MRP outlined by Binford (1977, 1985:580–581).

On the postprocessual side, Hodder (1982a, 1983) was an early advocate of ethnoarchaeology. Nonetheless, in just a few short years the honeymoon was over and the relationship turned rocky: "Ethnoarchaeological studies are of interest in their own right but they cannot contribute directly to our understanding of the past" (Hodder 1987a:424). But in the early 1990s, by the second edition of *Reading the Past*, we find evidence for a lukewarm reconciliation:

Should ethnoarchaeology not disappear, to be replaced by or integrated with the anthropology of material culture and social change?…In many ways [ethnoarchaeology] is a stop-gap, caused by the lack of anthropological concern with the issues central to archaeology…It seems likely, then, that ethnoarchaeology, ideally with a more 'anthropological' methodology, will retain a role in the immediate future. (Hodder 1991a:108)

By the beginning of the 1990s ethnoarchaeology no longer emphasized the importance of causal relationships specified by the MRP. The MRP explicitly challenged researchers to start with the archaeological record; that is, devise research questions that stem from specific archaeological patterns (e.g., Binford 1983c:391). In contrast, ethnoarchaeology, as Hodder suggested, became a "stop gap" version of material ethnography. Ethnoarchaeology was increasingly devoted to "salvage studies," justified because this-or-that culture or such-and-such behavior was disappearing fast. This fire-sale approach to ethnoarchaeology meant that the MRP's emphasis on archaeological relevance would have to be relaxed.

This shift in emphasis is well represented in the current literature on ceramic ethnoarchaeology (Arnold 2000). A single example will suffice. One of the best know ceramic ethnoarchaeological projects has been directed by William Longacre among the Kalinga of the Philippines (Longacre and Skibo 1994b). This longitudinal study has dramatically increased our knowledge of contemporary ceramic production and consumption. Moreover, Longacre (1970; Longacre and Ayres 1968) was an early advocate of the use of ethnographic information to understand the archaeological record. Nonetheless, much of the Kalinga research does not appear to be directed toward any particular archaeological problem or deposit, per se. For example, according to one participant, the real value of such studies is that "data from ethnographic settings cannot help but stimulate the archaeological imagination" (Stark 1994:197).

This minimizing of ethnoarchaeology's relevance to archaeology is also reflected in Longacre and Skibo's (1994a:xiii–xiv) complaint that archaeologists often pay scant attention to ethnoarchaeological research. This may be true, but rather than demonstrate how ethnoarchaeology directly contributes to archaeological practice, they take the archaeological community to task: "Certainly, sherds are unavoidable at many archaeological sites, but prehistorians must frame their questions in terms of whole vessels to address many behavioral topics" (Longacre and Skibo 1994a:xiv). Should archaeologists stop dealing directly with the archaeological record and begin to think more like ethnographers? This shift in focus may be comfortable for some scholars, but it represents a clear departure from the MRP's emphasis on the material record as originally outlined by Binford (1977, 1978, 1981).

The above comments are not offered to condemn the Kalinga research as bad ethnoarchaeology. Quite the contrary; this research is impressive and has immeasurably enriched our understanding of contemporary potters. The point is that ethnoarchaeology as currently practiced is not necessarily synonymous with middle-range research (also see David and Kramer [2001:54–61] on "interpretive ethnoarchaeology").

In sum, it should be clear that, despite the oft-cited comments by Kosso (1991) and Tschauner (1996), the MRP is not designed to apply ethnographic analogies to the past. Rather, the MRP is designed to establish causal relationships between behavior and archaeologically relevant patterns. Moreover, in the same way that hypothesis testing is not "hypothesis fitting," ethnoarchaeology and the MRP are not interchangeable. Much current ethnoarchaeology is in fact material ethnography and its relevance to the archaeological record is only a distant concern.

MAPPING THE PAST WITH A MIDDLE-RANGE DATUM

At this point you might be thinking "OK, so the MRP is not the New Archaeology of the 1960s and 1970s. And it's not the hermeneutics of postprocessualism. In fact, it's not even ethnoarchaeology. So what is it? And more to the point, how do we use it?"

The MRP is a method, nothing more. It provides researchers with a dependable instrument to investigate variation as reflected in the archaeological record. But keep in mind that variation is not particularly meaningful without reference to some kind of standard. Any two things may vary in multiple ways, so the important question is how to operationalize variation so that these differences can be explored effectively. The investigation of archaeological variation is most effectively realized with reference to a middle-range standard.

Most readers are familiar with the practice of mapping an archaeological site. The topographic variation across space is rendered intelligible by relating distance and elevation to a point of reference, the site's primary datum. And although a number of different datum points may serve the purpose, the most important requirement is that the position of any particular datum remains fixed, i.e., its location is constant. In this way the topographic representation obtained by using different datum points should be similar, assuming that comparable scales of measurement have been applied. In fact, one way to evaluate the accuracy of a map is to employ the same general techniques, only use a different datum as the point of reference. The degree to which the versions correspond is a measure of the accuracy of the rendition.

The role of the MRP is very much akin to the function of the site datum. The causal relationships derived from actualistic research underwrite our uniformitarian assumptions. These uniformitarian assumptions, in turn, serve as dependable points of reference. But in this case they are not spatial constants; rather, they are inferential constants. These points enable us to gauge archaeological variation in a behaviorally meaningful way. But, keep in mind that invoking these inferential datum points *does not* constitute a "test" of any hypothesis. As Binford (1981:290, original emphasis) notes, "middle-range theory plays no role in the *explanations* offered for the variability in the subject matter of interest." Such explanations require appeals to a separate body of general theory. The MRP simply provides an opportunity to monitor and evaluate departures from well-anchored points of reference. In this way we begin to "map" the behavioral circumstances that produced the archaeological record.

The MRP uses inferential standards to investigate behavioral variation as reflected in the material register. This point has been repeatedly misunderstood by critics who claim that the MRP is designed to expose cross-cultural generalizations or "universal laws of cultural process" (Hodder 1991a:107). This characterization is simply wrong, as the above discussion of ethnographic analogy should make clear. "Does the use of a datum point to map different archaeological sites mean that every site will look the same?" I don't think so. "But what about the 'contextual nature' of research—will the datum point operate differently in Mexico vs. Mali vs. Outer Mongolia?" I certainly hope not. "OK, but aren't there multiple ways to construct a culturally meaningful map?" Of course there are, but the reason we use different tools is because we need to complete different tasks. The last time I looked, my treasure map didn't help me navigate Chicago traffic and the "X" on my road atlas didn't mark King Solomon's mine.

The uniformitarian principles sought through the MRP do not insist that "everyone does the same thing" or even that "everyone does a certain thing the same way." The reliance on inferential standards simply recognizes that when certain activities occur, they produce an unambiguous, dependable material pattern. Again, the emphasis of the MRP has more to do with the creation of the archaeological record than the behavior, per se. Giving meaning to that behavior via explanation is a different activity entirely.

As a preliminary example of a middle-range program, consider the following. In the 1980s, as part of a team conducting archaeological research at Comoapan, Mexico, I participated in the survey and excavation a 4-ha complex of kilns (Arnold et al. 1993; Santley et al. 1989). Archaeologists often cited kilns to infer nonresidential pottery making (for a discussion see Stark 1985), so the presence of these features immediately raised questions about production scale and intensity. None-

theless, contemporary potters in this part of Mexico were using kilns as part of their domestic ceramic-making tradition. Clearly, the kilns themselves could not be indicative of the particular scale and organization of ceramic production activities. Thus, the question arose as to how we could differentiate kilns used as part of a larger-scale operation versus a series of individual firing facilities that had simply accumulated through the repeated use of an area.

In order to tackle this question I concentrated on how contemporary pottery making was spatially organized within the domestic context (Arnold 1990, 1991). I noted that the use of single kilns by individual potters in these residential settings resulted in a patterned association of features and material by-products. This pattern consisted of a lone firing facility associated with an adjacent midden of large sherds. A review of the ethnographic literature lent additional support to this particular distribution of kilns and the associated waster dump. Ultimately, I was satisfied that the link between the production behavior and the patten I had observed was robust (see Arnold 1991 for a thorough discussion of this linking process).

Taking this pattern back to the original archaeological deposit, I encountered a very different arrangement of kilns and middens. Rather than finding each kiln associated with its respective waster dump, kilns appeared to be clustered in groups of three to five facilities organized around a more centralized midden. Furthermore, this pattern was repeated across the entire area.

So how was this pattern to be interpreted? Based on additional information taken from studies of refuse management, task operations, and spatial organization, I argued that the archaeological remains resulted from multiple, co-occurring firing activities (Arnold 1991; Arnold et al. 1993). My interpretation of a nondomestic production context was further supported with reference to independent evidence derived from formal and stylistic characteristics of the ceramic assemblages associated with the respective kiln clusters.

The actualistic research I undertook gave me a standard against which I could evaluate the archaeological pattern. This was not a case of direct historical analogy, since the Comoapan pattern *deviated* from the one I observed among contemporary producers. My reliance on local potters was admittedly fortuitous, but it was in no way necessary to the study. Another ethnographic group who used kilns could have served. As an amusing aside, I originally proposed to compare the organization of domestic pottery making to that of local, larger-scale brick manufacture, but my funding proposal was rejected. Ironically, one of the reviewers felt that I was wasting my time, since the archaeological potters at Comoapan were not making bricks. While I was attempting to avoid a simple analogy, the reviewer apparently thought it was essential!

In sum, I used the ethnographically derived relationship between the spatial organization of domestic production and the archaeologically recoverable evidence of kilns and waster dumps as a standard. I employed that standard to monitor and evaluate variation in the archaeological record. I did not argue that the contemporary potters and the Precolumbian potters were behaving in a similar fashion; in fact, I concluded the exact opposite. Nor did I argue that the Precolumbian potters were involved in intensive production simply because they used kilns. The ethnographic record clearly refutes that conclusion. Instead, I undertook a middle-range exercise whereby causal connections established in the present were applied to an archaeological context. My conclusion, in turn, was supported with reference to independently derived evidence.

CONCLUSION

In this paper I have adopted an informal tone to discuss current misconceptions about the Middle-Range Program. I adopt this tone because I believe that many discussions of archaeological philosophy and theory are their own worst enemy. All to often they take on the flavor of a private country club—without the secret buzzwords or appropriate name-dropping your chance of gaining entry and

benefitting from the received wisdom is practically nil.

This situation is simply unnecessary and has produced as much harm as good. The viability of the MRP provides an excellent case in point. Although originally proposed as a form of science, it was never meant to be "rocket science." The concepts are not that problematic; in fact, archaeologists use middle-range methods without giving them a second thought. Studies that invoke use-wear analysis on lithics and ceramics are excellent examples. Investigations that rely on taphonomic processes present additional instances. Research based on neutron activation analysis and other elemental techniques provides a third case. These investigations rely on uniformitarian *assumptions* about the relationship between different phenomena. These uniformitarian links have been established in the present through actualistic research, whether conducted in a laboratory setting or "in the field." Thus, a middle-range approach is implicit in much of what passes for good, contemporary archaeological method.

So, what's the problem? Why the confusion? It seems that the MRP has become just one more negotiation in the bitter divorce between "humanistic" and "scientific" archaeologies. But rather than agree that the two parties' research goals are irreconcilably different, some self-appointed judges insist that "we all just get along." The MRP has been turned into the child whose best interests are served only if both parties kiss and make up. To force the issue and dismiss the suit, certain judges introduce doctored paternity data to link contextual archaeology with the MRP. On closer inspection no such bloodline exists. Perhaps it is time to invoke the wisdom of Solomon—I would lay even money that if the judges moved to cut the MRP down the middle, the deconstructionist daddies wouldn't bat an eye (e.g., Hodder 1991a: 109–109, 180).

The MRP offers a few basic principles. It says that archaeological research should address the material record ahead of inferred behavior. It says behavior should be linked to the material record via uniformitarian assumptions. It says that uniformitarian links should be established in contemporary settings. Finally, it says that these links should serve as points of reference to investigate behavioral variation in the past.

In sum, the MRP as originally proposed is an important archaeological method. All statements about the past rest on assumptions; given two competing statements, the fundamental question is how to evaluate the underlying assumptions. Some might use the scholar's credentials, others might prefer the scholar's creativity, and just about everyone will appeal to coherence and correspondence. The MRP opts for those assumptions with the greatest chance of holding steady between the present and the past. In the spirit of a more pragmatic archaeology, I'll bet those odds every time.

ACKNOWLEDGMENTS
Thanks to Christine and Todd VanPool for the invitation to contribute to their volume and for their encouraging comments regarding the direction of this paper. Others who also provided important feedback include Shannon Fie, Robert Pruecel, and an anonymous reviewer. The research discussed here was supported by grants from the National Science Foundation, Sigma Xi, the Heinz Foundation, and the University of New Mexico.

7

Biological Evolutionary Theory and Individual Decision-Making

JOHN KANTNER

The social sciences have been dogged by the assumption by various groups of practitioners that their paradigms need only be internally consistent, not answerable to our understanding of life in general—Nettle 1997:285

In a 1991 Distinguished Lecture in Archaeology for the American Anthropological Association, Elizabeth Brumfiel criticized what she called the "ecosystem approach" in American archaeology and asserted that scholars should instead focus more on "agent-centered perspectives" and recognize that "human actors, and not reified systems, are the agents of culture change" (Brumfiel 1992:559). Her criticism of the ecosystem approach especially concentrated on assumptions that human groups adapt to their environments through culture-based behavioral systems and that individuals play a limited role in influencing change. Brumfiel proposed that archaeologists should more actively consider how individual goal-oriented behavior within a social context can stimulate and shape sociocultural change.

Brumfiel's lecture is representative of a growing dissatisfaction over the past two decades with archaeological approaches that in some way appeal to biological evolutionary theory. While the so-called "ecosystem approach" has provided important insight into the interaction between human societies and their environments, emphases on diet and demography have obscured other inter-esting arenas of human behavior, such as intentional individual decision-making that influences nonsomatic behavior. The result has been an emerging belief that biological evolutionary theory is incapable of explaining some of the more interesting behaviors in which human individuals and groups engage, and subsequently many scholars are now pursuing other explanatory frameworks that arguably do not possess the same coherence as evolutionary theory. Certainly the cause has not been helped by the continuing emphasis on interpretations of neo-Darwinian evolutionary theory that either lack a comprehensive theoretical foundation, such as in the case of group adaptationism, or that are presented with too narrow a focus, as in the case of selectionism.

This chapter explores human individual agency and biological evolutionary theory with the goal of contributing to discussions of how the two can be integrated into a more cohesive approach for examining human sociocultural change. The chapter starts with a brief review of biological evolutionary theory and then examines three perspectives that are ostensibly founded upon ideas from the Darwinian theory of evolution by natural selection: group adaptationism, selectionism, and human behavioral ecology. The latter approach is argued to be a more effective foundation for accommodating human intentional behavior and modeling its affect on sociocultural change. To support this contention, the chapter concludes with two examples that illustrate how human behavioral ecology is an effective way to consider individual behavior within the context of biological evolutionary theory.

THE INDIVIDUAL IN EVOLUTIONARY THEORY

In recent decades, a number of specific approaches to explaining human sociocultural change have been derived from biological evolutionary theory. Particular emphasis has been placed on the Darwinian principle of natural selection, although considerable freedom has been taken in the interpretation of this principle and its importance for human sociocultural evolution. While the process of natural selection is based upon the individual as the unit of evolutionary change, some scholars have either ignored this important foundation of Darwinian theory or they have implicitly or explicitly promoted "multi-level selection" that allows for several different units of change. The result is a number of approaches, ranging from the oft-criticized adaptationist view to the uncompromising selectionist perspective, that claim roots in evolutionary theory but that disagree on the appropriate unit of evolutionary change. This lack of agreement merits further examination.

Evolutionary Theory

In modern biological evolutionary theory, several specific requirements must exist for evolutionary change of any kind to occur: (1) there must be traits on which some selection process operates; (2) there must be mechanisms to create trait variations; (3) there must be a process of trait inheritance; and (4) there must be a mechanism that results in the differential representation of traits (Durham 1991:21–22; Schmid 1987: 83–85; Smith and Winterhalder 1992:26; see also Schilcher and Tennant 1984:4–9). All evolutionary processes, from Lamarckian to natural selection to sexual selection, require each of these in order for any change to take place. In his theory of evolution by natural selection, Darwin, who had no knowledge of Mendelian genetics, was unclear on the mechanisms of trait generation, and he argued that inheritance was blended. Darwin did recognize, however, that traits were inherited from one's parents, and, most importantly, he regarded the process of natural selection as the most powerful process affecting differential reproduction.

The conditions for Darwinian evolution by natural selection to occur are most often outlined as follows:

1. Variation: There is variation in phenotypic traits among members of a population.

2. Inheritance: These traits are heritable to some degree, such that offspring are more like their parents with respect to these traits than they are like the population mean.

3. Differential reproductive success: Different variants tend to give rise to differing numbers of offspring in succeeding generations (Brandon 1990; see also Boone and Smith 1998:142).

Note that all three conditions must be true for evolution by natural selection to occur. Only if there is phenotypic variation and only if this variation is differentially inherited through reproduction from one generation to another will evolution be able to occur. However, as Brandon points out (1990:9–11), these conditions, while necessary, are not sufficient for natural selection to occur. If they were, then evolution would simply occur randomly, with no reference to environmental context. The critical principle of natural selection is that the traits are selected for because they make their bearers better adapted to their environment and increase their expected fitness. Only then does evolution by natural selection occur.

In the modern synthesis of neo-Darwinian evolutionary theory, the basic propositions for the theory of evolution by natural selection have been elaborated, particularly to accommodate our knowledge of genetics. Considerable effort has focused on identifying the traits on which a process of selection operates. In discussions of this issue, scholars have found it useful to distinguish between "replicators" and "interactors," which are abstractions of the traditional genotype-phenotype distinction (Dawkins 1982). A replicator is the specific entity of which copies are made in the process of transmission, such as a gene. The interactor, on the other hand, is the entity whose interaction with the environment actually results in differential replication. In the standard view of evolution by natural selection, the interactor is the individual organism that either dies or survives to pass on its replicators to the next generation through reproduction. However, the replicator-interactor distinction has been made in order to allow for other entities—such as memes and groups—to play a role in evolution by natural selection.

The replicator-interactor distinction opens the way for a balanced consideration of the role of group selection in neo-Darwinian evolutionary theory. After years of relegation to a minor role in evolutionary explanation, group selection has recently reemerged, most notably in D. S. Wilson's (e.g., 1998) consideration of how human groups with certain proportions of altruists could out-compete groups of nonaltruists (see also Soltis et al. 1995). The issue is important in various anthropological manifestations of evolutionary theory and therefore warrants reexamination. At the basic level, the term "group selection" can be confusing, for it usually refers to a unique unit of selection and not to a different process of selection, as the term "natural selection" does. Group selection is also manifested in a number of specific forms, in which the group is considered to be a replicator, an interactor, or even both at the same time (Brandon 1990:97). Several scholars (Brandon 1990:87–88; Maynard Smith 1988:128–129, 138–141) have proposed that group selection (through the process of natural selection) can occur only if the following conditions hold: (1) there is differential reproduction among groups such that group replicators are differentially transmitted from generation to generation; and (2) the interac-

tor—the group—"screens off," or supersedes, properties of other potential units of selection, such as the traits of individuals within the group.

The concept of group selection can be further clarified by examining the two ways that group fitness can be measured (Brandon 1990; Damuth and Heisler 1988). In the first approach, group fitness is considered to be an average of the fitnesses of individuals within the group, while in the second approach, the group fitness is measured only according to the differential reproduction of the groups themselves. In most studies of group selection (e.g., Boehm 1996; Wilson 1998), the first approach is used, with the argument that those groups that increase average individual fitness of group members are being selected for. However, this proposed process violates the necessary conditions for group selection described above; the differential reproduction of groups is not based on the selection of group properties. The replicative success of individual properties is not being "screened off," and therefore the group is neither the interactor nor the replicator. This is therefore not the natural selection of groups at all, but rather individual selection in which a property of the interactor—the individual—is its ability to organize into groups in such a way that all members receive mutual benefits. As Brandon notes (1990:115), this approach only considers "the growth of one group relative to another. It is well understood why the mere growth of one individual relative to another does not count as individual selection." This distinction is critical for evaluating anthropological approaches that claim a foundation in modern biological evolutionary theory.

Only the second way of measuring group fitness, in which only properties unique to the group (and not its members) are relevant, reveals a process of group selection that is consistent with neo-Darwinian evolutionary theory. Group traits must be properties that are unique to the group and that affect group rather than individual fitness, such as in the case of the sex ratio (Maynard Smith 1988:

203), or perhaps through trait frequencies shaped by cultural transmission (Boyd and Richerson 1985; Soltis et al. 1995; but see Palmer et al. 1995). Groups subject to natural selection at this level should also be isolated such that group properties do not flow between them (Brandon 1990:96; Pepper and Smuts 2000:70–71); if this flow of properties were to occur, the resulting changes would not be attributable to natural selection, just as the transfer of genetic material between individuals would not be natural selection, even though it would cause change. Finally, in order for group traits to be heritable, the reproduction of groups should involve a budding or fissioning process in which "offspring" groups consist of individuals randomly chosen from the original group. Even in the rare circumstances when these conditions are met, however, group selection may only be able to explain changes that take over 500–1,000 years (Soltis et al. 1995:481–482). Expecting that groups maintain isolation for that long seems untenable.

Efforts to expand Darwin's theory of evolution by natural selection have also focused on the second requirement of evolution stated at the beginning of this section: the mechanisms that create trait variations. Debate has often focused on the issue of the directed vs. undirected generation of variation. Many scholars have argued that evolution by natural selection necessarily requires that the generation of trait variations be undirected such that the process is uncorrelated with adaptive benefit (Rindos 1989c). Why this needs to be true is unclear. Genetic mutation is generally regarded as undirected, but examples do exist where mutations appear to be directed toward specific environmental conditions (e.g., Rosenberg 2001; Schilcher and Tennant 1984:79–82). And even if the generation of traits is directed, they are not therefore immune from processes of natural selection. For example, evolution by sexual selection—a directed mechanism—and evolution by natural selection—arguably undirected—have always been compatible processes. And in the case of human-induced artificial selection, we often have to go to great lengths to prevent natural selection from operating on the variation that we have created; releasing a toy poodle in an alligator-infested bayou would be sufficient evidence that natural selection will operate on directed variation. Clearly the mechanisms of directed variation are compatible with modern evolutionary theory and therefore do contribute in significant ways to explaining change.

The issues surrounding replicators vs. interactors and undirected vs. directed variation are symptomatic of a larger issue in modern evolutionary theory: overemphasis on the concepts of adaptation and evolution by natural selection. The role of this process in the history of life on earth is unquestionable, and clearly all evolutionary changes must in some way acknowledge the potential effect of natural selection on the resulting variation. But explanations of change should also consider other processes of variation-generation and variation-selection that have evolutionary consequences. This is especially needed for understanding human evolutionary histories. In anthropology, however, the explanation of evolutionary change has always been founded on some interpretation of the neo-Darwinian theory of evolution by natural selection. The following sections review three well-known theoretical perspectives employed in anthropology that rely on some formulation of Darwinian evolutionary theory.

Group Adaptationism

The adaptationist approach to explaining human sociocultural change has been much maligned over the past several years (e.g., Bettinger and Richerson 1996; Brumfiel 1992; Headland 1997; Maschner and Mithen 1996). The reasons for the dissatisfaction with this paradigm are varied, including considerable criticism emerging from post-modern intellectual trends in the discipline, but even from within the evolutionary sciences, three aspects of the adaptationist perspective have been challenged. The first concerns the adaptationist tendency to rely on assumptions that groups were the primary units of sociocultural change, or at least the only units that archaeologists can recognize and thus analyze. Criticism of the group selectionist perspective is discussed in detail above, and can perhaps be best summarized in the following statement: "Where individuals made the right decisions and survived, they have kin in the world today. Whether corporate groups failed has negligible influence on subsequent human evolution except insofar as it determined the fate of individuals" (Nettle 1997:284).

A second line of criticism directed at the adaptationist perspective concerns the concept of adaptation itself. In most applications of group adaptationism, properties of human groups are seen as "adaptations" to specific environmental conditions, such as climate-induced stress or inadequate information flow. The problem is that the terms "adaptive," "adaptation," and "adaptedness" have been used with considerable imprecision (Brandon 1990; Maynard Smith 1988; Schilcher and Tennant 1984). Defining "differential adaptedness" between entities is a particularly contentious issue. The term can refer to actual differential reproductive success, but this would not be able to distinguish differences generated through the process of natural selection from other processes, including chance, that can also produce different levels of reproduction. Differential adaptedness can also refer to the possession of specific properties that are clearly favored by natural selection in all circumstances, but the problem with this is that arguably no property would be advantageous for all evolutionary units in all environments. As Brandon (1990:13) points out, even fecundity is not selected for in all circumstances, so even higher reproduction is not automatically adaptive. The third and final definition of differential adaptedness is based on the identification of specific properties that increase the propensity of evolutionary units to survive and reproduce within a given environment. This last perspective avoids the problems of the first two definitions.

Another critical aspect of the third definition of adaptedness is that it makes the distinction between an "adaptation," which is

an ontogenetic property generated through evolutionary processes, from "adaptability," which is a behavioral process whereby an organism is able to change its phenotype in response to environmental changes (Schilcher and Tennant 1984:39–40). This point is critical, for it acknowledges that human cognitive capacity and our corresponding ability to learn and teach are themselves adaptations that increase individual adaptability, or phenotypic plasticity, to innumerable environmental circumstances. However, just as we would not see a chameleon's change from brown to green as a sudden adaptation resulting from evolutionary processes, it may be inappropriate to refer to human behavioral choices as adaptations. These are more than trivial semantic distinctions. Our cognitive mechanisms are adaptations that increase our propensity to survive and reproduce, but they also partially insulate ourselves from the immediate action of natural selection, just as the chameleon is immune from selective pressures to be either always green or always brown; it can be both as circumstances warrant. With humans, however, our cognitive processes are much more complex and flexible, and Brandon (1990:43) calls much of what humans do "epiphenomenal byproducts" of actual adaptations; the epiphenomena themselves are not adaptations in the evolutionary sense. In fact, individuals often pursue behaviors that can be adaptive, neutral, or counter-adaptive, and our decision-making often unwittingly but usually only briefly exposes us to natural selective pressures. Certainly, the teleological conclusion that what human groups do are adaptations is difficult to maintain from this perspective.

This discussion suggests that the adaptationist tendency to see most human group behavior as adaptations to changing environments might need reevaluation, at least insofar as these adaptations are regarded to be the product of natural selection. This leads to the third criticism of adaptationist approaches: an imprecise articulation with contemporary evolutionary theory. This is exemplified by a recent discussion of adaptation and evolution in which Dean (1996:27) states that "adaptation is an evolutionary outcome of selection in a Darwinian sense, although the adjective 'natural' is not appropriate in [the human cultural] context." A few sentences later, Dean further claims "the relevant traits are behaviors that are selected for or against depending on their contribution to the survival of groups or cultural systems." These are unclear interpretations of neo-Darwinian evolutionary theory, made more so by Dean's claim that "adaptation [refers] to the integration of behavioral, demographic, and environmental variability to help maintain social entities at existing levels of complexity." This perspective is not uncommon in anthropology. It is inconsistent with accepted interpretations of neo-Darwinian processes while at the same time it appeals to the authority of evolutionary theory, perhaps to avoid what many see as less palatable alternatives based on Lamarckian selection or inherent properties of human adaptability. The result is a perplexing perspective that articulates poorly with biological evolutionary theory and that by itself lacks coherence.

Selectionism

Selectionism is often referred to as "cultural selectionism" or more generally as "evolutionary archaeology," although the latter term inaccurately characterizes selectionism as the only evolutionary approach used in archaeology. The genesis of selectionism is usually attributed to the writings of Robert Dunnell, especially his seminal 1980 article, although an earlier paper in 1978 established the framework for his later work. Dunnell's views were a reaction to what he believed was the improper application of Darwinian evolutionary theory in archaeology (an accurate criticism, as discussed in the previous section). Dunnell denounced the progressive and transformational assumptions of unilineal typological theory that ostensibly regarded culture as a selective agent. He also argued that the then-prominent adaptationist explanations of change relied on Lamarckian concepts of directed variation and selection in which humans were seen as spontaneously

generating behavioral variation to solve specific problems. This was seen as a conflation of variation-generation and variation-selection mechanisms, which in neo-Darwinian formulations of evolutionary theory are usually kept distinct.

Selectionists call for a more rigorous application of neo-Darwinian evolutionary theory to archaeological explanation (Dunnell 1989; Lyman and O'Brien 1998). They accordingly regard change in human systems as the differential persistence of discrete cultural "variants." To avoid problems of developing behavioral interpretations of the archaeological record, the variants that selectionists typically emphasize are artifact varieties, which are seen as part of the extended human phenotype. In accordance with a strict interpretation of Darwinian theory that considers variation-generation to be undirected, selectionists regard the origins of variants as irrelevant. In selectionism, human individual intentionality is reduced to a variation-generating mechanism that has no role in the selective process and thus no explanatory potential (Lyman and O'Brien 1998:616–618). Instead, the differential replication of variants and their spread through time and space through the process of natural selection is emphasized. Selectionist explanation involves the identification of environmental factors that are responsible for favoring the perpetuation of specific variants of artifact classes (or, more rarely, behavioral options) by virtue of their "performance characteristics" (Braun 190:79–82; Dunnell 1980; Neff and Larson 1997). Similarly, some selectionist scholars have focused on determining the evolutionary fitness of a specific behavior by measuring its replicability (Leonard and Jones 1987; Teltser 1995c), thereby allowing them to circumvent the critical processes of vertical transmission and individual reproductive success that are the actual mechanisms of biological evolutionary change.

In comparison with the adaptationist approach, the theoretical rigor of the selectionist perspective is laudable. However, a number of potentially problematic interpretations of evolutionary theory should be addressed. First, the focus on "performance characteristics" or "design analysis" is a source of concern. To show that natural selection has occurred and produced an adaptation, evidence should be presented that demonstrates that the property in question has enhanced the adaptedness of the individual and, most importantly, that this has emerged through differential reproduction (Brandon 1990:165). Simply suggesting that a property could or *should* be an adaptation is insufficient, for its generation and perseverance may in fact have nothing to do with the process of natural selection. Similarly, "replicability" is a characteristic of individual traits that may or may not be related to evolution by natural selection. As previously discussed, fecundity and differential reproductive success are not automatically indicative of natural selection having taken place.

Another aspect of selectionist theory that is problematic is the unclear distinction between replicators and interactors (Boone and Smith 1998:143). Natural selection operates most directly on interactors—the phenotype—but the replicability and heritability of the replicators determine the effect of selection. In contemporary evolutionary theory, interactors can be physical traits, behaviors, or even artifacts, but of critical importance is the identification of the replicator, which is normally considered to be the individual organism. In selectionist theory, the replicator-interactor distinction is seldom made and the assumption often seems to be that an artifact variant fulfills both roles, analogous to the interpretation that each of a chameleon's different possible color states are separate evolutionary units that are independently selected for and differentially "replicate."

Lyman and O'Brien (1998:619, 2001a:408) contend that since paleobiologists don't worry about identifying gene replication, selectionists can focus on variant replicative success and avoid identifying exactly what it is that replicates. But this does matter very much (and of course paleobiologists do understand the behavior of the gene as a replicator). Certainly if the individual or gene is the relevant replicator, the process of natural se-

lection will be temporally constrained by the length of human life-spans and we would expect variant evolution (i.e., trends in material culture) to be much slower than the evidence otherwise suggests (Neff 2000). If, on the other hand, the "meme" or an analogous concept is seen as the relevant replicator, as is usually implied in selectionist work (O'Brien and Lyman 2000b:242), then a number of other complications arise. As Maynard Smith (1988:108) notes, the fact that a meme is necessarily a physical structure of the brain means that it can replicate merely by generating a phenotypic representation of itself, in which case differential replication would be promoted regardless of the selective environment. Meme evolution would therefore be primarily geared toward increasing its frequency of phenotypic expression by a single individual. For example, teaching as many people as possible how to make a certain projectile point would increase the variant's frequency regardless of any selective benefits that it might provide. Related issues include how best to accommodate the horizontal and oblique transmission of either memes or the selectionists' artifact variants (Boyd and Richerson 1985; Richerson and Boyd 1992).

All of the criticisms of selectionist theory discussed so far have focused on unresolved issues that are not necessarily insurmountable. A more fundamental issue, however, is the proper role of directed and undirected variation-generation in explanations of human sociocultural change. For selectionists, the genesis of the variation upon which natural selection operates is irrelevant, an odd perspective considering that they also expend considerable effort to promote the process of natural selection as the only "creative" evolutionary process (Rindos 1989c). Although they presumably acknowledge the individual as a critical unit of evolution, the ways that individuals create the behavioral variation that drives evolutionary processes are ignored, often under the dubious assumption that the generation of behavioral variation is analogous to random genetic mutation (e.g. Ramenofsky 1995:135–136). In essence, they treat humans as no different from any other organism with a direct ontogenetic link between genotype and phenotype, only acknowledging that the human phenotype is more complex. As we experience on a daily basis, individuals do consciously and intentionally create new artifacts and generate new behaviors, and they clearly pick and choose from among the myriad traits available to them (e.g., Axelrod 1984:83–84). Not only does this selective process shape the behavioral variation upon which natural selection can operate, but, as Boone and Smith point out (1998:152), this intentional decision-making *is* evolutionary change. To say that these processes are irrelevant to explanation begs the question of what it is that we are trying to explain. In the long run, natural selection presumably will winnow out those traits that are less successful within given contexts. But for much of human history, archaeologists are faced with very rapid, short-term changes that also merit explanation (Boehm 1996; Spencer 1997:223).

What the selectionists have done is confuse the universal applicability of evolution by natural selection with the universal explanatory power of this process; clearly the former is true, but the latter is not (Schilcher and Tennant 1984:63). Natural selection is simply not the only process that can cause evolutionary change in human societies (e.g., Durham 1992:341–350), and the paucity of solid selectionist applications may indicate that natural selection has little relevance to explaining most human cultural change. A good example illustrating the limited explanatory potential of selectionist theory can be seen in this quote from O'Brien and Holland (1995a:180):

> For whatever reason, anthropologists are incapable of shrugging free of intention as the ultimate explanatory device. Intention, however, explains nothing but how variation might be generated. Many early aviators must have leapt from cliffs, propelled by hopeful inventions and the intent of flying. Ultimately, it was the ability to overcome gravity—not intent—that determined which aviators survived to

pass their genes and inspiration on to others.

The problem is that many, if not most, anthropologists are more interested in explaining why someone wanted to fly in the first place, so much so that he or she was jumping off cliffs to try it. That people now fly and that only the successful methods of flying have persevered is simply not very interesting. The selectionist approach fails to justify why we should ignore the enormous array of intentional, individual human behaviors that clearly shape sociocultural changes.

Behavioral Ecology and Individual Decision-Making

In contrast with the adaptationist and selectionist approaches, behavioral ecology regards intentional, goal-oriented individual behavior as an important part of the phenotypic plasticity that defines human adaptability. This is not to deny that the evolutionary process of natural selection is important, both for the role it has played in shaping human cognitive abilities and its continuing influence in culling maladaptive traits from our behavioral repertoires. But behavioral ecology asserts that other variation-generating and variation-selecting processes besides natural selection can directly affect human evolutionary change. Several processes that are potentially complementary have been identified, including individual decision-making and cultural transmission (Boone and Smith 1998; Boyd and Richerson 1985; Durham 1991; Kelly 2000; Smith 2000; Smith and Winterhalder 1992). All of these approaches implicitly or explicitly recognize that evolution by natural selection has led to the development of specific cognitive processes that guide human learning and decision-making and that accordingly shape our individual and group behavior.

The primary influence of neo-Darwinian evolutionary theory on behavioral ecology is the underlying assumption that human cognition, no matter the specific mechanisms involved, has evolved such that it promotes individual self-interest (Boone and Smith 1998;

Smith and Winterhalder 1992). The contention is that the human mind is not a *tabula rasa* that merely directly copies other behaviors, but rather that it possesses some innate propensities that allow individuals to rationally choose behavioral options that have the best potential for achieving specific individual goals that in turn probabilistically promote reproductive success. The focus in behavioral ecology on individual self-interest is founded on the assumption that natural selection operates on the individual and therefore would not lead to mechanisms detrimental to the individual; if theories of the natural selection of groups discussed above are accepted as true, we would need to acknowledge that the fundamental mechanisms shaping human decision-making could promote group rather than self interest. But until group behavior is shown to be something more than mutualism, mechanisms that enhance individual self-interest are the recognized outcomes of our evolutionary past.

Demonstrating that humans actually behave rationally has been a problematic issue. Part of the problem is that human rationality cannot be expected to be identical across all individuals, even if it is innate. Humans obviously vary in their capacities for rationality, as measured in temporary or permanent differences in cognitive abilities (Feinman 1995: 262; Hayden 1995:20–21; Mithen 1989: 491). Other criticism has focused on specific "agent-based" modeling techniques that are accused of assuming that humans possess a "preposterously omniscient rationality" (Jochim 1983:162–164; Mithen 1989:488; Moore 1983:175–177). Critics have especially berated strict optimization models that predict how perfectly rational humans should interact with a presumably completely knowable physical environment. However, these approaches are often criticized for the wrong reasons. The assumption of rationality is not necessarily wrong, just the manner in which it is applied. This is because rationality is contingent on both the specific goals that individuals hope to achieve and the historical, physical, and social contexts in which they

are making their decisions. When models acknowledge these contingencies, they can better accommodate the "limited" or "culturally bound" rationality that best characterizes human decision-making (Cowgill 2000; Kelly 2000:66–67; Webster 1996). At the most basic level, the concept of rationality simply contends that humans act consistently when presented with the same goals in identical circumstances. Many of the cases of "irrational" behavior that critics point to as proof against universal human rationality are really examples of humans pursuing goals or utilities different from those that the critics expect. Whether these goals or utilities make sense from the perspective of somatic or reproductive maximization is a separate issue.

Critics of human behavioral ecology have also focused on the concept of maximization, which they believe is an inappropriate way to characterize human decision-making. Selectionists rightfully point out that the process of natural selection does not directly produce maximizing behavior (O'Brien and Holland 1995b:154–156). Rather, natural selection only promotes individual behaviors that perform relatively better than the behaviors engaged in by others. Of course, unless only one individual exists in any given context, this constant improvement produces behaviors that operate as if they are maximizing. And if actual maximizing behaviors or cognitive mechanisms were to emerge, natural selection would likely promote them. However, selectionists deny or ignore the possibility that human decision-making, having been shaped by natural selection, operates to increase or maximize somatic and reproductive fitness. This is because they see human behavior as serving exclusively to produce the variability on which natural selection operates; the role of decision-making in generating and selecting variation is disregarded.

Most of the criticism of the concept of maximization is based on the belief that it always refers to the acquisition of as many resources as possible. This is a misunderstanding of the concept. Maximization is dependent on the specific utility being measured. Different goals pursued in particular contexts will have a unique structure, or "utility function," that mediates the relationship between individual preferences and the actual quantities of a resource that are obtained and thereby determines how maximization is actually expressed (Boone 1992: 320–322; Fitzhugh 2001:129–132; Smith and Boyd 1990:169–173; Smith and Winterhalder 1992:46–49, 55–56; Winterhalder et al. 1999:304–306). In many cases, such as where storage is not possible, the maximization of one's utility will not equate with the acquisition of maximum quantities of a resource since at a certain point additional units of the resource are useless or even detrimental to the individual. Furthermore, if we accept that human decision-making is determined by proximal mechanisms shaped by our evolutionary history, then these mechanisms can be subverted for the maximization of utilities that do not directly influence our expected fitness. For example, our decision-making can be affected by ideological considerations that alter our utilities in ways that can even lead to behaviors that diminish our fitness. As an extreme example, one's utility could actually be to maximize someone else's utility, such that "rationally" maximizing one's own utility ends up reducing their own fitness. Such is the nature of human goal-oriented decision-making, which although shaped by natural selection is no longer ruled by it.

Comparisons can be made between the agent-based approach of human behavioral ecology and the increasingly popular paradigm of practice or agency theory (e.g., Dobres and Robb 2000b). Agency approaches reflect influence by Giddens (1984) and Bourdieu (1977) and are intended to overcome what are seen as flaws in methodological individualism—the foundation of neo-Darwinian theory—by acknowledging sociocultural structure, historical contingencies, and their dynamic influence on individual action. In practice, however, "purported case studies in agency theory actually constitute a retreat back to methodological individualism... Agents are typically seen as dominant individuals acting in their own self-interests" (Gillespie 2001:74). Most concrete archaeological examples of agency theory ultimately rely heavily on ecological explanations, and accordingly they look very much like human behavioral ecology without the neo-Darwinian foundations. Therefore, while agency theory has provided a needed evaluation of strictly ahistorical and acultural methodological individualism, I find it ultimately deficient in two related ways. First, as manifested in archaeology, agency theory appears to lack explicit modeling procedures. In most case studies, the analyst observes an example of social and political conflict and then situates this within the general guidelines of agency theory. Less clear is how variations in the expression of agency can be consistently explained. This leads to the second criticism: agency theory does not explicitly outline why humans should behave the way they do. If agency is present in all sociocultural contexts (e.g., Roscoe 1993:114; Webster 1996:610–611), does this not suggest some universal propensity for individualistic behavior? If this is true, it would seem that neo-Darwinian theory and human behavioral ecology, as long it is historically and contextually sensitive, should provide a more comprehensive approach for understanding and modeling agency that is consistent across disciplinary boundaries (see also Clark 2000).

To summarize, then, human behavioral ecology is based on the assumption that individual decision-making is guided by a number of specific adaptations that have been shaped by natural selection as a way to promote adaptability through rapid phenotypic plasticity. Decision-making is guided by innate self-interest and the promotion of somatic and reproductive success as measured proximally through utility maximization. Individuals are assumed to make rational, or consistent, decisions that maximize utility. In the long term, utility is likely to correlate with the probability for reproductive success, an assumption that has formed the foundation for much of the research in human behavioral ecology (e.g., Cronk 1991:29–41). However, a corollary of the indirect articulation between individual decision-making and individual reproductive success is that this relationship will not always be perfect, for the process of human rationalization is always susceptible to error, misguided utility, and manipulation. Furthermore, the choices available to individuals and the decisions they make depend on environmental, social, and historical constraints and especially on the expected actions and reactions of other individuals in the group. While the mechanisms of individual decision-making are designed to lead us to make "adaptive" behavioral choices, this need not always be the case. For some scholars, this disjunction between individual agency and neo-Darwinian explanation is reason enough to retreat to group adaptationist approaches (e.g., Braun 1991). Others, however, see this disjunction as the source for much of the interesting behavioral variability exhibited by humans both in the past and in the present (Bird 1997; Cronk 1999).

EXAMPLES FROM THE
SOUTHWESTERN UNITED STATES

Most of the debate over the role of intentional individual decision-making in evolutionary change has focused on theoretical issues, with less attention dedicated to developing studies that actually employ or evaluate the different approaches. Nowhere is this more true than in selectionist publications, which have only more recently dedicated any significant effort to actually demonstrate the efficacy of their perspective, often with very ambiguous results that bring up concerns of equifinality and teleology; as Kelly notes (2000:65), "stated bluntly, selectionist archaeology has yet to 'solve' any longstanding problems of prehistory." Accordingly, to avoid hypocrisy, two brief examples from the prehistoric Southwest are presented to demonstrate the validity of an approach based on human behavioral ecology and individual decision-making. The first example is "negative" in the sense that it presents a case study that primarily critiques some of the assumptions that underlie adaptationist and selectionist perspectives. The second example

is "positive" in that it provides a case study in which an understanding of individual agency founded on behavioral ecology is employed to explain prehistoric human behaviors that are not adaptations but that do comprise evolutionary change.

Community Definition and
Demographic Sustainability

Archaeologists focusing on the prehistoric Southwest have for some time been concerned with how best to define the concept of "community," both in the sense of a theoretical definition and as a physical entity of the archaeological record (e.g., Kolb and Snead 1997; Varien 1999). Clearly this is an important issue, for interpretations of community and group boundaries, mechanisms for their maintenance, community political organization, and the function of monumental architecture all depend on how communities are identified on the prehistoric landscape. The argument presented in this section is that interpretations that frequently appear in discussions of the topic are implicitly or explicitly based on questionable assumptions from adaptationist or selectionist theory.

In an important 1980 article, S. Plog attempted to determine the level of autonomy experienced by communities in the prehistoric Southwest. His discussion was based on what was probably an accurate belief that most archaeologists saw clusters of habitations as having been primarily autonomous from one another. To build a new understanding of community autonomy, Plog appealed to simulation research conducted by H. M. Wobst (1974, 1975) that concluded that a minimum of 175–475 people must participate in a mating network in order for the population to be demographically stable. Based on population density figures from various phases of Southwestern prehistory, Plog (1980:136) predicted changes in the sizes of territories within which, according to Plog's argument, communities could not have been autonomous. This information was in turn used to evaluate changing roles of stylistic variation in maintaining intercommunity boundaries.

Since Plog's article, the issue of demographic stability for defining community extent or group sustainability has emerged a number of times. For example, Powell (1988: 188–189) discusses the requirements of minimal mating networks in the summary volume of the Paleoenvironmental Group. In a 1994 volume on Southwestern communities, at least two of the articles (Adler 1994:99; Graves 1994:165) refer to demographic consequences of community size, with Graves noting that "the adaptive role of ceramic design boundaries is debatable, at least in a strict sense of the word, as promoting differential female or social group survivorship or ability to persist in a given region." Rautman (1996:199–200) argues that "all local groups are already presumably participating in some form of extra-local interaction, if only to provide social contacts that are necessary to maintain a mating network of sufficient size over time." More recently, in an excellent discussion of community definition, Kolb and Snead (1997:611) appeal to "demographic consistencies" and define a community as "a minimum demographic component comprised of a core of individuals…whose repeated interactions socially reproduce the group." While they do not define or illustrate what they mean by social reproduction, their discussion has been used as a foundation for interpreting the spatial scale of prehistoric Southwestern communities according to "the minimum number of people and geographic area that would be required to maintain a reproductively viable social unit" (Mahoney 2000:20).

What is important about these various statements on community and group definition is that they assume that a minimum number of individuals must exist in order for a community to sustain itself. Most of the statements refer to Wobst's 1974 simulation illustrating that in populations below a certain threshold, people will be unable to find "appropriate" mates and demographic stability will be challenged. The problem with these assumptions is that no clear mechanism is proposed whereby people recognize and maintain proper mating networks. Since many of these studies are informed by adaptationist viewpoints, presumably the belief is that a specific adaptive behavior will direct groups to maintain the proper demographic levels either internally or through the formation of adequately sized intercommunity mating networks. How is this adaptive behavior identified and selected? A selectionist perspective might appeal to the process of natural selection to ensure that demographic sustainability is maintained, but this process would almost certainly require many generations even in the unlikely event that contextual factors were stable; Wobst's simulations (1974:15–16) identified a demographic "half-life" of 180 years in which half of a minimum band of 25 people would cease to exist.

The issue that is important in this example is that no role is given to the process of human behavioral selection and decision-making. Individuals operating in group contexts are the ones creating and maintaining the sociopolitical networks that might allow for sustainable demographics, but it is not clear how they would know that communities of less than 175 people (or any other number) endanger demographic or social stability. Without innate mechanisms analogous to incest taboos and without enough time and contextual stability to allow for the operation of natural selection, how can we assume that demographic sustainability will be maintained by humans? We can't, and we probably should not use this assumption as a foundation for defining community boundaries or intergroup networks. Undoubtedly other decisions made by individuals in group contexts are more likely to reduce mating networks instead of sustain them, as illustrated by a number of studies of modern and historic populations from around the world in which factors from geographic isolation to ethnic endogamy have reduced the size of mating networks (e.g., Durham 1991:305–309; Mascie-Taylor and Boyce 1988; Narancic and Rudan 2001; Nelsen et al. 2001).

In the prehistoric Southwest, evidence does exist to suggest that adequate demographic networks were not always maintained and that their sizes varied considerably over time and from place to place. Osteological data are potentially useful for identifying situations in which mating networks were exceptionally small, for many heritable congenital defects can be identified through the analysis of skeletal remains. When there is a strong genetic component to the defects, their frequencies can help to determine whether mating networks were so small as to promote the appearance of genetic diseases or defects. No osteological analyses in the Southwest have directly considered this issue, but a few do provide relevant discussions. One example is a study conducted by W. D. Wade (1979, 1981) on a collection of Kayenta Anasazi remains from seven sites in northern Arizona. Wade focused on skeletal indicators of Klippel-Feil Syndrome (KFS), an inherited condition that has been linked to four dominant, recessive, and X-linked alleles. The clinical definition of the syndrome centers on the congenital fusion of parts of the vertebral column, especially C2–3, but a number of more serious symptoms ranging from dermatological problems to cardiovascular disorders are also associated. Extreme cases can result in death (Barnes 1994:67–71). In the skeletal assemblage that Wade analyzed, KFS was identified in an astounding 5 of 29 individuals and possibly as many as 8 of 40, most from one site; normal frequencies range from 1:42,000 to 3:700 births. Barnes's discussion (1994:70) of Wade's data leads her to conclude that "the high frequency of [KFS] suggests genetic isolation."

Other studies have also noted cases suggestive of KFS, although they were not identified as such. In his discussion of 38 individuals (many of which were incomplete) from the Chaco Canyon site of Bc59, Reed (1962) describes two skeletons that appear to exhibit evidence of KFS. He notes (Reed 1962: 246) that the symptoms he saw were "rare... but not unheard of in Southwestern Indian material" (see also Reed 1967). Site Bc59 was one of the more elaborate and comparatively wealthy "small houses" in Chaco Can-

yon—it was the location of a turquoise jewelry workshop (see the second case study below)—and perhaps mating networks were intentionally limited, as is often the case among elite members of society. Interestingly, Barnes's summary of axial defects in Southwestern skeletal populations (1994) describes numerous congenital defects in skeletal material from nearby Pueblo Bonito, although the data are anecdotal and not quantitative.

Barnes's analysis (1994) of late prehistoric Rio Grande populations has also identified high frequencies of KFS, or what she calls "block vertebrae." Small samples of skeletal material from Puye, Otowi, and Tsankawi exhibit frequencies of the disorder ranging from 5.6 percent to 15.4 percent, and Barnes further notes (1994:70–71) that cases of block vertebrae are known from other late prehistoric sites, including Las Humanas, Arroyo Hondo, Homol'ovi, Giusewa, Amoxiumqua, Hawikku, and Heshotauthla. The cases she identifies are relatively minor, but Barnes indicates that high frequencies of minor conditions likely indicate that severe, debilitating defects also existed, but that individuals with these defects would "rarely find their way into skeletal collections—primarily because of low neonatal survival rates" (Barnes 1994:320). Barnes suggests that village endogamy could be responsible for the distribution of KFS in the late prehistoric Southwest.

Other defects attributed to genetic origins have also been identified in abnormally high frequencies among late prehistoric skeletal populations. For example, in her analysis of skeletal material from the Tijeras Canyon project, Ferguson (1980) identified high frequencies of congenital defects, including spina bifida occulta, bipartite petallae, congenital scoliosis, and anatomical characteristics promoting hip dislocation. Changing frequencies of these defects over time are particularly interesting, for they appear to increase among the latest skeletal materials. The skeletal data may indicate that the intensive village aggregation characterizing the late occupation of Tijeras Canyon reduced mating networks and threatened demographic sustainability. Tijeras residents, as well as other late prehistoric villages, may have intentionally restricted marriage outside of the community to protect scarce village resources. Combined with the apparently abysmal health of the latest prehistoric inhabitants of Tijeras Canyon, it seems likely that these and related behaviors were not "adaptive" for maintaining group demographics, but they do reflect evolutionary changes that merit explanation.

The point of these examples is not to suggest that people in the prehistoric Southwest were consistently maladapted or "inbred," nor to offer well-tested explanations for why mating networks would be limited in particular cases. Rather, this discussion demonstrates that a priori assumptions of group adaptive behavior such as the maintenance of mating networks should not form the basis for identifying probable community boundaries or intergroup interaction networks. Individuals arguably cannot recognize these properties of the groups in which they live, and it is instead their decisions guided by their goals and utilities that shape their social interactions. These goals and utilities, in turn, are shaped by self-interest within the context of historical and contemporary contingencies. While the mechanisms that guide individual decision-making are adaptations that increase our adaptability, they are not omnipotent nor are they always directed to solving problems that enhance survivability or reproductive success. Even less often are they directed towards the promotion of group survivability or "reproductive" success.

Resource Monopolization, Package Size, and Turquoise

In the prehistory of the Southwest United States, the emergence and development of the Chaco Anasazi between A.D. 900 and 1150 remains a focus of continuing research (e.g., Kantner and Mahoney 2000; Mathien 2001; Wills 2000). This sociocultural tradition attracts the curiosity of both the general public and archaeologists alike due to the intriguing

patterns that have been identified. Massive great houses, live macaws from Mesoamerica, extensive roadways, and solar observatories are some of the material traits associated with the Chacoan "phenomenon" that have mystified scholars for a century. One of the features of the Chaco Anasazi that has received considerable attention was their apparent interest in turquoise, which appears in large quantities in many Chacoan sites; the vast majority of prehistoric turquoise recovered in the entire Southwest is from the alleged Chacoan center of Chaco Canyon, particularly in association with two extravagant burials (Neitzel 1989). While turquoise artifacts have been recovered from Southwestern sites that both predate and postdate the Chaco Anasazi tradition, scholars remain mystified as to why turquoise played such an important role in Chacoan society. In this section, a model derived from a behavioral ecological perspective with a focus on individual decision-making is presented and evaluated.

In other works firmly based in human behavioral ecology (Kantner 1996, 1999), I have proposed that the development of Chaco Anasazi sociocultural patterns were directly related to the actions of self-interested individuals whose activities were stimulated and structured by changing environmental contexts beginning around A.D. 900. Outlining the entire developmental model is beyond the scope of this chapter, but an important component that is seen as influencing the expression of individual self-interested behavior is the structure of available resources. In particular, the model proposes that the presence of resources that are either maximizable, monopolizable, or both can significantly influence sociopolitical change since they alter the structure of social interactions and allow some individuals to gain advantages not available to others. A maximizable resource is one that exhibits a linear or increasing utility function (Fig. 7.1a, b); the greater the quantity of the resource that one possesses, the more valuable it is to them (e.g., Boone 1992:320–322; Smith and Boyd

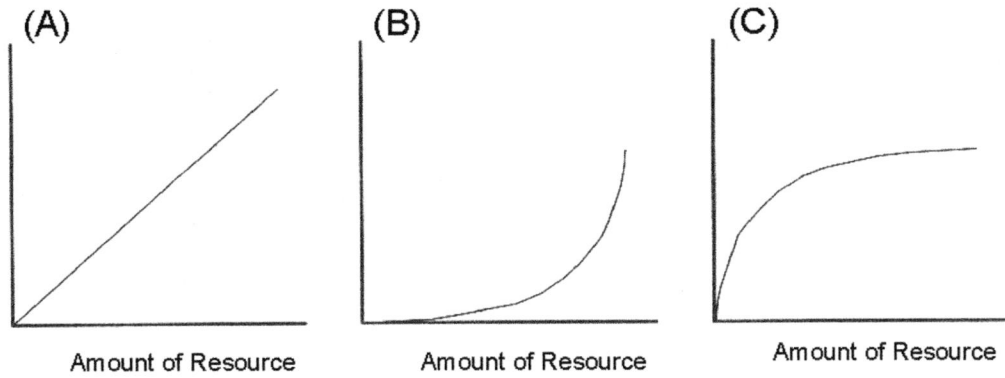

Figure 7.1. Examples of different functions that represent the relationships between quantifiable payoffs and either fitness, in the case of a "fitness function," or preferences, in the case of a "utility function": (a) illustrates a linear function, (b) is an increasing-returns function, and (c) is a diminishing-returns function.

1990:169–171; Winterhalder et al. 1999). An especially lucrative maximizable good is one that is amenable to investment. For example, a resource that can be used for creating obligations through balanced or incremental reciprocal exchange is potentially maximizable (Betzig 1988; Godelier 1982:31–32; Hayden and Gargett 1990:14; Modjeska 1991:238). A resource or its means of production is monopolizable if access to it can be restricted (Earle 1991:5–7; Kristiansen 1991:22; Modjeska 1982:63).

A number of studies based in behavioral ecology have considered how the monopolizability and maximizability of a resource can structure social behavior. For example, the storability and defensibility of a particular resource are seen as important factors that determine the role that the resource will play in social interactions. Because bulky and perishable items are harder to store for future use and less easy to defend (Hawkes 1992:238–294), a resource of this type can be characterized by a diminishing-returns utility function (Fig. 7.1c), in which, at a certain point, additional units will be useless since retaining them long enough to use would be costly. These resources face an additional problem in that individuals with few units may be willing to pay high costs to seize the resource from others; those possessing a surplus may find it too costly to deter such theft (Cashdan 1992:265). In Figure 7.2, for example, individual A has more of the resource than they can use, while individual B can still benefit by acquiring more. In this case, B will be willing to pay greater costs to gain more of the resource, while A will have little incentive to pay the cost of defending the resource from B. This situation illustrates the concept of "tolerated theft" that may explain many forms of resource sharing (Bliege Bird and Bird 1997; Fitzhugh 2001:135; Hawkes 1993:346; Smith and Boyd 1990:185); individual A may be willing to just give away some of the resource since it will do them more harm than good to continue to defend it against B. In other words, such a resource is difficult to monopolize and inequities in resource ownership difficult to maintain. In contrast, small and long-lasting items are easier to monopolize and can in fact increase such inequities and influence sociopolitical change.

In virtually all applications in human behavioral ecology, the resources that are considered are those that directly sustain somatic and reproductive functions. By their very nature, these items are subject to tolerated theft and therefore difficult to monopolize. However, because *any* desired resources that are monopolizable and maximizable can theoretically promote inequities, other goods can

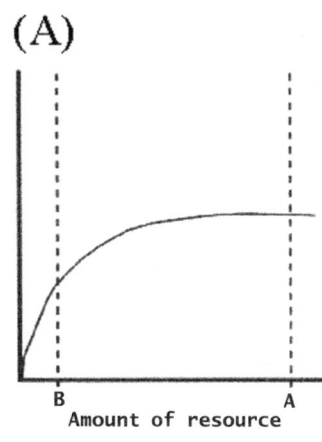

(B)

A ⟍ B	Seize Resource	Do Nothing
Defend Resource	V_b −C −V_a −C	0 0
Give Resource	V_b −V_a	V_b −V_a

Variables:
    V_a=value of resource to player A
    V_b=value of resouce to player B
    C=cost of injury
Solutions:
    given utility function in (A), the
    solution is for Player B to try to
    seize the resource and for Player A
    to just give it to B.

Figure 7.2. An example of conditions that can promote "tolerated theft": (a) illustrates the utility function shared by Players A and B in reference to some resource, showing that Player A has more of the resource than Player B; (b) shows the strategic game for their interaction when Player B wants some of Player A's resource. The rational choice in this situation is for Player A to give the resource to Player B rather than incur the costs of Player B trying to seize the resource.

also play important roles in economic and sociopolitical development. In particular, so-called "prestige" goods possess a variety of characteristics that make them especially amenable to the emergence of economic differentiation. Most are characterized by small "package size," which makes them more easily stored and defended and therefore less susceptible to tolerated theft (Hawkes 1992). Their roles as obligation-creating or prestige-enhancing gifts or directly as exchange items make them eminently maximizable (e.g., Gosden 1989; Levy 1993). They also resist discounting that would degrade their value and result in a diminishing-returns utility function unless used immediately (Green et al. 1995).

The problem with prestige goods is that they have no inherent value, for in and of themselves they do not enhance somatic or reproductive success. This is where the manipulability of the human decision-making process is important, for the perceived values of resources only indirectly articulate with any possible adaptive or maladaptive in-

fluences they may actually have on the individual. In my model for the development of the Chaco Anasazi (Kantner 1999), I argue that the essential route for assigning value to prestige items is by manipulating the historical ideological role that these items may have. Through this process, which is analogous to the "materialization of ideology" proposed by other scholars (DeMarrais et al. 1996; Helms 1994b), material value can be assigned to maximizable and monopolizable objects that have no inherent value. This manipulation can be (and in fact may always be) the first step in the creation of a prestige goods economy, which in turn can result in socioeconomic inequalities that promote sociopolitical change.

As a resource with distinctive visual characteristics, a limited natural distribution, and small "package size," turquoise would have been a perfect material for creating a prestige good that could serve the self-interest of certain individuals among the Chaco Anasazi. As a resource for augmenting socioeconomic inequities and sociopolitical differentiation,

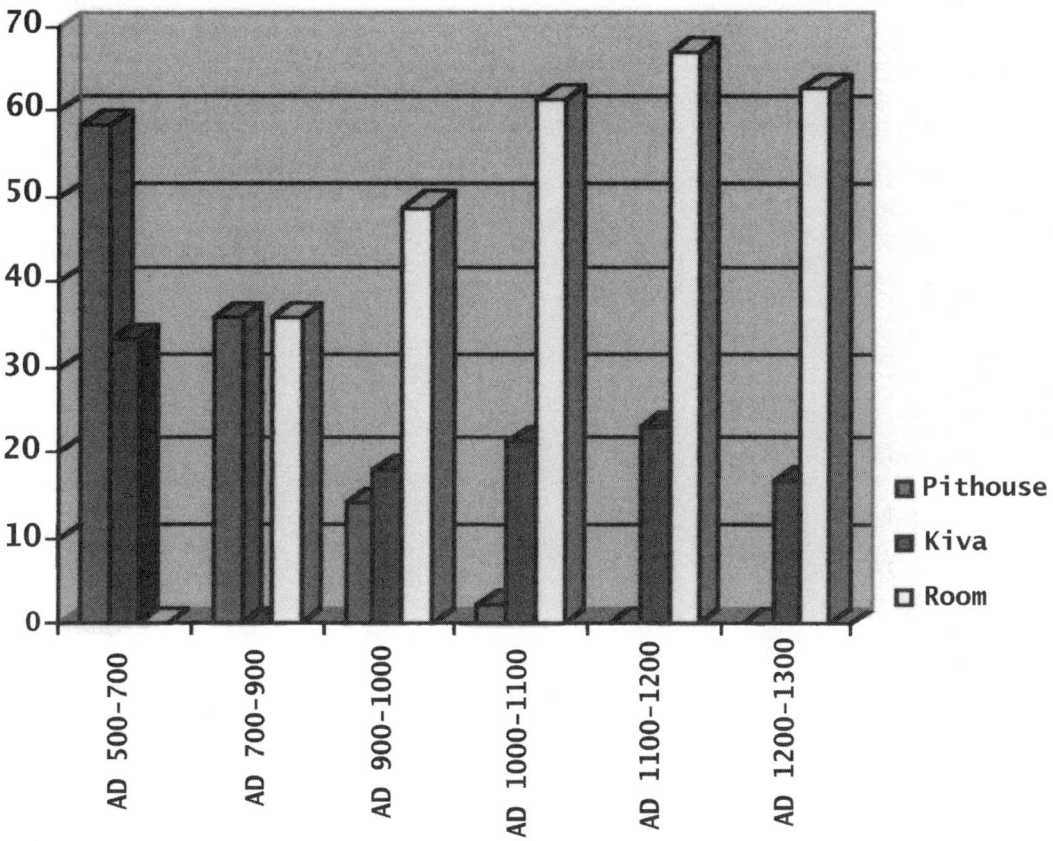

Figure 7.3. Frequencies of turquoise organized according to general context of recovery.

turquoise would have been substantially more effective than other common resources such as maize, which has virtually none of the characteristics that make it monopolizable or maximizable. However, for turquoise to have been amenable to manipulation of ideological value, it would have already needed a place in the ideological system prior to its development as a socioeconomic resource. Accordingly, the most likely individuals to "materialize" the ideological value of turquoise would have been those with ideological authority. The expectation, therefore, is that turquoise would have had a historical connection with the ideological realm, but that it would increasingly have served as a socioeconomic resource as sociopolitical complexity increased in Chacoan society.

As a preliminary evaluation of this behavioral ecological model for turquoise use in

Chaco Anasazi society, information on the date, context, and artifact form was collected for over 500 contexts in which turquoise has been recovered in the Greater San Juan Basin area surrounding Chaco Canyon. Data collected included the general context of recovery, the specific feature from which turquoise was recovered, and the artifact form. In subsequent analyses, contexts and artifact forms were further aggregated according to whether their function was secular, ritual, or otherwise. For example, turquoise recovered from ceremonial kivas or interred at the base of pilasters were distinguished from turquoise recovered from more clearly domestic contexts, such as storage cists in a pueblo room. Similarly, many of the turquoise artifacts were beads or pendants that most likely were designed to be personal adornment, while other artifact forms, such as mosaics and

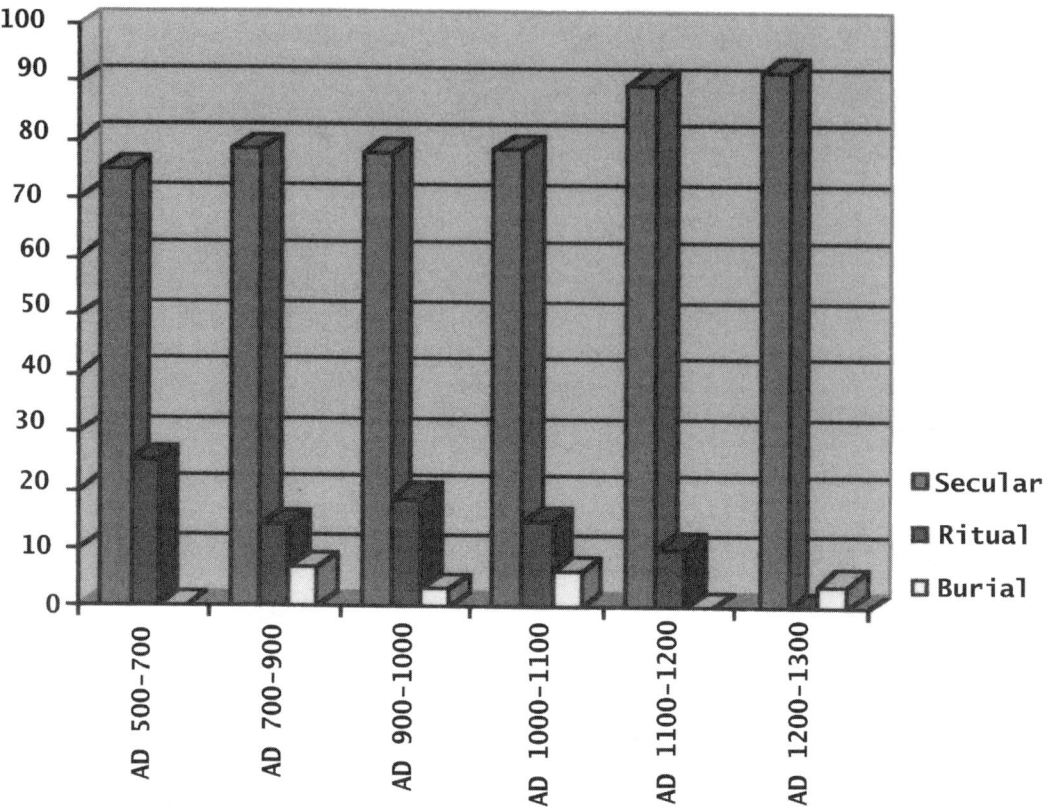

Figure 7.4. Frequencies of turquoise organized according to type of feature from which the artifacts were recovered.

inlays, appear to have had a more ritually oriented function. This classification of the data is subject to interpretation; for example, controversy continues on how to define a ceremonial kiva from a domestic pit structure (e.g., Lekson 1988). It is therefore gratifying that the data do exhibit interesting temporal patterning (also see Mathien 2001, who independently confirms these patterns).

An examination of changing frequencies of turquoise use by the Anasazi both before and during the Chaco era demonstrates that the patterning predicted by the behavioral model is tentatively confirmed by the data. Figure 7.3 displays changing frequencies of contexts in which turquoise has been recovered. It shows that over 30 percent of the contexts for Basketmaker III turquoise are interpreted to be ceremonial kivas. In contrast, as the Chaco tradition emerges, the frequency of turquoise from kivas declines while the

number of times that turquoise appears in pueblo rooms rapidly increases. Of course, the increase in rooms during Pueblo I reflects the growing use of above-ground architecture. It is also relevant to note that this particular aggregation of the data does not distinguish between those turquoise artifacts found in kiva fill and those interred in a niche in a kiva, each which would lead to different interpretations. Nevertheless, the relative decrease of turquoise in kiva contexts is intriguing. The data generally support the expectation of changing turquoise use from a ritual function to one that is more secular.

Fewer interpretive problems complicate other patterns in the turquoise data. Figure 7.4 displays frequencies demonstrating changes in the specific features from which turquoise artifacts were recovered. As predicted by the model, the relative frequency of turquoise found in ritually oriented features

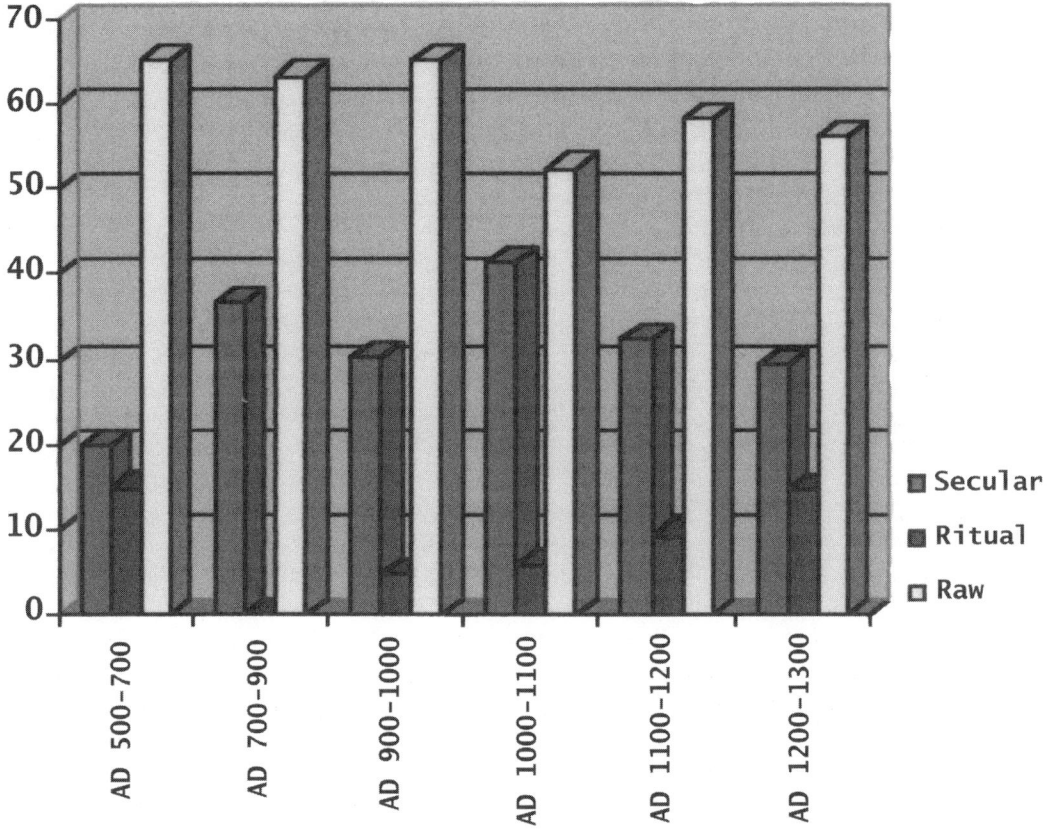

Figure 7.5. Frequencies of turquoise organized according to the artifact form.

declines over time, while the appearance of turquoise in secular contexts increases. Support for the model also comes from changing frequencies of artifact form (Fig. 7.5). This figure demonstrates a decrease in ritual turquoise objects from Basketmaker III to Pueblo II and a corresponding increase in secular items associated with personal adornment. Note that in the earlier Basketmaker and Pueblo I periods, many of the so-called "raw" turquoise artifacts (unworked or partially modified pieces) were actually recovered from ritual contexts, such as pieces found placed in kiva benches or at the bases of kiva posts. During Pueblo II, turquoise is still used in ritual contexts, but greater quantities of artifacts are in the form of beads, earrings, or pendants. Interestingly, and in accordance with the model, after the Chaco tradition falls apart and as Chaco Canyon is abandoned, the trend is reversed.

Although the sample sizes, especially for the earlier periods, are small, the data support the agent-based behavioral model of turquoise use. As predicted, turquoise apparently had an important religious function and ideological value during the earliest periods, when it was often buried in wall foundations, kiva benches, or the base of posts or pilasters (Mathien 2001). As the Chaco Anasazi sociopolitical tradition developed, the value of turquoise took on an increasingly secular value as an item of personal ownership. This is not to deny that it still had ceremonial value—its continued use in post-Chacoan ritual contexts suggests that the ceremonial value of turquoise was never lost—but it did begin to be unequally distributed in secular forms and context. Its small package size, limited availability, ease of storage and identification as personal property, and its preexisting ideological value would have made it the perfect material for maximization and monopolization. Accordingly, during the height of Chaco development during Pueblo II, turquoise was likely important in the structuring of socioeconomic and political relationships. This interpretation is greatly facilitated by the perspective of human behavioral ecology and its focus on individual decision-making in social contexts and how self-interested behavior can structure sociocultural change. Adaptationist or selectionist perspectives would find it more difficult to explain this kind of evolutionary change.

CONCLUSIONS

Human behavioral ecology contends that individuals make decisions according to the goals they are trying to achieve and the utilities and currencies that they employ to evaluate their options. While goal-oriented behavior is ultimately tied to adaptive behavioral mechanisms that enhance human adaptability, proximal manifestations of these mechanisms are often only distantly related to individual adaptation. Decision-making processes can even be structured by utilities and currencies that are maladaptive for the individual or detrimental to group preservation. Decision-making mechanisms can also be manipulated in order to achieve the ends of the few to the detriment of the many. Ultimately, the process of natural selection is responsible for shaping the cognitive mechanisms that drive individual behavior, and it also continues to affect human behavioral variability over longer time spans. But our decision-making mechanisms guide much of the short-term behavioral changes that interest anthropologists and that merit explanation.

This perspective challenges both the adaptationist and selectionist positions, for both minimize the role that individual intentional behavior plays in sociocultural evolutionary change. In the case of the adaptationist approach, the implicit focus on group selection and methodological collectivism is hard to sustain considering what we know of individual human behavior. And the perspective's selective adoption of certain aspects of neo-Darwinian natural selection theory leads to an incoherent approach to explaining human sociocultural phenomena. In contrast, the selectionist perspective is so rigorously focused on the theory of evolution by natural selection that individual human decision-making is all but ignored. Advocates of selectionism disregard the argument that our evolved adaptability allows individuals to pursue behaviors that by their very nature are designed to promote rapid evolutionary change.

Ultimately, much of the disagreement regarding the proper role of biological evolutionary theory in anthropological explanations of change can be attributed to the imprecise use of concepts from natural selection theory. Particularly abused are terms such as "adaptive," "adapted," and "adaptation." As discussed in this paper, in biological circles, these terms are explicitly distinct from one another and very cautiously applied. This conceptual rigor has not carried over to anthropology. Instead, the tendency has been to regard everything that humans do as an adaptation of some sort, and therefore all we need to do to explain why things change is to identify the selective pressures that made the new behaviors adaptive. The resulting scenarios cannot help but be teleological and accommodative. Extreme examples of this kind of interpretation are those that cannot be tied directly to a clear adaptive function and therefore are explained as "wasteful behaviors" that are adaptive because they impede human reproductive efforts (e.g., Graves and Ladefoged 1995). Such explanations beg questions of causality.

The perspective advocated in this paper does not deny the relevant force of natural selection in constraining human adaptability, but to attribute everything to this evolutionary process seems an untenable position for an anthropologist to take, for it really offers no help in explaining the behaviors that surround us on a daily basis. But, as they say, the proof is in the pudding, and it is hoped that the examples presented in this paper illustrate how human behavioral ecology and agent-based modeling can contribute to our understanding of human behavior and evolutionary sociocultural change.

ACKNOWLEDGMENTS

This chapter was originally prepared for the symposium "Method and Theory 2000" organized by Todd VanPool and Christine Van-Pool for the 1999 SAA annual meeting in Chicago, Illinois. I am grateful for having been included in the list of prestigious participants. Special thanks to the following people for their comments and guidance: Todd Van-Pool, Christine VanPool, Ron Hobgood, Kevin Vaughn, Frank Williams, Bob Preucel, and an anonymous reviewer. Thanks also to Jameela Turay for assisting me with some of the research. As always, all inadequacies are my responsibility.

8

Agency and Evolution: The Role of Intended and Unintended Consequences of Action

TODD L. VANPOOL AND CHRISTINE S. VANPOOL

One of the earliest and most sustained critiques of an evolutionary approach to archaeology is that it fails to treat humans as intelligent creatures with decision-making capabilities. According to such critiques, evolutionary archaeology (hereafter referred to as EA) is accused of employing a reductionistic approach to behavior in which the humanity of humans is rejected, and human behavior is considered little more than conditioned responses to external stimuli. In other words, an evolutionary approach is accused of reducing humans to biological automatons who mindlessly wander landscapes while processes such as natural selection mechanistically control their behavior. For example, Bruce Trigger (1989:306) argues that an EA approach "carries to an extreme the denial that consciousness and intentionality play a significant role in shaping human behavior." George Cowgill (2000:52; see also Clark 2000) echoes Trigger when he states:

> I am highly critical of the "strict selectionist" [Evolutionary Archaeological] version, associated especially with Robert Dunnell and his students...A crucial aspect of strict selectionism is that individual intentions have no explanatory power, at least not on the scale appropriate for archaeology. This is diametrically opposed to my view...The mind-set of strict selectionism diverts attention from contexts, resources, and interests, but

that is exactly where attention should be focused, at least for short- and medium-term phenomena. Conflicting interests, conditioned by the different contexts of different individuals, are a major factor in intentions to reproduce or to alter existing socio-cultural contexts.

In contrast to the alleged reductionism of an EA approach, many authors explicitly focus on human "agency" and advocate what has come to be termed praxis or practice theory (e.g., Bell 1992; Clark 1999; Cowgill 2000; Dobres 1995; Dobres and Hoffman 1994; Pauketat 2000a, 2000b; Wobst 1996). This perspective explicitly recognizes that humans are decision-making entities, and seeks to understand human behavior by identifying the totality of underlying motives and social factors that led humans to behave as they did.

In this discussion, we seek to challenge the suggestion that EA is incompatible with an agency-based understanding of human behavior. Specifically, we argue that evolutionary archaeologists can gain valuable insight into the generation and continuation of behavioral variation using an agency-based approach. We further contend that those using agency-based approaches can gain valuable insight into the effects of both unintended and intended consequences of human behavior from the work of evolutionary archaeologists, and can thereby better understand how agency affects the continuation of social structures. In fact, we contend that an agency-based evolutionary archaeology provides a more complete and realistic perspective of human behavior by combining the best insights of both approaches, and thereby provides a more complete approach for addressing a greater variety of questions concerning the past.

Our discussion is divided into two sections. First, we provide an introduction to the theoretical underpinnings of agency-based and EA approaches, and demonstrate that they are not fundamentally incompatible. In particular, we highlight the fact that agency-based approaches have heretofore been unable to successfully address the role of unintended consequences and unacknowledged conditions of action on the continuation of social systems, whereas EA has heretofore considered the differences between intended and unintended consequences and acknowledged and unacknowledged conditions of action moot. We then demonstrate that an EA approach identifies one of the mechanisms through which unintended consequences and unacknowledged conditions of action feed back into behavioral systems. It thereby provides a more complete understanding of the impacts of human agency on the continuation of social systems and relationships than is possible without it. In contrast, an agency-based approach provides great insight into the origin and nature of variation, a topic that EA has largely ignored.

In the second section, we illustrate the utility of an agency-based EA by providing an explanatory narrative of cultural changes in the Casas Grandes region of Northwest Mexico and the American Southwest. We contend that our approach provides a foundation for a more complete explanation of the complexity of cultural change than would be possible using either approach in isolation.

AGENCY

In their introductory chapter to *Agency in Archaeology*, Dobres and Robb (2000a:3) correctly observe that the term agency is a new "buzz word" in archaeology. The varied intellectual backgrounds and approaches of the contributors to their volume certainly attest to their point by underscoring both the current importance of the concept and the fact that researchers using a variety of theoretical perspectives find the concept useful.

Following Dobres and Robb (2000a:4–5), we suggest most agency-based researchers share at least seven basic premises despite the diversity in their intellectual backgrounds. First, nearly all agency-based perspectives reject any approach that reduces human behavior to "behavioral systems," "adaptive responses," or "evolutionary lineages." For example, Clark (1999:131; see also Brumfiel 1992; Gero 2000:38; Wobst 2000:40, 44–45) argues such "reductionistic" approaches provide so limited a view of behavior that "we are left with neither humans nor behavior. What remains are bipedal biological units, with moderate mobility and trophic capabilities, which ambulate through resource patches of various densities and caloric potentialities to harvest and digest vitamins, starches, proteins, and assorted trace elements in order to maintain biological viability."

Second, social structures are viewed as the product of the behavioral relationships between individuals created during everyday material production. Social institutions and formalized social relationships such as caste or class systems are thus the product of the interaction between individuals within a group (e.g., Pauketat 2000b).

Third, researchers using agency-based approaches generally reject concepts such as free will and individual volition, partly because they argue humans cannot choose the social and material contexts of action and are therefore constrained in their behavior, and partly because the behavior of individuals is influenced by the social structure within which they operate (e.g., Wobst 2000:47–48). The effect of the surrounding social system on an individual's behavior is frequently unacknowledged, according to many agency-based approaches, a premise that further undermines the idea that individual humans consciously and rationally choose how they wish to behave.

Fourth, structural institutions and conditions such as governmental systems and power inequities are considered to be largely the product of material contexts and relationships. Social institutions are therefore propagated by the differential access to resources and the subsequent effects this has on the production of material goods (e.g., Saitta 1999).

Fifth, structural institutions that compose a social structure create a material world that is observed by individuals, and therefore affects their behavior (e.g., Johnson 2000). Sixth, society is partly the effect of previous social conditions, and as a result social history is an important factor shaping human behavior and social structure (e.g., Cobb 1998:200–204; Hodder 1987b:vii). Finally, most researchers using the concept of agency hold that humans are actors whose behavior can only be understood in terms of their motives expressed within their social context (e.g., Dobres and Robbs 2000a:9; Wobst 2000:40).

Taken together the seven principles produce a view of human behavior in which humans effect and are affected by their material surroundings, create and reproduce social institutions through their interaction with each other and their material surroundings, and operate within these social institutions in accordance with their motives. Humans are thus both the products and the creators of social structures (Wobst 2000:40–42).

An additional similarity is that most researchers using agency-based approaches employ a perspective that is inspired by, and is in general agreement with Giddens (1984; see Cowgill 2000:51; Robb 1999:4–5; Wobst 1999:124–125, 2000:40). The foundation of Giddens's theoretical system is the premise that humans are "social actors," defined as individuals who have agency, that is, who behave in accordance with their desire to affect the outcome of future events (Cohen 1987; Giddens 1984:2). Giddens also argues hu-

man behavior is more than an accumulation of individual, random acts; it is instead a series of acts historically connected by the conscious monitoring of the effects of past action and the social contexts of current action. According to Giddens (1984), this view implies several important correlates. First, it suggests that humans have knowledge of the context of their behavior such that they *think* they can predict the outcome of future events. This ability, which Giddens (1984:2) calls reflexivity, not only includes some form of self-consciousness, but also includes the ability to monitor, albeit imperfectly, ongoing changes in social interaction with other actors. Actors therefore evaluate their changing social circumstances and the results of their past acts, and alter their current actions accordingly. Additionally, humans act purposefully. Individual actors act because they have intent or a motive, and their behavior can only be understood in terms of their motives.

Giddens's system can be illustrated using the example of a young girl living at Pecos Pueblo in the American Southwest during the early 1400s who makes a ceramic pot to use as a toy. According to Giddens's scheme, the girl is a social actor who: (1) is a member of a social organization that includes knowledge of the construction of ceramic vessels, and (2) has the desire to produce a pot for use during play. The production of the pot is an act that can only be understood as a product of the young girl's agency, that is, the construction of the pot is explainable as an expression of the young girl's motives in her social context.

However, there is more to understanding the girl's behavior than simply understanding her motivation to have a pot. Giddens's structuration theory views an actor's behavior as a continuous chain of action and cognition (Giddens 1984:3) because humans monitor their social surroundings and change their actions as dictated by their motives and desires. Various aspects of the social structure with which the girl is associated, perhaps including rules regarding a sexual division of labor and appropriate behavior of children,

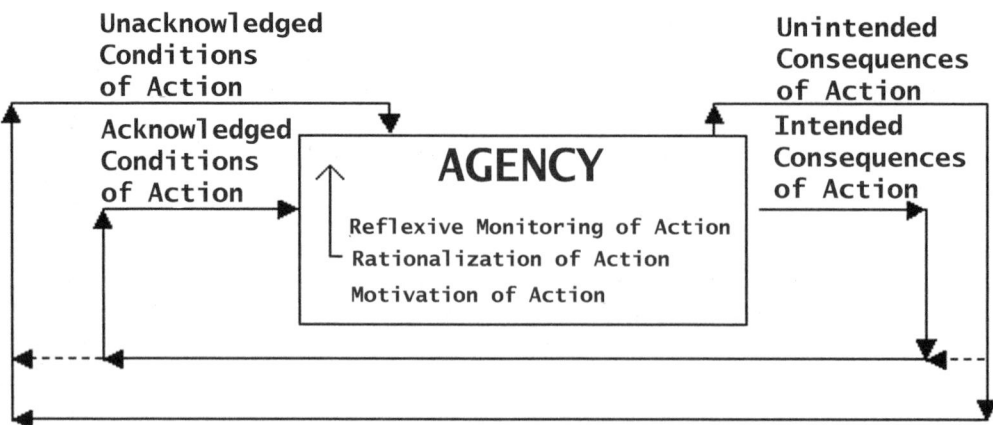

Figure 8.1. A schematic of Gidden's Structuration Theory illustrating that intended and unintended consequences of action can become acknowledged and unacknowledged conditions of action, which in turn affect an individual's agency through his/her motives and reflexive monitoring of contexts and action.

influence her behavior. Thus, the pot's fabrication cannot be reduced to a single moment in which the young girl formed the vessel to use as a toy, but is instead a small segment in the entire series of social interactions that both influenced and were created by the action of the child.

Furthermore, the child likely monitors how others respond to her pot through reflexivity, perhaps taking pride when the construction of the vessel is praised, or identifying mistakes she made when flaws in the vessel's construction are brought to her attention. She may also hear others discussing ceramic production, and may compare her own efforts and experiences to theirs. When the child desires to produce more vessels, she will likely mimic the traits of her first vessel that brought praise and incorporate the suggestions generated by her previous mistakes. Her future production of ceramics thus cannot be fully understood without reference to her reflexive monitoring of the effects of previous action and her social surroundings. Her behavior is therefore part of a series of acts historically linked by the conscious monitoring of the past effects of her behavior and the present contexts of action.

Giddens (1984:3) argues that the concept of a continuous chain of action, which he calls *durée*, prevents archaeologists and other social scientists from reducing human behav-

ior to synchronic or discontinuous actions and intentions. Instead, human behavior should be viewed as history, in which each act blends into others and in which actors take into account the context of their behavior.

While actors act to produce desired outcomes, Giddens (1984) explicitly acknowledges that their behavior can produce unforeseen effects. For example, the young girl may use a lead-based glaze causing her to contract lead poisoning despite the fact that she did not intend on becoming ill. She could also have a mishap during the firing process that causes her to be severely burned, although that was not her intent. Obviously then, actions can produce unintended consequences (Giddens 1984:8) that can influence the future action of the actor or other actors through *durée* (see also McCall 1999). Of course, not all unintended consequences are harmful. The girl may unintentionally increase her social status by showing an exceptional ability in manufacturing ceramics, or she could gain increased skill in ceramic production even though that is not her goal. The act of producing a toy may consequently have a variety of effects that are unforeseen and unintended by the girl. According to Giddens (1984:10–11, 282, 344–346), unintended consequences bring up an important aspect of human action. While consequences are created by actions and are only possible within the context of the act, the consequences of action are not actually under the control of an actor or even a group of actors.

As a result of reflexive monitoring of the consequences of their action, actors may realize their action had unintended consequences. However, some unintended consequences may not be evident to them. For example, discussion of the girl's pot may influence the behavior of one of the girl's friends without the girl ever being aware that her behavior had the unintended consequence of influencing her friend. Likewise, the child might decorate her pot with symbolically important designs that reaffirm her membership to particular social groups and thereby help reinforce the social significance of these social structures to herself and those who view the pot. This reaffirmation may then influence her behavior and the behavior of others without their conscious knowledge that it is doing so. The consequences of behavior can therefore feed back into the context of action to create unacknowledged conditions of action (Fig. 8.1), that is, conditions that affect an actor's behavior but that are not consciously considered by the actor. While an actor may not even be aware of the unintended consequences and the unacknowledged condition of action, they are still as much a product of the actor's agency as are the intended consequences (Giddens 1984:8–9).

We contend that an agency-based approach is a worthwhile framework for archaeological research, insofar that it provides a means of modeling human behavior, but that it is incomplete as it is generally applied because it does not provide a means of understanding the complex effects of unacknowledged conditions and unintended consequences of action. Giddens and others who use his concept of agency emphasize the importance of unintended consequences and unacknowledged conditions of action, but they have been unable to develop effective methods to deal with the long-term effects of such processes. Nor have they been able to demonstrate how such factors affect the replication of social structures (Dobres and Robb 2000a:10–12). Giddens (1984:13–14)

himself suggests, with reservations, that functional analysis, such as that undertaken by Bronislaw Malinowski (1944) or Marvin Harris (1966), may be useful in this role. For example, a structural-functionalist analysis like that advocated by Malinowski (1944), which demonstrates that the production of ceramic pots by young girls is an important component of the teaching process of future ceramic producers, might illustrate the general role that specific unintended consequences and unacknowledged conditions of action play in a social system. However, Giddens (1984:12–13) warns against blindly applying functional analysis to understand and explain unintended consequences or unacknowledged conditions of behavior, because human behavior can only be understood in terms of the *durée* of the actors, not at the level of society. Functional analyses therefore beg the question of why actors reproduce the action that creates the functional consequence, which can only be answered by reference to the conscious goals and intentions of the individual actors as viewed through their reflexivity (Giddens 1984:12–13).

Still, Giddens's suggestion that functionalism might be useful when dealing with unintended consequences and unacknowledged conditions of action is more than a courteous bow to researchers who use other perspectives. It is a realization on Giddens's part that his and similar systems that employ the concept of agency do not allow for the adequate analysis of either of these issues, because their relationship to agency, the cornerstone of his approach, is inherently unspecified (see Dobres and Robb 2000a:12). In other words, structuration theory provides no explicit mechanism for understanding the effects of unintended consequences, because they cannot be directly explained through agency except as unforeseen accidents. Likewise, unacknowledged conditions of action do not directly affect the reflexivity and action of individuals, and therefore their relationship to agency is ambiguous.

In practice, functionalist analysis has not proven useful for addressing unintended consequences and unacknowledged conditions

generally emphasizes "unintended consequences

of action as Giddens hoped. We argue this is because functionalist approaches in anthropology are synchronic (Barrett 1996:61, 67) whereas agency-based approaches are inherently historic (see also Hodder 1987b:vii). In other words, functional approaches are incompatible with the historical viewpoint required by Giddens's concept of reflexivity. Functionalist approaches describe the operation of a system *at a given time,* but are unable to address questions related to why behaviors, structures, and systems form and change *through time,* which is generally the fundamental question those using agency wish to address.

We argue, in contrast, that an evolutionary approach can benefit an agency-based perspective by specifying how unintended consequences and unacknowledged conditions of action affect agency. An evolutionary perspective is both historic and functionalist. As a result, it provides a compatible framework for identifying the effects of certain types of unintended consequences and unacknowledged conditions of action. This point is more fully developed below.

EVOLUTIONARY ARCHAEOLOGY

The corpus of evolutionary archaeology research has grown substantially since the early 1980s and now presents a number of well-developed theoretical premises and applications (see for example O'Brien and Lyman 2000b and 2002c, and papers in Hurt and Rakita 2001 and O'Brien 1996a). We will not provide a complete summary of EA, but instead refer interested readers to any of the overviews available (e.g., Leonard 2001; Lyman and O'Brien 1998; O'Brien and Lyman 2000b, 2002c). In this context, we will only discuss the issues relevant to the role of intentionality and natural selection in affecting human behavior.

The Three Premises of Natural Selection
As discussed by Dunnell (1980:62–63), Leonard and Reed (1993:649–651), Lewonton (1970:1, 1974), and Rindos (1989a:11), three basic premises are required to apply the concept of natural selection regardless of the

subject matter being studied or the questions being asked. These are: (1) the presence of variation that results in differences in the reproductive fitness (the ability to survive and reproduce) of individuals, (2) the ability of future generations or other individuals to inherit the variation, and (3) the generation of the variation independently of natural selection.

Human behavior undeniably possesses the first two characteristics. The effect of an individual's behavior on his or her survival and reproductive success is unquestionable, and is easily seen in our own society in discussions of the effects of drunk driving, the impact of diet and prenatal care on the health of newborns, and the use of contraceptives. It is equally certain that similar factors affected the reproduction and survival of individuals in the past (Bentley 1996; Bentley et al. 1993; Merbs and Miller 1985; Ramenofsky 1987).

For example, Buikstra et al. (1986:540) demonstrate that a major change in fertility in Late Woodland and Mississippian populations of west-central Illinois is associated with a shift from smaller ceramic cooking vessels with sand temper and thick walls to larger cooking pots with shell temper and thin walls. Their argument rests on the observation that the thinner walled vessels, made possible through the use of shell temper, have greater thermal conductivity and increased resistance to thermal shock when compared to the sand-tempered ceramics. The attributes of the shell-tempered ceramics allowed starchy seeds to be boiled, which provided a suitable weaning food. The availability of weaning food allowed early weaning, which led to a decrease in the length of nursing, that in turn caused a reduction in the average length of postpartum amenorrhea (the period during which a female does not ovulate because of low body fat content caused by prolonged nursing). This in turn led to a decrease in the spacing of births, which subsequently resulted in an increase in the number of children. In short, the development of shell-tempered ceramics, a simple change in the design of ceramic cooking vessels that intu-

I love this! yep it's also agency & unintended consequence.

itively would not appear to have any significant consequence on human reproduction, allowed a change in food processing and preparation that caused a significant increase in fertility. The history of human development is surely replete with similar cases in which subtle changes in behavior and the associated technology substantially affected individuals' survival and reproductive success (e.g., Merbs and Miller 1985).

Second, it is undeniable that behavioral information is heritable (Rindos 1989a:6–7, 11–13). The very fact that you can read this sentence demonstrates this point. If information and its behavioral correlates, including artifacts, could not be transmitted to other individuals, all forms of scholarly discourse would be impossible.

The actual mechanism of behavioral transmission is still debated (e.g., Boyd and Richerson 1985; Cullen 1993; Dunnell 1995; Hewlett et al. 2002; Neff 2000; Schiffer 1996). However, it is certain that the transmission of behavioral-cultural traits does occur, and simply knowing this is sufficient for applying an evolutionary framework (Dunnell 1978a:197, 1980:66). This point is illustrated by the fact that it was not until the late 1930s and 1940s with the development of the "New Evolutionary Synthesis" (Mayr 1988: 525–554, 1996) that biologists using Darwinian evolution began to fully understand the role genes play in the evolution of physiological traits. Until that time, they were satisfied in knowing that the traits they studied were heritable in some way.

The third requirement, that behavioral variation is generated independently of natural selection, is more problematic, especially among those using agency-based approaches. It is undeniable that there is tremendous variation in human behavior through time and across space. This variation has been the subject matter of archaeological and anthropological analyses since their inception, and anthropologists and archaeologists have used a variety of means to deal with it. They have compiled huge data sets, such as the Human Resource Area Files and the *Ethnographic Atlas* (Driver and Massey 1957; Ember and

Ember 1995; Murdock 1967; Murdock and Provost 1973), created "culture areas" (Kidder 1924; Kroeber 1939; Willey and Phillips 1958), identified tool kits (Binford 1968) and activity areas (Binford 1983d:144–192), and focused on class structures (McGuire 1992b), gender differences (Joyce 1993), and the social differences of individuals (Blanton 1995). Regardless of how they have dealt with it, every theoretical approach, including agency-based approaches and EA, has as its fundamental goal the understanding and explanation of this variation.

Still, the premise that such behavioral variation is generated independently of natural selection superficially seems to imply that human behavior is randomly generated and is devoid of intentionality. Critics of EA, including those who use a concept of agency, have been quick to point out that human behavior is not generated randomly, but is instead produced by humans reacting to their environment in nonrandom ways to accomplish tasks that are important to them (e.g., Arnold 1999:106–109; Boone and Smith 1998:S148–S149; Spencer 1997:222–225, 227–231). For example, Cowgill (2000:52) states, "The source of biological variation is genetic mutation, and mutations are independent of selection pressures. This is emphatically not the case with human intentions as a source of sociocultural variation, because these intentions are significantly related to the contexts and perceived interests of individuals."

Evolutionary archaeologists agree with their critics that human behavior is nonrandom and purposive. In fact, evolutionary archaeologists would uniformly agree that when faced with the choice of eating rocks or a nicely grilled T-bone steak, far more humans would choose the steak, and that such an association would be nonrandom.

Still, evolutionary archaeologists, including ourselves, contend that the premise that variation in human behavior is generated *independently of natural selection* is reasonable, and that the criticism of EA by authors such as Boone and Smith (1998:S148–S149; see also Gould 1996:221) is based on a subtle yet profound confusion between the statement "variation must be generated independently of natural selection" and the phrase "variation must be generated randomly." Phenotypic variation that is evolutionarily important need not be, nor is it ever, generated completely randomly, even in biological contexts (Dawkins 1987:306–308; Rindos 1989a:12–13). At the very least, the variation that is possible is constrained by evolutionary changes in the past (see Smith et al. 1985 and Stearns 1986:40 for a discussion of developmental constraints in genetic evolution). Additionally, Dawkins (1996:81–82) points out that the generation of variation does not even need to be completely independent of the action of the selective forces to meet the requirements of Darwinian evolution (see also Mayr 1997:100). To illustrate this point, he suggests that a gene exists in a hypothetical world that increases the rate of genetic mutation when an animal is under environmental stress, and that the resulting mutations are biased towards being reproductively beneficial when facing certain types of stresses. He observes that the development of the mutations and the effects of the environment on their continuation are still separate events, that is, that change is still a two-step process of (1) the generation of variation, and (2) its sorting by natural selection. Natural selection within a Darwinian framework is therefore still responsible for the changes in the frequency of variation and the continuation of the mutations, even if the generation of variation is in some way tied to the pressures from the environment. As long as the variation is generated first, i.e., independently of natural selection, and then acted upon by natural selection, Darwinian evolution is the means through which evolutionary change occurs (Mayr 1997:100).

Evolutionary archaeologists would of course readily agree with Cowgill's (2000:52) observation that humans intentionally respond to their surroundings using discursive reasoning, although they would likely echo Dobres and Robb's (2000a:4) warning that humans are "socially embedded, imperfect,

and often impractical people." Human behavior absolutely is not random; humans work, save valuable resources as possible, optimize their resources as they feel is appropriate, seek to gain additional resources through social cooperation or force, frequently plan for the future, and otherwise try to intentionally adapt to their surrounding environment. However, evolutionary archaeologists contend that the behavior of humans is random *with respect to the selective environment*; while humans seek power, operate within social structures, or even consciously try to "adapt" to their environment to increase their reproductive success, they cannot accurately understand the present or future selective environments, i.e., social and natural factors, that affect their evolutionary success. In short, evolutionary archaeologists suggest that there are unacknowledged conditions of action and unintended consequences of action that affect human behavior as a result of natural selection and other evolutionary processes.

For example, in a hypothetical group, three general agricultural strategies are evident: farmers who plant their crops at high elevations, farmers who plant their crops on flood plains, and farmers who plant small plots in a variety of locations. The farmers who plant their crops in high elevations may have excellent crops during years with high rainfall, but will not have good yields during dry years. In contrast, the farmers who plant on the flood plains will have excellent yields during years with low rainfall, but will loose their crops to flooding during wet years. Finally, the farmers who plant crops in both areas will be guaranteed of losing some crops, but are also assured that some of their crops will produce.

Farmers using these various strategies obviously intend to plant crops, otherwise they would not do so. The planting is not a random act made by automatons unaware of what they are doing. Likewise, the farmers each plant their crops in different locales, trying to match the type of crop with appropriate areas so that they can have a good

So typically they think randomness equivalent to "purposive" but with unintended consequences

Actually that assumes a certain type of societal organization & demonstrates why evolutionary and get tricky at micro level

harvest. Obviously, these decisions are not random either; each farmer makes slightly different choices when planting based on factors such as past experience, differential access to land, religious or social prohibitions, environmental differences in the cultivated areas (e.g., soil type, slope, run-off characteristics), and any of a number of other factors related to the environment, individual preferences, and social structures.

In the terms of agency-based approaches, each farmer in this hypothetical group is an agent who acts and thereby demonstrates intentionality, although the farmers may not be consciously aware of many of the factors that influence their choice to use a particular strategy. Each of these farmers' strategies will result in good crops, with the right rainfall patterns. However, none of these farmers can predict the weather, causing many of the consequences of their behavior to be unknown and beyond their control.

One of the strategies will provide a higher yield on average over time. The use of this strategy will therefore be favored by natural selection in our hypothetical environment, because the increased yields will result in better nutrition and consequently in increased average reproductive success. High rainfall will cause strategies focused on higher elevations to be "selected for." Low rainfall will cause floodplain farming to be favored. Unpredictable and variable rainfall will favor a mixed strategy. The success and subsequent evolutionary consequences of the farming strategy is independent of the individual farmer's intention, and the origin of the variation in farming strategies is independent of the forces of natural selection, even though the farmers are consciously attempting to ensure their crop's success. The generation of variation is therefore separate from, and prior to, the operation of natural selection, just as required by a Darwinian approach.

An objection could be raised that humans can recognize at least the most obvious selective forces, and intentionally "adapt" to them, thereby creating variation that is directed by the environment. For example, on a cold day, people know that they need to wear a coat, or they will become hypothermic and possibly freeze to death. We do not have two groups of individuals, those who wear coats and those who do not, who go out and then have differential persistence of their behavioral traits resulting from their survival. Instead, we have rational agents who evaluate their environmental context and react to it in ways that are consistent with their motives and social structures. Likewise, farmers in the hypothetical environment described above may quickly realize that one farming strategy is superior to the other strategies, and will therefore adopt it. Consequently, the presence and use of coats or a particular agricultural strategy is explainable by agency, not the direct action of natural selection or some other evolutionary process.

There is obvious truth to such arguments; humans have extremely flexible behavior and useful problem-solving abilities that they use when confronted with difficulties (see Rindos 1989b:28). People do know when they need to wear coats, but this observation does not demonstrate that *the selective environment directs the generation of variation* and thereby does not invalidate a Darwinian approach to understanding human behavior. On the contrary, even when operating within the same social structures and environmental contexts and when employing the same problem-solving strategies, humans frequently derive different solutions to their problems (e.g., different styles of coats made from different materials and produced in different ways). Their motives may explain why they seek to solve problems (e.g., they are cold), and, in a superficial way, why behavior changes (e.g., they wear coats), but motives and intentionality ultimately do not explain why specific solutions are effective and therefore persist for extended periods of time. In other words, intentionality and an actor's motives explains why humans want to wear coats, or grow domesticates, or have healthy children, or make pots, but it does not satisfactorily explain the structure of the coat an individual might wear, the structure of the

This is just a rehash of old function/style dichotomy

[handwritten margin notes:] "The obvious idea that there is a place where agency "finishes" & unintended consequences "begin"" / "put this in"

agricultural system, or the totality of factors that affect an actor's reproductive success.

Thus, EA does not deny human intentionality, the importance of motives, or the extreme effect that social structures can have on human actors. To the contrary, evolutionary archaeologists embrace these concepts and take them as givens. However, they suggest that there is necessarily more to the human story than just intended consequences and acknowledged conditions of action. As Rindos (1989b:31) observes:

> We need not claim that these specific human characteristics such as decision-making, experimentation, or cultural bias must be excluded from consideration in understanding the genesis of the original variant behaviors that were to form the foundations for the evolution of new cultural traits. We need only claim that these processes *in and of themselves* were insufficient to generate the evolved systems [emphasis in original].

So how do natural selection and other evolutionary processes affect an individual's agency? Evolutionary archaeologists such as Leonard and Jones (1987) observe that there is no one-to-one correlation between the reproduction of individuals and the replicative success of artifacts and other cultural traits. This realization has led some authors such as Blackmore (1999), Cullen (1993), and Neff (2000) to the commonsensical position that there is no relationship between human reproduction and the transmission of cultural traits (see also Shanks and Tilley 1988:154–155). They argue instead that cultural traits can spread within a population even if they reduce the average reproductive success of the individuals who possess them.

Although it is true that humans can adopt new cultural traits quickly, it is incorrect that maladaptive traits can have the same replicative success as selectively beneficial traits. As discussed by those using agency-based approaches, the *durée* of individuals gives society an underlying structure, which necessarily influences humans and their agency, and limits the types of cultural and behavioral changes they will adopt. Again as specified by those using agency-based approaches, it is the action of individuals that propagates and recreates these underlying structures. Natural selection will therefore cause structures and cultural traits that have negative consequences on the reproductive success of individuals to become less frequent over time when compared to other structures and cultural traits for the simple reason that those who possess traits that are being selected against will have less opportunity to transmit their social structures to others, especially given that much cultural transmission in nonindustrial groups occurs primarily within kinship and linguistic groups (Renfrew 1992).

A particularly facile example illustrates the impact of natural selection on agency and the continuation of social structures. A religious group called the United Society of Believers in Christ's Second Appearing, or more commonly the Shakers, began in the Manchester area of England as an offshoot of the Quakers in the mid-1700s and moved to the New York area of the United States in 1774 (Stein 1992:2–4). Their social structure included complete celibacy, a cultural trait that has obvious impacts on their reproductive success. All new adherents to the Shakers were of necessity converts. The Shakers grew to their largest membership of between 4,000 and 6,000 members in the 1830s (Foster 1991:17; Melton 1996:604) but number fewer than 25 today (Melton 1996:604). While the social structure associated with the Shaker religion does continue to this day, and does continue to affect and be reproduced by the agency of the group's members, its frequency has declined relative to other social structures as a result of the action of natural selection. A large portion of the explanation of this decline must rest on the general lack of reproductive success of its members, which has hampered the transmission of the religion to additional individuals.

The Shaker example is a rather extreme illustration of the action of natural selection, but the same point is evident in the practice of cannibalism among the Foré of the highlands of New Guinea, the example cited by authors such as Blackmore (1999:34) as evidence that cultural traits spread irrespective of their reproductive consequences. The ceremonial consumption of deceased relatives at their funeral led to the development of kuru, a fatal degenerative disease that was devastating the Foré. Although the practice of ritual cannibalism had a clear and negative impact on the reproductive success of the members of the Foré, Blackmore (1999:34) notes that Cavalli-Sforza and Feldman (1981) demonstrate mathematically that the cultural trait could continue to spread even if it eliminated 50 percent of the host population. From this, Blackmore (1999:34) concludes that even cultural traits with extremely negative impacts on reproductive success can spread relatively unchecked throughout a closed population.

Blackmore's (1999:34) observation is correct, but completely ignores the fact that the number of Foré was rapidly decreasing *in comparison with other groups,* and that they would have almost certainly ceased to exist as an ethnic group were it not for governmental intervention and the elimination of cannibalism as a social structure (Lindenbaum 1979:89–99). Thus, the practice of cannibalism could have spread within the closed population of the Foré, but the consequences of the differential reproductive success understood through the concept of natural selection did and would have continued to affect the continuation of the Foré social structure and would have led to its decreased frequency and perhaps even its eventual elimination. Likewise, any attempt to understand the archaeological record of the contact period that ignores the effects of European diseases on the native populations is inherently naïve (Leonard 1993; Ramenofsky 1987, 1995). The archaeological record reflects *both* the replicative success of cultural traits and the reproductive success of individuals. The influence of differential reproductive success will quite possibly be unacknowledged by the people who are affected by and

who reproduce social systems, but its impact is undeniable; reproductive success is a very significant component of the continuation of social systems.

Ultimately, then, both evolutionary archaeologists and agency-based approaches agree that humans are not omniscient and practical economizers, but are instead imperfect decision-makers who are not conscious of all of the factors that affect their behavior. Some unintended consequences of human action affect the reproductive success of individuals, which further affect actors' behavior and the continuation of social structures. The effects of such differences in reproductive success "might be imperceptible at any given moment but accumulate irrevocably over generations," to borrow the words of Dobres and Robb (2000a:11), but their effects are undeniable.

At best, humans' intentions may help create useful variation that will lead to successful evolutionary adaptations, but, as illustrated by the Shakers and the Foré, an individual's intentions does not guarantee his or her evolutionary success or the success of his or her social structures. Although it is possible that reproductive consequences are acknowledged conditions of action, evolutionary archaeologists do not suggest that humans generally adopt a technology or behavior because they believe it will increase their inclusive fitness and general reproductive success. Instead, evolutionary archaeologists realize that people adopt a behavior because of some benefit the actors perceive they will accrue (e.g., increased social status, more food, warmer houses, healthier children, or more spare time). But the operation of natural selection can and in many instances will become an unacknowledged condition of action.

THE FUNDAMENTAL COMPATIBILITY BETWEEN EVOLUTIONARY ARCHAEOLOGY AND AGENCY-BASED RESEARCH

As previously mentioned, Giddens (1984:12–14) acknowledges the difficulty of dealing

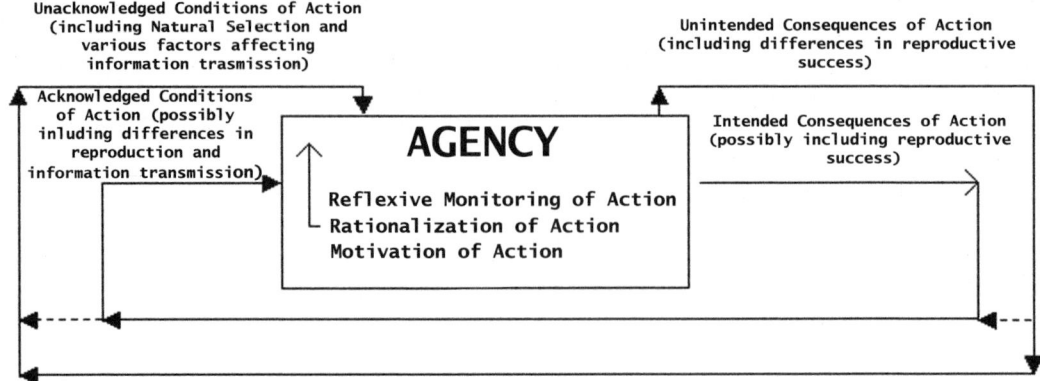

Figure 8.2. A schematic of an agency-based evolutionary archaeology in which the role of reproductive differences as an unintended consequence of action and evolutionary processes such as natural selection as unacknowledged conditions of action is illustrated.

with the affects of unintended consequences and unacknowledged conditions of action within an agency-based approach. With the notable exception of Marxist-style studies of the role of ideology as a means of legitimizing social status (e.g., Pauketat 2000b), those who use Giddens's system have also failed to solve this difficulty (Dobres and Robb 2000a:11). We contend this is because they have not developed a historically based functional approach that can specify how unintended consequences and unacknowledged conditions of action affect agency. In contrast, evolutionary archaeologists have developed a historical, functional framework for identifying the behavioral effects of differential reproductive success (natural selection) and the nuances of differential information transmission (drift; e.g., Neiman 1995; O'Brien and Lyman 2000b:257–271). However, they have generally failed to consider the role that agency plays in producing variation and creating the social environment, despite the fact that the social environment is an important component of an individual's selective environment.

Evolutionary archaeologists have failed to address the behavioral effects of human agency and aspects of social systems such as class structure, whereas those using agency-based approaches have failed to consider the impact of the natural environment, differen-

tial rates of reproduction, and factors affecting information transfer and the generation of behavioral variation such as population size (see Neiman 1995). Neither approach adequately addresses the total complexity of the factors that influence and ultimately explain past human behavior. We argue, however, that sharing the insight provided by both perspectives in order to create an agency-based evolutionary approach can present a more complete understanding of the factors that influence and are produced by human behavior.

We propose that the compatibility between agency-based approaches and EA is derived from their historical perspectives and their fundamentally similar views of the nature of unintended consequences and unacknowledged conditions of human behavior. This point is illustrated in Figure 8.2. Unlike Figure 8.1, we have labeled the lines representing unintended consequences and unacknowledged conditions of action using Darwinian evolutionary principles. The inclusion of the evolutionary terminology is possible because human behavior will feed back into the behavioral system in accordance with evolutionary principles (e.g., natural selection and drift). In particular, the evolutionary principle of natural selection is applicable to those intended and unintended consequences of human behavior that impact the survival and reproduction of individuals in some way, and the differences in reproductive success then become either acknowledged or unacknowledged conditions of future action. The effect of increased reproductive success on the agency of actors and long-term patterns of action can be *and in fact must be* understood within a historical, evolutionary perspective. Evolutionary theory can therefore fulfill the role that Giddens assigned to functionalism because it provides an explicit system illustrating how unintended consequences and unacknowledged conditions of action feed back into a behavioral system using a historical framework.

The schematic also illustrates how differences in reproductive success can be generated by agency, social structures, and intended consequences. As a result, agency-based approaches provide a historical framework for understanding how factors such as social inequality, class differences, and, more generally, intended consequences of action and acknowledged condition of action feed into the evolutionary system.

The compatibility of agency-based approaches and EA can be illustrated using the previously introduced example of the young girl from Pecos Pueblo. The role of the girl's agency in the creation of her pot has already been demonstrated, but how can an EA approach help archaeologists understand the factors that affected both her behavior and the general continuation of the social structures she acted within and helped produce? The use of ceramic vessels clearly has profound positive reproductive consequences in many environments as previously illustrated in our discussion of the work of Buikstra and others (1986). As a result, individuals who create and are affected by social structures that provide them with the benefits of ceramic vessels will be favored by natural selection in such environments over those who act within alternate social systems. Assuming that the hypothetical young girl is in an environment where the use of ceramics positively affects reproductive success, which is almost certainly the case in the American Southwest given the importance of ceramics in process-ing domesticated crops (Crown and Wills 1995:175–176, 180), natural selection would favor the continuation of social structures that included pottery manufacture. As a result, a significant reason why the hypothetical young girl was acting within a system that included ceramic production and perhaps even encouraged her to learn and become proficient with ceramic manufacture is attributable to the action of natural selection. Furthermore, an EA approach can identify factors such as population size that affect information transfer and the generation of behavioral variation, which consequently affect the girl's agency, probably as unacknowledged conditions of action and unintended consequences of behavior.

A synergy between agency-based approaches and EA will have several beneficial effects. First, it will help evolutionary archaeologists better understand the sources of variation in human behavior. EA has almost completely ignored the generation of behavioral variation (Schiffer 1996:655), although researchers such as Neiman (1995) are beginning to address this topic. The reason for this oversight is that evolutionary archaeologists have simply not considered it an important issue. As Dunnell (1978a:197) states, "the specific origin or invention of new elements becomes a trivial inquiry," because new behavioral variants are developed independent of natural selection and other evolutionary processes. Thus, evolutionary archaeologists have been able to apply Darwinian evolution to the archaeological record without knowing why or how the variation in the record is created, just as early evolutionary biologists could apply Darwinian evolution without knowledge of genetics and mutation.

However, we agree with Schiffer (1996:655) that "like modern evolutionary biologists, archaeologists should regard variation and its sources as subjects worthy of explanation." Understanding why humans attempt to solve particular problems is an important component of explaining the origin and nature of the solutions that evolution eventually favors. Borrowing the example from Kantner (Chapter 7), understanding why humans wanted to fly is an important component of understanding why humans have created the variation in flying machines that they have, and hence in explaining why they developed working flying machines with the particular characteristics that they did. Agency-based approaches provide the necessary means of addressing such questions by allowing an understanding of proximate social factors that affect the generation and continuation (replicative success in Leonard and Jones's [1987] terms) of various artifacts. Thus, such research is beneficial to an evolutionary perspective because it can describe the cause and origin of the behavioral variation that natural selection affects.

An agency-based approach can also help evolutionary archaeologists understand the mechanisms underlying the evolutionary process of drift, that is, the random differential persistence of selectively neutral (stylistic in Dunnell's [1978a] terms) variation (Neiman 1995; Price 1996:322–324). Within a Darwinian framework, drift is simply a description of random differences in the successful transmission of variation. EA can describe many of the factors that affect drift (e.g., population size), but it is fundamentally unable to explain changes in selectively neutral traits. For example, if the decoration on children's pots used as toys is stylistic, then changes in their decoration cannot be explained through the direct action of natural selection (Hurt et al. 2001), and instead must be based on an identification of the specific and unique features that led to the differential transmission of the designs. Although EA does understand and can model many factors such as the affects of population size and the intensity of interaction that are reflected in drift (Neiman 1995; Lipo et al. 1997), evolutionary archaeologists also understand that a large portion of the factors affecting information transfer are specific to each particular social context. Drift is consequently a nonexplanation, in some ways admitting that the frequency of selectively neutral traits changes for myriad reasons that are not related to natural selection, some of which can be modeled using general principles but some of which

cannot. It therefore begs the question of why the observed change occurred. An agency-based approach can provide the requisite answer by providing an understanding of the source of behavioral variation and proximate explanations for the continuation of these traits, such as changing social tastes, the reinforcement of dominant ideologies, or the successful challenging of dominant ideologies through social resistance (see Cowgill 2000: 52). This will in turn allow a more nuanced understanding of the role of social factors in the evolutionary study of style and its influence on the replicative success of artifacts.

Likewise, those using agency theory have argued that archaeologists should be careful of assigning a social meaning to everything in the archaeological record (Shanks and Hodder 1995:17–18). They observe that some portion of the record must reflect human interaction with the natural environment, and therefore reflect the necessity of adaptation. Sometimes a pot is just a pot (Hodder 1991c: 10). However, archaeologists using agency-based approaches have failed to formalize the nature and mechanisms of the interaction of the environment and the individual, a task that is central to recent EA research (e.g., Dunnell 1989; Leonard 1989; Leonard and Reed 1993; Maxwell 2000). EA can therefore help agency-based approaches by identifying those aspects of human behavior that reflect the interaction between behavior and the natural environment, and how such action helps propagate particular social structures.

Furthermore, the effects of evolutionary processes as specified using EA provides an avenue for those using agency theory to successfully understand how agency and unacknowledged conditions of action/unintended consequences of action affect long-term social change. Within an EA framework, social structures and social relationships (which are the products of agency) that correspond with increased reproductive success would be expected to become more common through time when compared to other alternate social structures. As will be further illustrated in the example presented below, natural selection

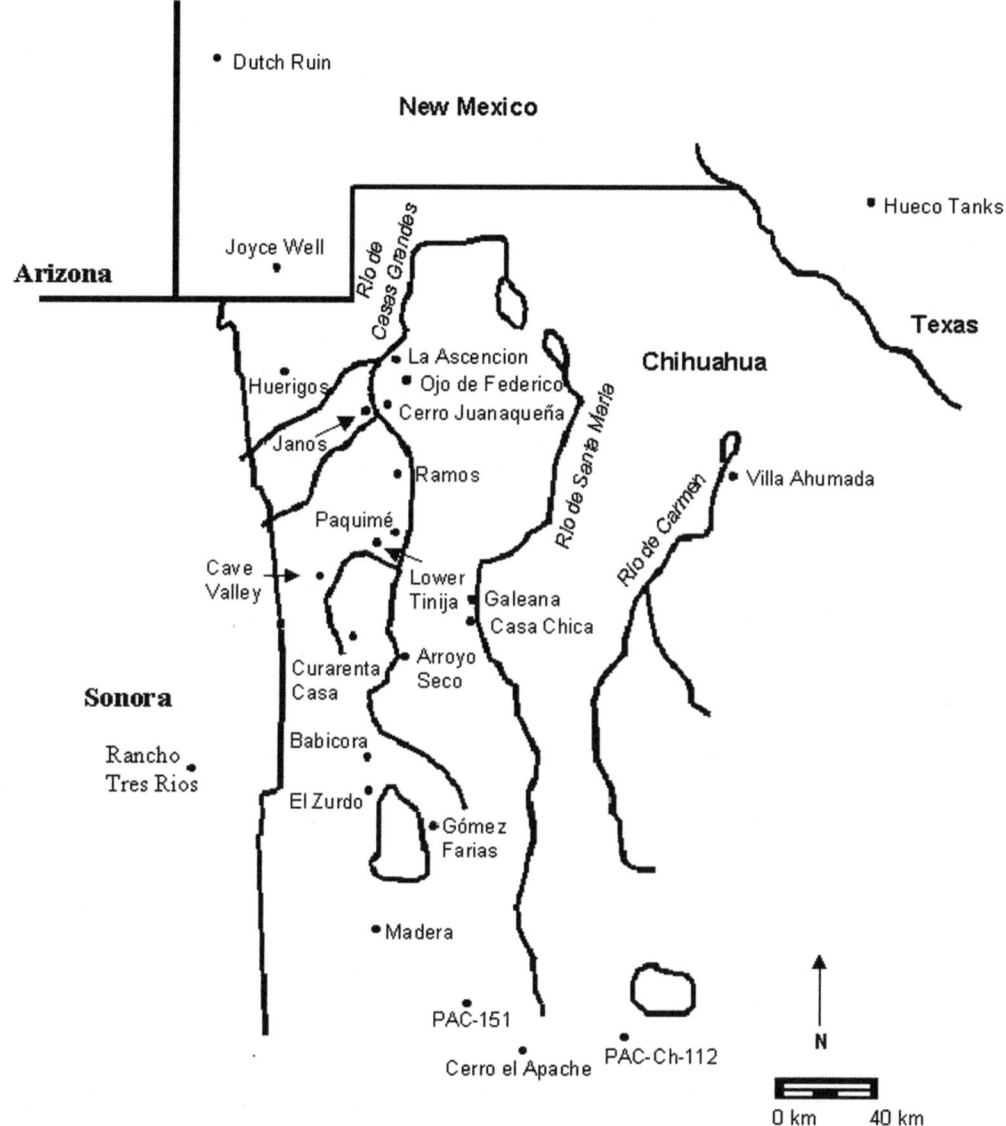

Figure 8.3. The Casas Grandes region of Northwestern Mexico and the U.S. Southwest.

would thereby create unacknowledged or possibly acknowledge conditions of action that would favor the continuation of the expression of agency that underlies the propagation of these selectively beneficial structures.

A synergy between agency-based approaches and EA will allow a richer and more complete view of the human behavior reflected by the archaeological record. Each approach has its own inherent weaknesses in addressing certain types of questions and dealing with certain components of the archaeological record, but they augment each other nicely. By combining the two approaches, evolutionary archaeologists will gain a means of understanding the source and origin of variation while those using agency-based approaches will gain a means of understanding the impact of unintended consequences and unacknowledged condition of action. Far from being incompatible, they can work in tandem to create a better understanding of the past. We will illustrate this point by considering the reasons for population aggregation and the concomitant development of a symbolically rich, hierarchical political system in the Casas Grandes region of northern Chihuahua, Mexico, between A.D. 1200 and 1450.

AGENCY, EVOLUTION, AND THE CASAS GRANDES REGION

During the shift from the Viejo period (A.D. 900–1200) to the Medio period (A.D. 1200–1450), the settlement patterns within the Casas Grandes region of northern Chihuahua, Mexico, and the adjoining portion of the American Southwest (Fig. 8.3) shifted from small, scattered settlements to large, aggregated towns surrounded by smaller outlying communities (Hendrickson 2001: 38; Phillips 1989:381–384). Concomitant with the shift in settlement patterns are significant changes in ceramic decoration, architecture, burial patterns, and other aspects of material culture that indicate a period of rapid cultural change and increased social and ceremonial elaboration (Di Peso 1974:2: 289–335; Fish and Fish 1999; Phillips 1989: 381–384; Rakita 2001:32–66, 269–332; Schaafsma and Riley 1999). These trends are perhaps best illustrated at the site of Paquimé, also called Casas Grandes, the largest and the most extensively excavated site dating to the Medio period.

Paquimé is a series of adobe pueblo-like room blocks covering 1 km in area. It is on the floodplain of the Rio Casas Grandes (Fig. 8.3), and is associated with two large I-shaped ball courts, a T-shaped ball court, numerous enclosed and opened plazas, and ceremonial mounds including the Mound of the Cross, the Mound of the Serpent, the Mound of the Heroes, the Mound of the Bird, and the Mound of the Offerings (Di Peso et al. 1974:5). The Amerind Foundation, the National Science Foundation, and the Instituto Nacional de Antropología e Historia sponsored excavation of Paquimé under the direction of Charles C. Di Peso during the late 1950s and early 1960s. Forty-two

percent of the site was excavated, and large quantities of shell, flaked stone, ceramics, and human burials were recovered.

Turquoise from the American Southwest, copper bells from western Mexico, and shells from the Gulfs of California and Mexico reflect trade with distant regions (Bradley 1999; Di Peso 1974:2:627–629; Kelley 1986; Lekson 1999; Vargas 1995, 2001). The treatment of the dead and the presence of monumental architecture have been interpreted as evidence of a complex and well-defined social hierarchy (Di Peso 1974:2:634–638; Di Peso et al. 1974:8; Rakita 2001:314–329; Ravesloot 1988). Additionally, architectural features such as macaw and turkey pens, the stockpiling of artifacts such as shell beads, and the production of morphologically standardized artifacts such as metates provided evidence of large-scale and centralized production/husbandry of various items and animals (Breitburg 1993; Minnis 1988; VanPool and Leonard 2002; Whalen and Minnis 2001:178–179). Well-formed trough metates with large grinding surfaces and specialized milling rooms used for maize processing also suggest a heavy reliance on maize agriculture when compared to preceding Viejo period settlements, a conclusion further supported by the ubiquity of maize in Medio period sites, the presence of large agricultural features in surrounding Medio period communities, and the isotopic carbon analysis of skeletal materials from the region (Di Peso et al. 1974:8:308–316; Doolittle 1993; Herold 1965; Hill 1992; VanPool and Leonard 2002; Whalen and Minnis 2001:71–72).

In addition to the shift in settlement patterns and the increased reliance on maize, the symbolic system of the Casas Grandes region as reflected by ceramic iconography and monumental architecture changed during the transition from the Viejo to the Medio period. Decorated Viejo period ceramics included textured wares, which have decorations in the form of designs inscribed into the vessel, and painted red-on-brown ceramics. The Medio period ceramics, which are generally called Chihuahuan Polychromes, are polychromes characterized by red and black

Figure 8.4. Viejo period red-on-brown jar. (Catalogue No. 8381/11, courtesy of Museum of Indian Art and Culture, Museum of New Mexico, Santa Fe.)

designs on a white or buff background (Brand 1933; Kidder 1916; Sayles 1936). The transition from bichrome to polychrome ceramics occurs across the American Southwest and northwestern Mexico during the thirteenth century A.D., but the differences between the Viejo period and Medio period ceramics are more profound than the color of their decorations.

To begin with, the layouts and designs of the Medio period ceramics are more complex than the Viejo period ceramics; Viejo period layouts are generally simple banding around the neck and body of the vessel, but Medio period layouts are generally divided into halves and then frequently halved again (Brooks 1973; Hendrickson 2000:36, 2001; Kidder 1916:261–262; VanPool and VanPool 2002). In addition, Viejo period painted ceramics are generally decorated with linear bands of geometric designs repeated three, five, seven, or twelve times (e.g., Fig. 8.4), whereas Medio period polychromes are generally decorated with interlocking black, red, and, less frequently, white elements (Fig. 8.5a). The interlocking geometrics give the Medio period designs a yin-yang impression

that is further emphasized by alternating the relationship of the colors between each panel (e.g., a panel decorated with a red step over a black step will be followed by a panel with a black step over a red one). These designs reflect an emphasis on duality and balance between red, black, and white designs, which is absent during the preceding Viejo period. Duality is also emphasized by the frequent presence of "twinned" heads on animal icons and effigies (Fig. 8.5b).

Horned serpent imagery also became much more prominent on the Medio period Chihuahuan polychromes than on the preceding Viejo period ceramics (Di Peso 1974: 2:88–92; VanPool et al. 2000). The "half spade" macaw/horned serpent motif, which Fenner (in Di Peso et al. 1974:6:99) called the "hallmark of the Chihuahuan polychromes," is perhaps the single most common motif on Chihuahuan polychromes, despite the fact that it is completely absent from the Viejo period red-on-brown pottery. The prominence of the horned serpent as a general motif suggests that the horned serpent was a central component of the Medio period Casas Grandes symbolic system, but not of the Viejo period. The presence of a horned serpent effigy mound (which had a stone engraved with a horned serpent as its eye), further reflects the social and ritual significance of horned serpent imagery in the Casas Grandes system.

In addition, Medio period ceramics are decorated with depictions of ritual activities that are not evident on Viejo period pottery. For example, males are depicted smoking, dancing, and conducting other activities that have been interpreted as ritually significant (Di Peso 1974:2:570–571; VanPool 2002; Woosley 2001:177–178). These males are characterized by specific stances and are associated with symbols such as horned serpent headdresses that are not shared by other male effigy figures or females (Figs. 8.5c and 8.5d). VanPool (2002:42–43) argues these differences indicate that the individuals depicted conducting ritual activities actually represent a distinct group of shamans who smoked hallucinogens, danced, and probably fasted to

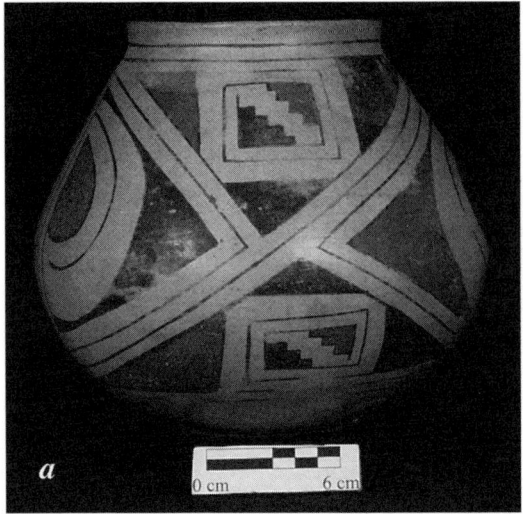

Figure 8.5. Medio period ceramics: (a) Medio period Ramos Polychrome with interlocking step motif. (Catalogue No. 59-9-797, courtesy of Wilderness Park Museum, El Paso.) (b) Medio period Villa Ahumada Polychrome double-headed effigy jar. (Catalogue No. 79.40.4, courtesy of Maxwell Museum, University of New Mexico, Albuquerque.) (c) Medio period Ramos Polychrome with male figure wearing a horned serpent headdress. (Catalogue No. A 36.85.18, courtesy of El Paso Centennial Museum, University of Texas at El Paso.) (d) Medio period Ramos male smoker effigy vessel. (Adapted from Di Peso [1974:570].)

induce trances (see also Di Peso 1974:2:570–571). During their trances, the Casas Grandes shamans underwent a "classic shamanic journey" (Myerhoff 1976; Sharon 1993) consisting of traveling from this world to the spirit world, communicating with supernatural entities in order to secure some action or to gain knowledge, and then returning to this world. Paraphernalia such as tobacco pipes that are associated with the ritual activities of these individuals are found in restricted areas at Paquimé, such as the House of the Walk-in Well, an architectural feature that Di Peso et al. (1974:7:305–306) and Walker and MaGahee (2001) argue is ritually significant using other lines of evidence (VanPool 2002:43). Although Rakita (2001:293–294) does report evidence for a limited form of shamanism in the Viejo period, it is not institutionalized and does not match the Medio period shamanic practice in terms of its standardization. Likewise, similar designs and activities are not found on Viejo period ceramics to our knowledge, nor are identifiable special "ritual" areas such as ball courts and ceremonial mounds evident in the Viejo period sites that have been excavated (Kelley et al. 1999:76; MacWilliams 2001).

Horned serpent imagery is further heavily integrated into all parts of the shamanic iconography, and is present during every step of the shamanic journey, including being represented as one of three supernatural beings that the shaman interacted with in the spirit world. In addition, burials identified by Ravesloot (1988) and Rakita (2001) as the most elite burials at Paquimé are associated with serpent iconography, prompting VanPool (2002) to argue that horned serpent imagery and the associated cosmological system is tied to both shamanism and social status.

Taken together, the modifications in the symbolic, architectural, and settlement systems indicate that the underlying social structures of the prehistoric inhabitants of the Casas Grandes region changed substantially during the transition from the Viejo to the Medio periods. These changes emphasized duality, new ritual activities conducted by a limited number of individuals, and a social hierarchy (Rakita 2001; VanPool 2001, 2002). Such transitions are precisely the type of changes that archaeologists using EA and agency-based approaches are interested in addressing.

An EA approach is ideal for explaining changes in settlement patterns and subsistence, factors that have strong implications for reproductive success, but is likely to be less intuitively satisfying when seeking to explain the changes in ceramic decoration and the development of social hierarchy. Agency-based approaches are a fruitful means of explaining the development of social inequality and the changes in symbolism, but will likely have less success in explaining the continued replication of the settlement and subsistence patterns, other than to say that they contin

ued because the actors in some way perceived them as "working." They each, therefore, can provide interesting insights into aspects of the changes in the Casas Grandes region, but ultimately leave important components of the shift unexplained.

Given that the various changes in the social structure are obviously interrelated somehow, both perspectives are therefore inadequate for explaining the general development in the Casas Grandes region, because they consider only part of the entire range of the factors that affected the development and continuation of the Medio period Casas Grandes cultural system. However, when taken together, we contend they strengthen each other, allowing for the formation of a more satisfying and complete explanation of the substantial social shifts. We begin the creation of this explanation by noting that population aggregation from A.D. 1200 to 1450 is not limited to the Casas Grandes region. In fact, similar changes in settlement patterns are evident throughout the American Southwest (Adler 1996; Adler et al. 1996).

Leonard and Reed (1993) argue that the population aggregation across the Greater Southwest is a consequence of decreased rainfall and the subsequent reduction of arable land. According to Leonard and Reed (1993:653), agricultural production in the American Southwest and Northwest Mexico is controlled by three variables: the amount of land cultivated, the amount of available water, and the amount of labor invested in agricultural production. They further argue that decreased rainfall led to both a decrease in the available moisture and a decrease in arable land during periods of the prehistoric occupation of the American Southwest. As a result, an increasing amount of labor had to be invested in the remaining arable land in order to maintain or increase agricultural production. According to Leonard and Reed (1993), the increased labor force of aggregated communities allowed for greater labor investment in nearby arable lands than is possible in dispersed settlements. Given the importance of agricultural production to the subsistence of the prehistoric occupants of

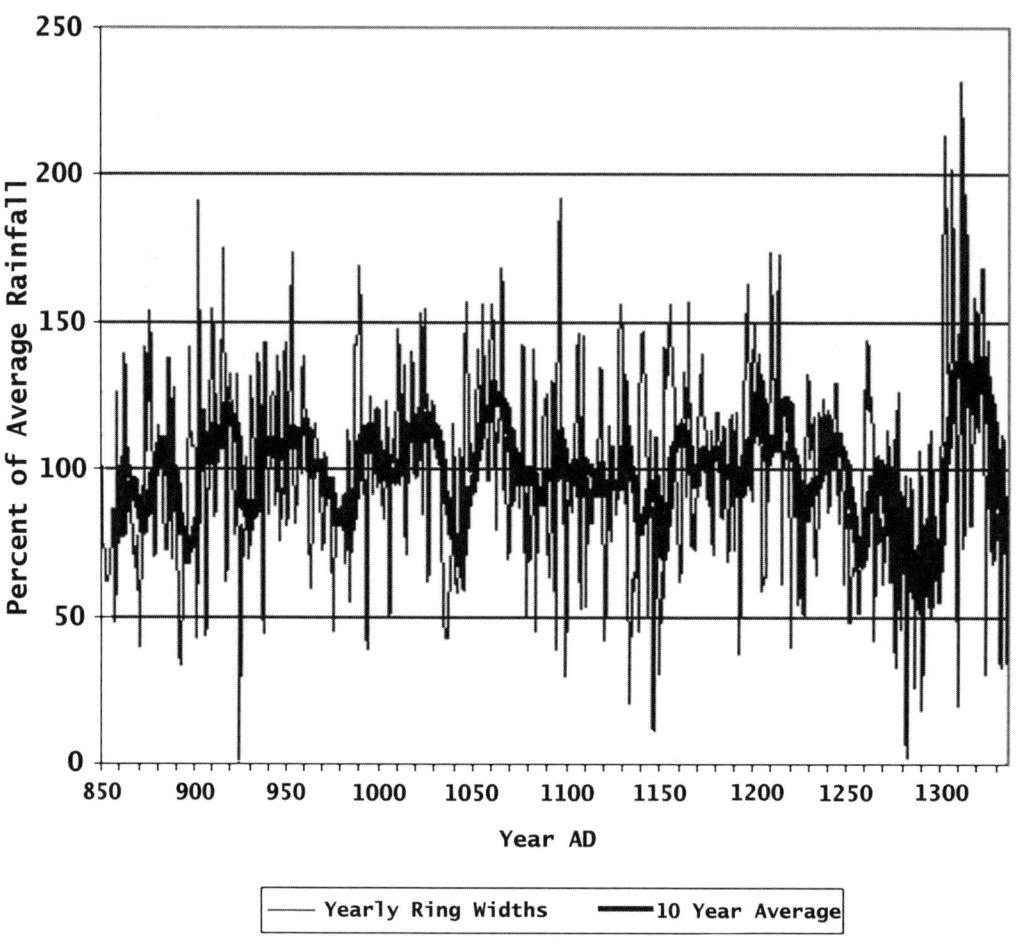

Figure 8.6. Yearly dendroclimatological data from Paquimé, Chihuahua, for the years from A.D. 850 to A.D. 1336.

the Southwest, Leonard and Reed (1993) argue that natural selection therefore favored the formation of large aggregated communities near arable land during periods of low rainfall.

Leonard and Reed (1993:653–658) illustrate the utility of their EA model by explaining population aggregation in the Chaco and Zuni areas, but they argue their model is applicable to the remainder of the American Southwest and Northwest Mexico. We agree; the similarities in the environment, geography, and agricultural systems across the region, especially within the Chihuahuan Desert, which encompasses much of New Mexico and Chihuahua (Brown 1994), support their argument.

Cordell (1997:365–428) and Dean et al. (1985:540–542, 546) documented a general decrease in precipitation throughout the Southwest during the thirteenth and fourteenth centuries A.D., which corresponded with the general formation of aggregated communities in many areas including northwestern Chihuahua. Dendroclimatological data reported by Scott (1966) indicate that this decrease in effective precipitation extended into the Casas Grandes region. Scott

(1966:63) compared the growth rings of trees used in the construction of Paquimé for each year between A.D. 850 and 1336 to the average growth ring for all of the years combined. He thereby provided a relative measure of the amount of growth of the trees, and by extension, an estimate of the effective precipitation for each year, with 100 percent reflecting an average year of rainfall. Figure 8.6 reports a 10-year moving average of the tree-ring widths.

During the Viejo period (from A.D. 850 to 1200), the precipitation levels fluctuated around 100 percent. However, after A.D. 1200, the amount of precipitation decreased significantly, especially between A.D. 1230 and 1300. There were 49 years of drought between A.D. 1230 and 1300, with growth rings for some years demonstrating only 2 percent of their normal growth. A brief increase in precipitation began shortly after 1300, but only lasted for about 20 years. By 1336, the 10-year average of the tree-ring widths had returned to about 70 percent of normal, and the actual widths for tree rings representing the year 1336 were only 30 percent of normal. This decrease in rainfall was consistent with the decrease of rainfall throughout the American Southwest, which is not surprising, given the geographical proximity of Chihuahua and New Mexico and the fact that both the states of Chihuahua and New Mexico have similar biomes (Brown 1994; Dean 1996).

In addition, the yearly variation in rainfall increased 25 percent after A.D. 1200 when compared to the variation in rainfall before A.D. 1200. Thus, the Medio period occupants of the Casas Grandes region were faced with less effective precipitation and greater variation in yearly rainfall, when compared to the earlier inhabitants. The general decline in precipitation and the decrease in arable land would have affected the people inhabiting the Casas Grandes region during the thirteenth and fourteenth centuries, just as it affected those living in the American Southwest.

The limited natural resources of southern New Mexico and northern Chihuahua prevented even moderately sized populations from subsisting on a strictly hunting and gathering lifestyle (Cruz Antillón and Maxwell 1999:47–50; see Hard and Roney 1998 for a discussion of the use of domesticated plants during the Archaic period occupation of the region). Consequently, individuals within the region would have recognized, probably with considerable alarm, the decreased agricultural production caused by reduced precipitation and arable land during the twelfth and thirteenth centuries. The reduced agricultural productivity became an acknowledged condition of action, at least to the extent that individuals realized that they could not produce adequate amounts of food using the existing agricultural systems. Their reflexive monitoring of their past experience would have caused them to realize that increased labor investment in agriculturally productive land would increase agricultural production, or at least hold it constant in the face of less favorable environmental conditions. As a result, we suggest many individuals consciously shifted their settlement patterns and agricultural strategies to increase their productive output. They formed larger communities, allowing them to pool their labor, near land that could be successfully cultivated. The initial impetuous of population aggregation in the Casas Grandes region was thus probably the reflexive monitoring of agricultural production in the face of changing environmental contexts, and the application of agency to create the intended consequence of increasing agricultural production, or at least hold it steady.

Some individuals undoubtedly chose to join aggregated communities, but others tried alternate strategies, such as maintaining the dispersed agricultural system or using broad-spectrum hunting and gathering (Di Peso 1974:2:331–332; MacWilliams 2001; Phillips 1989:383; Schaafsma and Riley 1999:237–239). Behavioral variation in subsistence strategies was thus present. This variation undoubtedly affected nutrition and, by extension, reproductive success. As illustrated by the miles of irrigation canals around sites such as Paquimé (Doolittle 1993), aggregated communities would have been able to invest more labor into agriculturally productive land, and would therefore have had increased agricultural production relative to other groups. Their access to crops would have resulted in better nutrition when compared to others employing different agricultural-subsistence strategies, which in turn would have caused individuals within the aggregated communities to have greater reproductive success in general, assuming that their social system was structured to allow them access to the crops they raised (see Bongaarts and Potter 1983; Campbell and Wood 1988; Ellison 1991; Nag 1968; Warren 1983 for a discussion of the effects of nutrition on fertility and other aspects of reproductive success).

As a result, natural selection would have favored individuals in larger communities over those who either maintained the previous agricultural system of dispersed, isolated communities or who used alternate systems such as broad-spectrum hunting and gathering. The choice to join aggregated communities and to pool agricultural labor into productive areas would have thus lead to the unintended consequence of increased reproductive success through time relative to those who made other choices. This is not to say that the health and subsequent reproductive success of individuals in the aggregated communities was superior to those who lived in the earlier Viejo period settlements. Quite to the contrary, the health of individuals in pre-industrial aggregated communities is often quite poor (Armelagos 1990:129–133), and the heavy reliance on maize and other domesticates at Paquimé and other Casas Grandes aggregated communities may have had negative health consequences when compare to the possibly more diverse Viejo period diet (Palkovich 1984). However, we do argue based on the evidence of a 70 percent decrease in precipitation across northwestern Mexico and the increased reliance on domesticates (Braniff 1994; Whalen and Minnis 2001:70–74) that a diverse diet with only limited reliance on domesticates was not generally feasible during the Medio period, and, consequently, that those who had greater access to domesticates also had better nutrition.

We also do not argue that aggregated communities were *the best possible* settlement and agricultural strategies in the Medio period occupation of the Casas Grandes region. There may have been a better strategy employed somewhere else in the world. However, we do argue that the aggregation of populations and the pooling of agricultural labor were the most evolutionarily successful settlement and agricultural strategies present during the Medio period occupation.

The differential reproductive success of those employing different agricultural and settlement strategies became either an acknowledged or an unacknowledged condition of action that favored the continuation of aggregated settlement patterns. If the differences in reproductive success became an acknowledged condition of action, actors engaged in other subsistence systems would likely have abandoned their own systems and joined or formed aggregated settlements, if possible. If it was an unacknowledged condition of action, those involved in other subsistence strategies would have probably continued to pursue their own subsistence strategies, assuming there was no other acknowledged condition of action that encouraged them to join the aggregated communities. Regardless, natural selection would have then cause the proportional frequency of those employing these other strategies to decrease relative to individuals in aggregated communities.

However, the large populations in aggregated communities would have led to the unintended consequence of increased scalar stress (Johnson 1982), that is, increased social conflict, when compared to the smaller communities. The existing social structures would have been inadequate to deal with the scalar stress, and the increased social conflict would have likely become an acknowledged condition of action. As Johnson (1982) observes, scalar stress within a group is generally reduced by either dividing the group into two or more new groups, or by adding another level of social hierarchy and thereby decreasing the number of individuals making certain kinds of decisions. The prehistoric inhabitants of Paquimé and the other aggregated sites clearly adopted the latter solution by initiating and accepting changes in their daily interactions, including changes in power relationships with the development of a social hierarchy and "leaders" (Di Peso 1974: 2:291–315; Rakita 2001:319–328; Ravesloot 1988).

For example, the changing social structure emphasizing community integration was manifested in Paquimé's architecture. Paquimé was initially built as at least nine and perhaps as many as twenty separate pueblo-like structures, each with their own independent plaza area, but was remodeled during the middle of the Medio period into contiguous, multistory apartment-like structures with large public architecture, such as the platform mounds and ballcourts. Wilcox (1999) argues that the changes in architecture reflect a shift from an emphasis on the integration of the smaller groups inhabiting each individual room block to an emphasis on integrating the entire community. In particular, Wilcox (1999:102) argues the public architecture served as "the locus of *community* solidarity" (emphasis in original).

Furthermore, the development of a social hierarchy and the emphasis on reducing social stress through community integration was reflected in the symbolic and ritual systems. Intentional alterations of the symbolic and ritual systems included the introduction and emphasis of symbols of authority and leadership, and the adjustment of ritual practice to reflect and emphasize the newly formed social relations (Rakita 2001:331–332). The symbolic system was likely further consciously manipulated by the emerging elites to legitimize their decision-making authority as the leaders of their society (see Helms 1988, 1999; Trigger 1990; Walker and Lucero 2000). For example, religious symbols, such as the horned serpent motif, the double-horned serpent icon, and the double-headed diamond macaw motif (Fig. 8.7) were introduced during the Medio period and were frequently associated with a limited group of male shamans. Exposure to this symbol on the ceramics and as a large mound

Figure 8.7. Medio period Ramos Polychrome with a double-headed macaw icon. (Catalogue No. 65.24.8, courtesy of Maxwell Museum, University of New Mexico, Albuquerque.)

at Paquimé, and its association with certain individuals, would have served as a continual reminder of the religious-social-political structure and would have constantly produced emotional responses that prompted learned behaviors (Mach 1993). In addition to the new symbols, symbols used on Viejo period ceramics such as scrolls, triangles, and running bands continued to be used, perhaps to emphasize a connection to the peoples' past history. These symbols would have tied into new religious structures, especially the Earth Fertility Cult and the Ancestor Worship Cult identified at Paquimé by Rakita (2001).

Given the prominence of the horned serpent motifs and their direct association with a subset of the Casas Grandes population (Schaafsma 1998; VanPool 2002), the elites at Paquimé probably propagandized their relationship with the supernatural horned serpent, and through myths, ethics, rules, rituals, and ceremonies involving their deity, consciously negotiated how people perceived them, the horned serpent and other symbols, and the associated social structure in general (see Walker and Lucero 2000). The desired meanings likely had a behavioral component, and thus reinforced a social norm of how one should interact with the symbols and within the society as a whole. In other words, the elites applied their agency and manipulated the behavior of their followers in order to affect the social structure and create the intended consequence of legitimizing their authority, increasing their social power, reinforcing the symbolic and ritual system (in which they probably believed), and fostering desired "proper" behaviors.

Other changes in the symbolic system may have unintentionally reflected the new social system. Such alterations likely included changes in the orientation and relationship between symbols that reflected the changed meaning and relationships of the subjects that the symbols reflected. As previously mentioned, Viejo period ceramics are decorated with running bands generally composed of a series of repeated design elements (three, five, or seven times), whereas Medio period ceramics are highly structured and emphasize dualities (VanPool and VanPool 2002). The systematic focus of duality in Medio period polychromes as seen in design layout, elements, and icons, and the twinning of icons indicate that there was a shift in the rules and grammar of the artistic tradition in the region. We contend that the highly structured relationships between symbols reflected changes in the deep cultural experience or *durée* of the people. The iconography suggests that the deep cultural experience was manipulated from a freedom in structure during the Viejo period to a highly organized structure with well-defined rules concerning how elements relate to each other. This change in the ceramics probably reflected the formation of more structured and well-defined rules concerning the interaction of individuals as well, and each member of the society understood at some level the roles of these dualities and the implication of the associated rules of conduct. In other words, social norms and codes of behavior were reinforced through iconography, and the well-defined system of rules fostered "proper" behavior and thereby reduced the social conflict resulting from a larger number of people trying to live together. This manipulation of the symbolic system also took the form of the adoption of new ritual activity such as ceremonial ballgames, changes in burials patterns, and the building of new public architecture.

The intended and unintended consequences of the changes in the symbols, rituals, and architecture of Paquimé was the reaffirmation of, and potentially the limited resistance to, the social system, which was consistent with, and the product of, the development of social hierarchy associated with aggregated communities. These new ritual and symbolic systems manipulated the rules and social fabric of the society so that social conflict could be lessened, allowing the community to remain intact. The continuation of these social systems would have been indirectly favored by natural selection, which favored individuals living in aggregated communities (see Hurt et al. 2001 for a discussion of evolutionary sorting).

To summarize, then, we argue that the apparent rapid shift in the general social structure of the Casas Grandes region, which included changes in settlement, subsistence, social-political organization, symbols, and ritual activity, is an unintended consequence of the aggregation of populations resulting from the conscious efforts of people to maintain or increase their current agricultural production in the face of declining agricultural potential in many areas. Natural selection favored those individuals who successfully maintained their agricultural productivity, thereby acting as a probably unacknowledged condition favoring those agents (people) who formed larger communities. The increased social conflict, an unintended consequence of population aggregation, changed the social context of action, likely became an acknowledged condition of action, and led to the development of social hierarchies and changes in the symbolic structure as individuals applied their agency to develop a social structure consistent with the requirements of the aggregated communities. The new social system produced acknowledged and unacknowledged consequences of action that included a more hierarchical social power structure, changes in ritual practice, and changes in iconography and architecture. Because natural selection favored those who participated in aggregated communities, it favored by extension those who had social structures consistent with the larger aggregated communities. It thereby became an unacknowledged factor favoring the continuation of the modified Casas Grandes social structure.

CONCLUSIONS

The apparent incommensurability between agency-based approaches and EA masks a structural compatibility between them. Any evolutionary approach that ignores the problem-solving ability of humans and the fact that their behavior is affected by their social contexts and personal motivations is incomplete. However, any agency-based approach that ignores the unintended consequences of behavior as well as the unacknowledged conditions of action that affect the differential transfer of cultural information cannot accurately account for the form and the continuation of social structures or the factors that affect an individual's behavior.

By sharing the insights of both groups of archaeologists, however, a more accurate and useful understanding of the archaeological record is possible. Clearly, the factors that influenced human behavior in the past are numerous, and the explanation of past behavior that relies on "single factor" explanations are almost certainly incomplete. By combining agency and evolutionary approaches, the interplay between human agency and the evolutionary nature of cultural information systems can be understood. We have illustrated the potential of this agency-based EA approach by providing an explanatory narrative of cultural changes in the Casas Grandes region of northwestern Mexico and the American Southwest that considers the interplay between the various aspects of human behavior. We ultimately argue that such explanations hold more potential for archaeologists than alternate approaches.

ACKNOWLEDGMENTS

We thank Elizabeth Bagwell, Garth Bawden, Marcel Harmon, Erica Hill, Robert D. Leonard, Thomas Patterson, Robert Preucel, Gordon F. M. Rakita, Sue Ruth, and an anonymous reviewer for their comments on previous drafts of this paper.

9

Resolving Phylogeny: Evolutionary Archaeology's Fundamental Issue

MICHAEL J. O'BRIEN AND R. LEE LYMAN

An increasing number of archaeologists are showing interest in employing Darwinian evolutionary theory to explain variation in the material record. Several historical reviews of evolutionism in Americanist archaeology (Dunnell 1980; O'Brien 1996a, 1996b; O'Brien and Holland 1990) devote considerable space to the differences between Darwinian biological evolutionism and the cultural evolutionism of White (1949, 1959), Steward (1955), and others, but often ignored is the fact that some culture historians in the first half of the twentieth century (Colton and Hargrave 1937; Kidder 1915, 1932; Kroeber 1931) acknowledged, if only metaphorically, the applicability of Darwinian evolutionism to the study of prehistory (Lyman and O'Brien 1997, 2001b; Lyman et al. 1997; O'Brien and Lyman 1998, 1999b). Kidder (1932), a leading culture historian of the period 1910–1940, found some of the concepts embedded in Darwinian evolutionism—descent with modification and extinction—quite appropriate when discussing artifact lineages. Throughout his career Kidder focused on documenting variation—the singular issue that underlies any Darwinian study—and attempting to explain it. To Kidder, variation in such things as pottery was not fundamentally different from genetically controlled variation. Rather, there simply was more of it being produced as a result of the almost limitless imagination of humans and their enormous capacity for effecting change in their social and physical environment.

Kidder's views are important because they indicate how at least one archaeologist working in the early decades of the twentieth century conceived of the phenomena he was studying: Cultures evolved; a historically documented culture had a developmental heritage, or historical lineage, and it was the archaeologist's job to describe that lineage and to determine why it had taken the form that it did. But Kidder (1932) correctly indicated that archaeology lacked both the basic data and a theory consisting of cultural processes parallel to the biological ones of genetic inheritance and natural selection to help explain a culture's lineage in evolutionary terms. Without the means to document variation and then to link that variation to applicable theory, which dictates how and why we measure the variation, so-called explanations of how and why things change—the epitome of evolutionism—are simply untestable interpretations about the past.

Kidder realized that compiling the data and retooling Darwinian evolutionism so it was directly applicable to the archaeological record would take some concerted work, but few archaeologists were inspired by Kidder's call to action. Although chronologies of artifact types and larger units variously termed cultures, phases, complexes, and the like have been constructed, tested, refined, empirically verified, and are now available for many areas of the Americas, these have the status of being mere historical sequences. They may or may not comprise lineages, and thus explanations of them in the sort of evolutionary terms Kidder used are notably lacking. Any serious effort to make Darwinian evolutionism applicable to the archaeological record must be grounded in trying to resolve phylogeny. Our objective here is to outline a few of the many conceptual and methodological issues that must be addressed before such a resolution can occur.

MODERN EVOLUTIONARY ARCHAEOLOGY AND PHYLOGENY

Kidder's contemporaries, such as Gladwin (1936), argued that because cultural evolution occurred much more rapidly than biological evolution, Darwin's ideas were not applicable to the archaeological record—a point of view that reached its zenith with the oft-quoted statement by Brew (1946:53) that "phylogenetic relationships do not exist between inanimate objects." This pervasive sentiment effectively squelched any efforts to move beyond chronological ordering of artifacts and toward the development of a theoretical perspective on why some artifacts from different geographic areas closely resembled each other. In the absence of theory that might explain such similarities, culture historians borrowed common anthropological notions such as diffusion and trade to account for the similarities. As with their anthropological colleagues, culture historians viewed cultural evolution and biological evolution as entirely uncoupled phenomena. Darwinian evolutionism was viewed as applicable to the biological side of humans, but it was seen as irrelevant to the cultural side. Filling the void was White's (1949, 1959) brand of cultural evolutionism, with its emphasis on culture as humankind's extrasomatic means of adaptation. Whitean evolutionism became the cornerstone of processual archaeology in the 1960s. Although some processualists occasionally made reference to Darwinian evolutionism, it wasn't until publication of Dunnell's (1978a) "Style

and Function: A Fundamental Dichotomy" that there was an incipient programmatic statement on how to write that particular kind of evolutionism in strictly archaeological terms. Few people paid serious attention to that article, primarily because it addressed two mainstays of archaeology—style and function—in terms that were uncommon in the archaeological literature. This was especially true with respect to how Dunnell treated style. We return to this point below.

Dunnell's early work (1978a, 1978b, 1980) was followed by occasional articles throughout the 1980s (e.g., Dunnell 1989; Leonard and Jones 1987; Meltzer 1981; O'Brien 1987; Rindos 1989c), but it was not until the 1990s that evolutionary archaeology attracted more than modest interest. During that decade the number of articles and books grew exponentially and continues to grow. Some of these focus on method or on rewriting evolutionary theory in archaeological terms (Bettinger et al. 1996; Hunt et al. 2001; Neff 1992; Neff and Larson 1997; O'Brien 1996a; O'Brien and Holland 1990, 1992; Teltser 1995a), but many are case studies of how Darwinian evolutionism can be applied to particular portions of the archaeological record (e.g., Allen 1996; Aranyosi 1999; Bettinger and Eerkens 1997, 1999; Cochrane 2001; Dunnell and Feathers 1991; Hamilton 1999; Hughes 1998; Leonard and Reed 1993, 1996; Lipo 2001; Lipo et al. 1997; Madsen et al. 1999; Maxwell 1995; McGimsey 1995; Neff et al. 1997; Neiman 1995; O'Brien et al. 1994; Pfeffer 2001; VanPool 2001; Vaughan 2001).

Despite the advances made in adapting Darwinian evolutionism to archaeology, we agree with Schiffer (1996) that more case studies are needed in which evolutionism has been shown to produce explanations that are on par with or superior to those produced by other intellectual programs. Further, until recently (e.g., Lipo and Madsen 1999; Lipo et al. 1997; Lyman and O'Brien 1998, 2000b; Neiman 1995; O'Brien and Lyman 2000b), evolutionary archaeologists have been largely silent about the processes that generate the enormous variation in the archaeological record. As we point out in detail elsewhere (O'Brien and Lyman 2000a, 2002a), for evolutionary archaeology to be more than an intellectual novelty—something ignored by the majority of the discipline (Preucel 1999)—those with an interest in the approach need to be clear about such basic issues as what it is that evolves (Dunnell 1995; Lyman and O'Brien 1998) and how evolutionary change is to be measured (Lyman and O'Brien 1999, 2000b; O'Brien and Lyman 2000b). And as has been made clear (Bettinger and Richerson 1996; Bettinger et al. 1996; Schiffer 1996, 2000), evolutionary archaeologists are going to have to be more accommodating of other intellectual approaches that incorporate elements of Darwinian theory, such as behavioralism (Schiffer 1996, 1999), human evolutionary ecology (Boone and Smith 1998; Broughton and O'Connell 1999; Winterhalder and Smith 2000), and even cognitive science (Mithen 1996).

These are a few of the challenges that evolutionary archaeology has ahead of it, but there is another challenge, and it comes from the inside. Lest it be assumed that evolutionary archaeology itself is a well-integrated approach over which there is universal agreement, we point out that considerable disagreement exists within evolutionary archaeology over fundamental issues such as whether artifactual units can be used to examine human fitness. Neff (1999, 2000, 2001), for example, is of the opinion that although artifacts can be examined in terms of artifact fitness—how well one kind of artifact outreplicates another kind—that particular kind of fitness may have no bearing on human reproductive success. We wonder if that view, which is simply a recasting of Gladwin's (1936) observation that culture change can be faster than genetic change, will be used as a reason to discard *all* aspects of Darwinism from archaeological research, as it was used to that end in the 1930s and 1940s (Lyman and O'Brien 1997). We therefore prefer to think that the "replicative success" (Leonard and Jones 1987) of an artifact type may be driven by natural selection working on the replicators (humans), by natural selection working on the interactors (artifacts), by the vagaries of transmission, or by some combination thereof such that one evolutionary process or the other applies at different times (Lyman and O'Brien 1998, 2001a; O'Brien and Lyman 2002b). We agree with Neff's central contention that the problem of which one works at which time is less straightforward than has previously been assumed.

Such internal wrangling should render as moot any claims that evolutionary archaeology is flawed because it is scientistic or because it makes a claim of corporate affiliation (Wylie 2000). The approach is not scientistic—it does not advocate one and only one approach to scientific investigation (here, the problem seems to reside in differences of opinion regarding the role of *theory* in scientific endeavors)—and neither is there a corporate affiliation. We believe evolutionary archaeology is pluralistic (O'Brien and Lyman 2000b), but we do not believe that all intellectual programs that exist in Americanist archaeology are of equal weight when the subject is Darwinian evolution (Lyman and O'Brien 1998; O'Brien et al. 1998). We believe there is much to be learned from the disciplines of evolutionary biology and paleobiology (Lyman and O'Brien 2000a, 2000b; O'Brien and Lyman 1999a, 2000b), and we have learned much from the successes and failures of the much-maligned paradigm of culture history (e.g., Lyman and O'Brien 2002; Lyman et al. 1997; O'Brien and Lyman 1998, 1999b), although some critics (e.g., Longacre 1999) have missed the latter point. We do, however, find metaphysical shortcomings in how evolution has generally been approached in archaeology, and we have offered alternatives (O'Brien and Lyman 2000b). Some archaeologists (e.g., Bettinger et al. 1996; Boone and Smith 1998; Schiffer 1996) have found what they consider to be weaknesses in our approach and have offered additional alternatives. Metaphysical, theoretical, and methodological differences of opinion are to be expected, if not demanded, in any scientific approach to problem solving (Bell 1982). That these differences over evolutionary archaeology exist and can be debated is a sure sign that whatever is going on, it certainly is not scientistic.

The attempt to integrate Darwinian evolutionism into archaeology reminds us in no small measure of how things were in evolutionary biology in the Synthesis days of the late 1930s and 1940s, when there was deep theoretical and methodological division among geneticists, neontologists, and paleontologist (see Mayr and Provine 1980). For example, Simpson worked for over two decades to show that paleontology could make significant contributions to the Darwinian theory emerging from the Synthesis rather than being simply a source of confirmation of that theory. Simpson's (1944) *Tempo and Mode in Evolution* provided both a statement on the applicability of the new evolutionism to the fossil record and a methodological synthesis of how paleontologists could examine that record and provide unique insights into the evolutionary process. Reviewers of the book (e.g., Hubbs 1945; Huxley 1945; Wright 1945), however, were not impressed, and most biologists and paleontologists ignored the implications of the differences between microevolution and macroevolution—paleontology being uniquely capable of revealing aspects of the latter—that Simpson underscored (Laporte 2000). Only in the last quarter century has Simpson's original vision been vindicated (Eldredge 1985).

The parallels between Americanist archaeology and paleontology are both remarkable and perhaps expectable. Like paleontology, Americanist archaeology has long struggled for legitimacy within its parent discipline. Since its birth in the late nineteenth century, and despite occasional pleas or encouragement for archaeologists to "shrive yourselves of the notion that the units which you seek to reconstruct must match the units in social organization which contemporary ethnographers have attempted to tell you exist" (Harris 1968:360), archaeology remained for the most part "the tail on an ethnological kite"

(Steward 1942:341). To do more than serve as mere technicians who retrieve broken pots and arrowheads from layers of sediment in the service of historical reconstruction, as Service (1964) put it, archaeologists—in part because they were told to do so by anthropologists—adopted ethnological theory as the center piece of their explanatory tool kit. For their part, archaeologists were uneasy to make the break from anthropology, with most agreeing at least in principle with Taylor's (1948) detailed arguments that archaeology must strive to be less of a descriptive taxonomic enterprise and more anthropologically oriented and also agreeing with Phillips's (1955:246–247) admonition that "New World archaeology is anthropology or it is nothing." The latter became the rallying cry of processual archaeologists of the 1960s (e.g., Binford 1962; Flannery 1967).

Paleontology struggled to make itself heard throughout the years preceding and following the Synthesis, but it was in some ways more successful than archaeology has been. Paleontologists developed ways to adapt—not merely adopt—biologically based evolutionary theory to the unique aspects of the fossil record—its lack of direct evidence of genetic transmission, behavior, physiology, and so on—in the process developing what came to be known as "paleobiology." Archaeologists in the 1960s and 1970s followed exactly the opposite strategy and developed what came to be known as "anthropological archaeology." They transferred ethnological theories of various sorts to the archaeological record without any adaptation of those theories to the vagaries and nuances of the material record. This strategy required that the archaeological record be converted to an ethnological-like record, and thus ethnoarchaeology, formation-process studies, and middle-range theory grew in importance. As Watson (1995) documents, the culprit seems to reside in the adoption of "culture" as a keystone concept within anthropological archaeology (see Bennett [1998] for an outline of some of the attendant problems).

Evolutionary archaeology today in many respects is in a period similar to that of evolutionary biology in the 1970s when paleobiologists (e.g., Eldredge 1971; Eldredge and Gould 1972; Stanley 1975) proposed a new way to look at the fossil record that involved some retooling of biological evolutionary theory to fit the fossil record. Despite more than two decades of squabbling, the success of their endeavors is abundantly apparent (see review in Eldredge 1995). Evolutionary archaeology is a bit past the middle of the squabbling period, but certain challenges remain. Nonetheless, we suspect that in the next few years evolutionary archaeology's success (or failure) should be assured. The fits and starts that evolutionary archaeology is going through will, we believe, produce a synthesis of its own (O'Brien and Lyman 2002b). The theory requisite to archaeology, unabashedly conceived of as a science concerning the historical development of peoples and their cultures, has been around since 1859, the year Darwin penned *On the Origin of Species*. The basic problem for archaeology is that, as has been pointed out several times (O'Brien and Holland 1990; Rindos 1989c), Darwin did not write a theory that can be applied directly to the study of the archaeological record.

This is problematic for archaeology, but only if we fall into the trap of believing that precisely the same theoretical postulates, not to mention the same methods and techniques, that an evolutionary biologist employs must somehow be retrofitted for archaeological applicability. Such a belief is nonsensical, although this point was never made clear in the early evolutionary-archaeology literature. Despite differences between evolutionary biology and evolutionary archaeology, there are a few tenets that they undeniably hold in common: (1) variation exists, (2) that variation is heritable, and (3) some variants do better in certain environments than do other variants. Thus, in the simplest of terms, Darwinian evolutionism is a framework for explaining change as the differential persistence of variation (Campbell 1970; Endler 1986; Lewontin 1970, 1977). If the differential production of heritable variation, of whatever sort, is central to Darwinian evolutionism,

then that particular evolutionism is a body of theory and method built around the subject of *change*, not simply difference and similarity:

> The continuity implied in the terms change and persistence bespeaks a fundamental assumption: the phenomena being examined are historically and empirically related to one another (Alland 1973:3). It is also critically important to note that evolution views change as a *selective*, and not as a *transformational*, process. Variability is conceived as discrete. Change is accomplished by alteration of the frequency of discrete variants rather than alterations in the form of a particular variant. This characteristic places rather severe constraints on the application of evolutionary theory, although perhaps not as severe as it may appear on first reading. (Dunnell 1980:38)

Evolutionists study populations of things; in biology the populations are organisms, and in archaeology the populations are artifacts. As Jones et al. (1995:28) put it, it is "the differential representation of variation at all scales among artifacts" for which evolutionary archaeology seeks explanations. Evolutionary archaeology rests on the premise that because they were parts of past phenotypes, objects occurring in the archaeological record were molded by the same evolutionary processes as were the somatic features of their makers and users (Dunnell 1989; Leonard and Jones 1987; O'Brien and Holland 1990, 1992, 1995a, 1995b). This premise has been viewed by some (Larson 2000; Maschner 1998) as problematic, but we do not share this view. That artifacts, along with the behaviors that created them, are phenotypic is nonproblematic to most biologists, who routinely view such things as a bird's nest and a beaver's dam as phenotypic traits (Dawkins 1982; Turner 2000; von Frisch and von Frisch 1974). Neither is it problematic to paleobiologists, who rely on the hard parts of phenotypes to study the evolution of extinct organisms and the lineages of which they were a part. Further, paleobiologists use trace fossils—casts, burrows, and the like—as proxies for phenotypic characters and behaviors. Human-manufactured tools can be used similarly.

Darwinian evolutionary theory concerns how and why particular variants look as they do and behave as they do, where behavior is manifest as a varying frequency distribution across space and time. From an evolutionary perspective, change is measured "in terms of frequency changes in analytically discrete variants rather than the transformation of a variant" into another variant (Teltser 1995b: 53). This perspective on change runs counter to the way change normally is viewed archaeologically—that is, as a gradual or sudden transformation of a variant from one state to another. The distinction between change, which is the more or less gradual *replacement* of one variant by a phylogenically related variant, and transformation is important to recognize. As Gould (1986) put it, in Darwinian evolutionism history matters. Selection, drift, gene flow, and all the other evolutionary processes are important factors in modern Darwinian explanations, but without history they are simply processes and mechanisms with little to do and nothing to produce. Darwin's theory of descent with modification was based solidly on the notion of common ancestry. What is "descent with modification" if not a historical statement? History, when applied to anything organismic, implies the existence of lineages. The cornerstone of evolutionary archaeology, then, is resolving lineages of artifacts—an old concept in archaeology but one that has had but limited success. The problem, as we will see, is in demonstrating heritable continuity between forms as opposed to simply historical continuity, the latter being merely a sequence of forms as opposed to a lineage of related forms. How does one demonstrate that two or more phenomena are indeed parts of a lineage?

CONSTRUCTING ARCHAEOLOGICAL PHYLOGENIES

The place to begin is with systematics, which we take to be both the study of diversity of the phenomena of interest, irrespective of the scale or kind of phenomena, and the sorting of that diversity into sets such that like goes with like. The phenomena may comprise discrete objects such as projectile points or organisms; they may comprise the bits of temper in ceramics or the genes in organisms; or they may comprise assemblages of tools or populations of organisms variously termed faunas, floras, or communities. The goal of systematics in biology (Mayr 1942), paleobiology (Simpson 1961), and archaeology (Dunnell 1986; Ramenofsky and Steffen 1998) has always been to sort specimens into sets of individuals that are in some sense similar. Each set should be internally homogeneous such that within-group variation is analytically meaningless and between-group variation meaningful. Either the term *affinity* or the term *relationship* is typically used to indicate that some kind of relation exists between similar specimens within a group or between groups of specimens.

The kind of relation specified when one states that every specimen of kind A has an affinity with every other specimen of that kind, and that specimens of kind A have a different affinity with those of kind B, often is of a particular sort. Multiple kinds of things may be affines because they are close in time, in function, in symbolism, in ancestry, or in terms of something else. Specifying and measuring a *particular* kind of affinity is the ultimate goal of systematics, irrespective of discipline. This point is critical. If we are interested in ancestral-descendant affinity, this is quite different than functional affinity. We cannot assume that the kinds used to identify the latter will automatically tell us something about the former. In fact, there is every reason to suspect they will not (Allen 1996; Beck 1995b, 1998; Meltzer 1981). This was one of the points Dunnell (1978a) made in his seminal paper, but it was not made clearly enough and was lost in the ensuing debate over style and function.

The goal of systematics is realized by *classification*, which is the creation of new units and the modification and revision of old units by stipulating the necessary and sufficient conditions for membership within a unit. A *unit* is a conceptual entity that serves as a standard of measurement. An inch is a unit constructed explicitly to measure linear distance; the degrees found on a compass are conceptual units constructed explicitly for the measurement of orientation. As conceptual entities, units must be defined explicitly. Units can be specified at any scale. They can comprise one or multiple attributes of characteristics of a discrete object, of discrete objects, or of sets of discrete objects of various kinds. All sciences require that units for describing the phenomena under study be specified, but this requirement is not always readily met. Lewontin (1974:8) put it this way: "[T]he problem of theory building is a constant interaction between constructing laws and finding an appropriate set of descriptive [units] such that laws can be constructed. We cannot go out and describe the world any old way we please and then sit back and demand that an explanatory and predictive theory be built on that description." Hull (1970:32) used similar wording when he noted that the "two processes of constructing classifications and of discovering scientific laws and formulating scientific theories must be carried on together." Others (e.g., Hughes and Labandeira 1995) have recognized this critical point as well.

No one should argue with the statement that to be useful a classification must allow one to do some analytical work. The implications of this are several, and they are profound. One implication, noted above, is that a classification constructed for one purpose may not perform satisfactorily when used for another purpose (O'Brien and Lyman 2002a). A second implication is that a set of phenomena can be classified in a virtually infinite number of ways, although we are aware of very few examples of a collection of artifacts being classified in more than one way even when the collection is used to answer disparate analytical questions. A third implication is that the analytical validity of the units produced by classification must be testable. In particular, do they measure the kind of affinity sought?

Fifty years ago culture historians had as their main objective determining the chronology of occupation of a locality. Their classification procedure was to sort, by visual inspection, a pile of similar artifacts—usually sherds or projectile points—into smaller piles in which all items in a pile were more or less alike in terms of features considered chronologically diagnostic, and different than items in all the other piles in terms of the same features. One problem was the "more or less." When did the differences become important enough to start another pile? Arguments on this point raged for years in the literature, and similar problems arose in paleontology. Culture historians were well aware of the necessity of testing their hypothesized chronologies, recognizing that if their sorting did not measure the passage of time—that is, the individual piles of artifacts did not have particular temporal affinities—then they had to revise their classification. When the chronological test was passed, each pile—a *type*—was named, and a description of the type was written.

Although this classification method is suited for its purpose—to determine chronology—it more often than not fails when applied to any detailed investigation of small-scale changes over time. Not only is it completely subjective in that it places all decisions in the eyes of the classifier, it hides any small (and maybe important) changes in the "more or less alike." The type description is based either on an outstanding specimen or on an average specimen and, with discovery of more specimens within the "more or less" range, the description may require revision. Over the years, this has led to the inclusion of specimens in types that some archaeologists have argued should not be included and to the naming of new types that are identical to existing types. Units (types) constructed in this manner are descriptive in that the *general appearance* of a specimen is captured by the unit definition. These units are useful for communicative purposes so that when a particular object is said to be, say, a "pickup truck," everyone knows basically what is being discussed, but such descriptive units are oftentimes not useful for analytical purposes.

There must be some explanatory theory that guides analysis because it is theory and its derivative propositions that suggest which attributes should be measured and the requisite scale of resolution at which they should be measured. In paleontology an example would be the choice of millimeters not only to describe the size of a series of teeth of a mammalian species but to monitor variation in the size of those teeth over time and/or space in order to measure evolutionary change. One could choose color to describe a set of fossils, but color may not reflect the behaviors of the represented organisms. The construction of units useful for analysis, then, must consider the critical question: What must we measure in order to perform the required analysis?

Analytical units are *classes*—conceptual (as opposed to empirical) units of measurement. Combinations of character states define classes and are specified by the analyst. Classes can be univariate or multivariate. An advantage to multivariate classes attends the fact that morphospace is multidimensional—they allow simultaneous consideration of the values taken by "state, meristic, and metric variables" (Gould 1991:420) within a set of specimens, but *only* if they are constructed in a particular way. The procedure for constructing multivariate classes was spelled out independently by Shaw (1969) in paleontology and Dunnell (1971) in archaeology and termed "paradigmatic classification" by the latter. Morphospace is defined by a number of mutually exclusive characters, each with a set of states. Multivariate classes are defined by the intersection of characters—that is, by combinations of particular character states. The number of characters (and the number of states within a character) included in a particular classification is unrestricted.

To create a paradigmatic classification, the classifier lists all characters—length, width, color, and so forth—that he or she views as analytically important. Note the last part of that sentence. *Only* those characters that are viewed as analytically important are considered. This *might* mean that color is considered, but it might not. Color could be of

Table 9.1. Shaw's (1969) Paradigmatic Classification of Conodont Morphology

Character 1: outer platform lobe development	
State L:	lobed
State U:	unlobed
Character 2: outer platform cross-sectional shape	
State F:	flat
State A:	arched
Character 3: blade and ridge (inner platform) plan	
State N:	nonparallel
State P:	parallel
State D:	divergent anteriorly
Character 4: inner platform profile	
State T:	triangular
State R:	rounded
State A:	alate

analytical importance in one study and unimportant in another. In the latter case, it would be excluded from consideration. For each character used in the classification, the classifier lists the states in which each character might appear. It is the combination of character states, one state from each character, that creates classes.

Classes can be constructed at various scales. A class can comprise a single character of a discrete object, a particular combination of character states of a discrete object, or multiple kinds of discrete objects (say, the taxa comprising a fauna). When constructing a classification with a paradigmatic structure it is important to ensure that all characters are of the same scale. This ensures that, for example, species are not being compared with families or projectile points with all chipped-stone artifacts. To repeat a point made earlier, paradigmatic classes can be constructed such that, using Gould's (1991) terms, one or more characters concern "meristic" variables (frequency), one or more characters concern "metric" variables (size), and one or more characters concern "state" variables (shape).

As an example of paradigmatic classification, we can examine Shaw's classification of

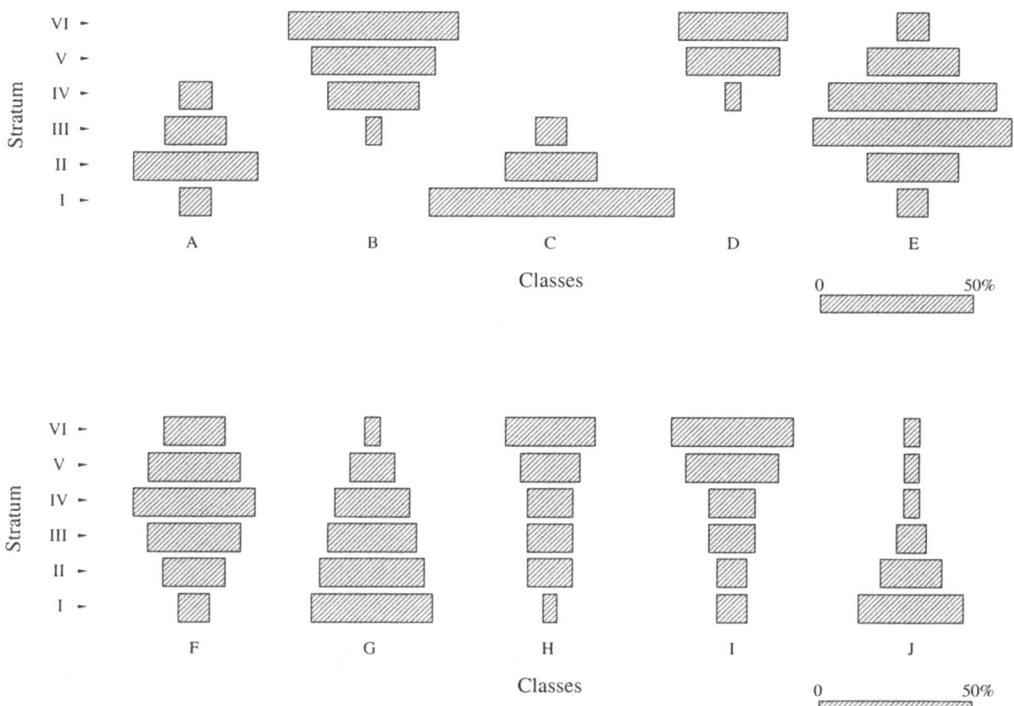

Figure 9.1. Examples of centered-bar graphs produced by percentage stratigraphy. There are six assemblages, one from each stratum (I–VI), in both the upper and lower examples. In this fictional example, change is faster and turnover more rapid among classes in the upper graph than among classes in the lower graph.

conodonts—toothlike phosphatic structures from now-extinct small, eel-like organisms. Shaw specified four characters, two of which included two states and two of which included three states (Table 9.1). Multiplication of the number of states per character ($2 \times 2 \times 3 \times 3$) indicates 36 classes exist within Shaw's classification. For example, the class LFNT is a conodont with a lobed outer platform, outer platform cross section flat, nonparallel blade and ridge, and triangular inner platform profile. In paradigmatic classification it is unnecessary for all classes to have empirical members; empty morphospace is just as important analytically as filled morphospace is. How might such units be used analytically to monitor variation?

Archaeology has nearly a century-long history of graphing culture change (Lyman et al. 1998), rather consistently graphing it as change over time in terms of the relative fre-

quencies of specimens within kinds, usually specified as *types*. Paleontology has a similar history. One graphic technique for monitoring change within lineages involves construction of a percentage-stratigraphy graph (Lyman et al. 1997, 1998), which comprises a set of columns of horizontal bars of various widths centered and stacked one atop another. Bar width signifies the relative abundance of a class within a set of stratigraphically associated specimens comprising multiple classes. Each row of bars represents a spatio-temporally unique assemblage, and each column represents a distinct class. The classes comprise variants of a more general category. Relative frequencies of classes are plotted against their stratigraphic proveniences. Character polarity (temporal order of character or character-state appearance) is dictated by superposition, with time passing from bottom to top along the vertical axis of

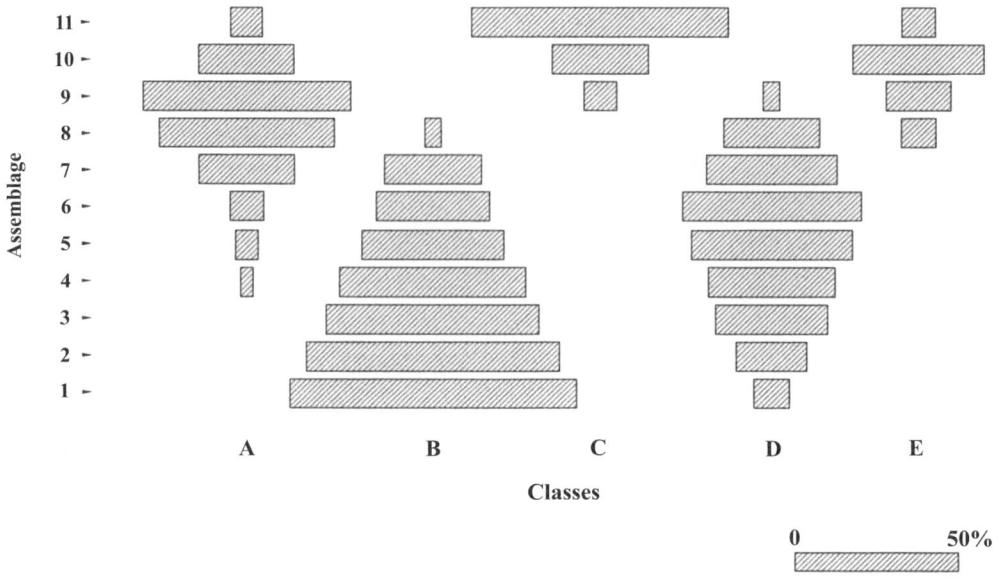

Figure 9.2. Hypothetical frequency seriation of 11 artifact assemblages using 5 artifact classes. Assemblages are ordered on the basis of artifact-class percentages, with bars summing to 100 percent for each assemblage. Only relative chronological ordering can be achieved through frequency seriation; further, time can run in either direction through the ordered assemblages.

the graph. What is shown in a percentage-stratigraphy graph is the history of the relative frequency of each of several classes of a particular category (e.g., conodonts, projectile points) over time.

Two examples of percentage-stratigraphy graphs (based on fictional data) employing classes are shown in Figure 9.1. As implied in this figure, relative rates of change can be monitored. Assuming the same strata are shown in both graphs, classes A–E (say, members of one taxonomic family) in the upper graph turn over much more rapidly than classes F–J (members of a second family) in the lower graph. Relative frequencies of classes within a family are plotted in both; values in each row of each graph sum to 100 percent. Say classes A–E represent classes of conodont morphology, as shown in Table 9.2. Because each class comprises an explicitly specified unique combination of character states, multiple classes may include the same character state, allowing the analyst to determine which classes have affinities on the

basis of shared character states. In Table 9.2 all classes share the same state (N) of the third character (blade and ridge plan), classes 1 and 2 share three (of four) character states (L, F, N), classes 3 and 4 share three character states (U, F, N), classes 1 and 5 share two character states (N, T), and classes 3 and 5 share three character states (U, N, T). Changes (or lack thereof) in the allometric relations of various character states are revealed. For example, outer platform lobe development (character 1) and outer platform shape (character 2) do not appear to display any such relation.

The rate of change from one character state to another within a character can also be monitored, and, importantly, because each class is multidimensional, mosaic evolution can be monitored (Table 9.3). Blade and ridge plan (character 3) remains stable across the five taxa (it always is nonparallel [N in Table 9.1]) and thus is not shown in Table 9.3. The inner platform profile (character 4) changes from triangular (T) to rounded (R)

Table 9.2. Relative Frequencies of Classes and Character States Plotted in Upper Graph of Figure 9.1

Stratum	1 (LFNT)	2 (LFNR)	3 (UFNT)	4 (UFNR)	5 (UANT)
VI	0	55	0	35	10
V	0	40	0	30	30
IV	10	30	0	5	55
III	20	5	10	0	65
II	40	0	30	0	30
I	10	0	80	0	10

Classes[a]

[a]Class definitions from Table 9.1.

Table 9.3. Relative Frequencies of Character States for Conodont Characters 1, 2, and 4

Stratum	Character 1		Character 2		Character 4	
	L	U	F	A	T	R
VI	55	45	90	10	10	90
V	40	60	70	30	30	70
IV	40	60	45	55	65	35
III	25	75	35	65	95	5
II	40	60	70	30	100	0
I	10	90	90	10	100	0

rather rapidly as we move up through the column. The flat (F) cross-sectional shape of the outer platform (character 2) decreases and then increases in relative frequency, and the development of the outer platform (character 1) changes from a higher unlobed relative frequency in the lower strata to a higher lobed relative frequency in stratum VI. Deciding which class or combination of classes might represent a species or higher taxon, if such a result is desired, can be accomplished by statistical determination of which character-state combinations (classes) occur more frequently than random chance allows or by stasis of character-state combinations over time. The same procedure, of course, can be used for artifacts.

As important as percentage-stratigraphy graphs are for monitoring change, how can we be sure that that change is between specimens that are directly related? In other words, how can we be sure that we are seeing heritable continuity as opposed to merely historical continuity? The answer is, we can't. We might be more sure if the pattern of change were replicated at numerous locales, but all such replicability confirms is the temporal sequence, not an evolutionary sequence. One means of searching for the latter is by monitoring change through frequency seriation (Fig. 9.2), invented by Kroeber (1916) to examine culture change around Zuñi Pueblo, New Mexico. Paleobiologists who have studied evolutionary change in lineages of organisms have taken notice of these graphs (e.g., Gould et al. 1987; Uhen 1996), although it is clear they do not fully grasp the epistemological differences between them and similar graphs they themselves have constructed. Frequency seriation provides one means of building hypotheses of heritable continuity precisely because it measures transmission (Lipo 2001; Lipo and Madsen 2001; Lipo et al. 1997; Lyman 2001; Neiman 1995; O'Brien and Lyman 1999b, 2000b; Teltser 1995b).

If frequency seriation in fact measures transmission, then the frequency distribution of each class over time will display a unimodal curve (Lipo and Madsen 2001; Lipo et al. 1997). *That* is the implication of frequency seriation as a test of heritable continuity (O'Brien and Lyman 2000b). The use of classes of artifacts representing what are referred to as "historical types" ensures heritable continuity at the scale of classes of artifacts because items are definitionally identical. The use of multiple classes of the same category of artifacts—projectile points, say—and their "overlapping," or occurrence in multiple assemblages, insures heritable continuity at the scale of the tradition of the artifact category (Lyman and O'Brien 2000a).

The phylogenetic implications of the hierarchical structure of the Linnaean taxonomy in biology are transferable to a similar hierarchical alignment of historical types of artifacts. For example, "pottery" can be aligned with a biological family, "types" of pottery with biological genera, and "varieties" of pottery with biological species. This is more or less what Gladwin (Gladwin and Gladwin 1930, 1934) and Colton and Hargrave (1937) proposed when they published major statements on the phylogenetic implications of pottery types. Gladwin (1936) shortly thereafter abandoned his scheme and mostly escaped criticism, but Colton and Hargrave did not (Lyman et al. 1997). Although Colton's knowledge of Darwinian evolution—he was a biologist by training—no doubt underpinned their scheme, the key to it was in the supposition that related forms were related because they were similar. As we discuss below, it should have been the other way around. The problem was that Colton and Hargrave offered no explicit theoretical argument and no empirical tests for their belief that the similarities were of the homologous sort. No one else at the time could offer an argument either, and Colton and Hargrave were blasted by archaeologists such as Brew (1946), who were not amused with their overtly biological scheme. Frequency seriation comprises a technique for testing hypotheses of relatedness.

A FURTHER WORD ON UNITS: HOMOLOGY AND ANALOGY

Evolutionary archaeologists have argued that, according to Darwinian theory, two kinds of units must be constructed so as to allow the measurement of two kinds of variation among artifacts (Dunnell 1978a; Lyman 2001; Lyman and O'Brien 1998; O'Brien and Holland 1990). Units that measure stylistic (adaptively neutral) variants allow the detection of transmission (e.g., Lipo and Madsen 2001; Lipo et al. 1997), a process that must be monitored to ensure that heritable continuity is being measured. As well, units that measure functional, or adaptive, variants must be constructed, as these contribute significantly to the writing and explanation of evolutionary history as it is driven by natural selection (e.g., O'Brien et al. 1994). The distribution of stylistic variants, because they are adaptively neutral and thus do not affect fitness, should, theoretically, oftentimes be different from the distribution of functional forms over time and space. Stylistic features measure interaction, transmission, and inheritance, whereas functional features will *sometimes* measure transmission as mediated by natural selection and other times measure adaptational difference alone (Beck 1995a; Meltzer 1981). As opposed to the continuous, unimodal frequency distribution exhibited by stylistic characters, functional characters can display one of several distributions. They might display a sharp rise in popularity followed by a steep decline (O'Brien and Holland 1990, 1992) as they are quickly replaced by other functional characters; they might display unimodal frequency distributions similar to those of stylistic characters; or they might display discontinuous, multimodal frequency distributions as a result of convergence or fluctuation in the selective environment. This brings us to an important point—the equation of style with homology and the equation of function with analogy. No other single issue has done more to confuse the style-function dichotomy in the archaeological literature than these seemingly straightforward equations.

In the case of style and homology, an equation is justified, but in the case of function and analogy it is not. Functional characters can be either analogous or homologous, which is why we noted above that functional forms *sometimes* measure transmission as mediated by natural selection and other times measure adaptational change alone. Homologous characters result from common ancestry. If we are sure that the characters with which we are dealing are homologous, then the phenomena exhibiting those characters are by definition related back through a common ancestor. In archaeology, the objects are related because of cultural transmission of various kinds (Boyd and Richerson 1985). But this tells us nothing about whether the homologous characters are functional or stylistic. O'Brien and Leonard (2001:5) state, "Do not be misled by the use of the term 'function' in defining what an analog is.... The key to whether a feature is homologous or analogous is strictly a matter of its history." A better way of putting it would be, "Although analogous characters can *always* be assumed to be functional, the reverse is not always true. Functional characters can be either homologous *or* analogous." In archaeology we assume that such things as decorations on pots are so complex that the probability of duplication by chance is small. If we find, say, two ceramic vessels containing identical decoration, we conclude that they are from the same tradition, or line of cultural heredity. They are homologous. We would normally not suspect that two completely independent groups of people arrived at *exactly* the same way of decorating their vessels, given the myriad possibilities available. There is no reason to suspect that we will *never* find such an example, but the more parsimonious explanation of such a phenomenon is that the vessels share a common developmental history and are from the same tradition.

Evolutionary archaeologists have emphasized the usefulness of stylistic traits for chronological purposes, making it appear as if those traits are the only kind that have such use, but this again masks the real issue: Is a character or set of characters homologous or analogous? If only stylistic characters or sets of characters (styles) can be used, then changes in, say, the hafting elements of projectile points, which we not only assume to be functional but can demonstrate empirically to be functional (Hughes 1998), would be useless as a basis for measuring the passage of time. This decidedly is not the case, as countless studies have shown (e.g., Beck 1995a, 1995b, 1998; Thomas and Bierwirth 1983; Wilhelmsen 2001).

We discuss elsewhere (Lyman 2001; O'Brien and Leonard 2001; O'Brien and Lyman 2000b) the hows and whys of constructing and testing stylistic and functional units, and a recent book on the subject (Hurt and Rakita 2001) adds substantially to the discussion. The matter, cast in slightly different terms, assumes center stage when we turn to another method of reconstructing phylogenetic histories, namely cladistics (see below). Here the focus is on first distinguishing between analogous and homologous characters, and second on distinguishing between two kinds of homologous characters: shared derived characters, or synapomorphies, and shared ancestral (primitive) characters, or symplesiomorphies. The easiest way of thinking about synapomorphies is to define them as homologous characters held in common by two or more taxa and their immediate ancestor but no other taxon. In contrast, symplesiomorphies are homologous characters held in common by an entire set of related lineages. Figure 9.3 illustrates the differences between ancestral and derived characters and how each occurs within a phylogenetic tree. If two phenomena share one or more synapomorphies, they are *by definition* phylogenetically related. The analytical challenge is to identify such characters. The distinction between homologous and analogous characters has long been noted by both processual archaeologists (Binford 1968b; Spencer 1992) and evolutionary archaeologists (Dunnell 1978a; Lyman 2001; O'Brien and Holland 1990, 1992), as it was by culture historians (Kroeber 1931; Steward 1929; Woods 1934), but only recently has interest been paid to the critical distinction between synapomorphies

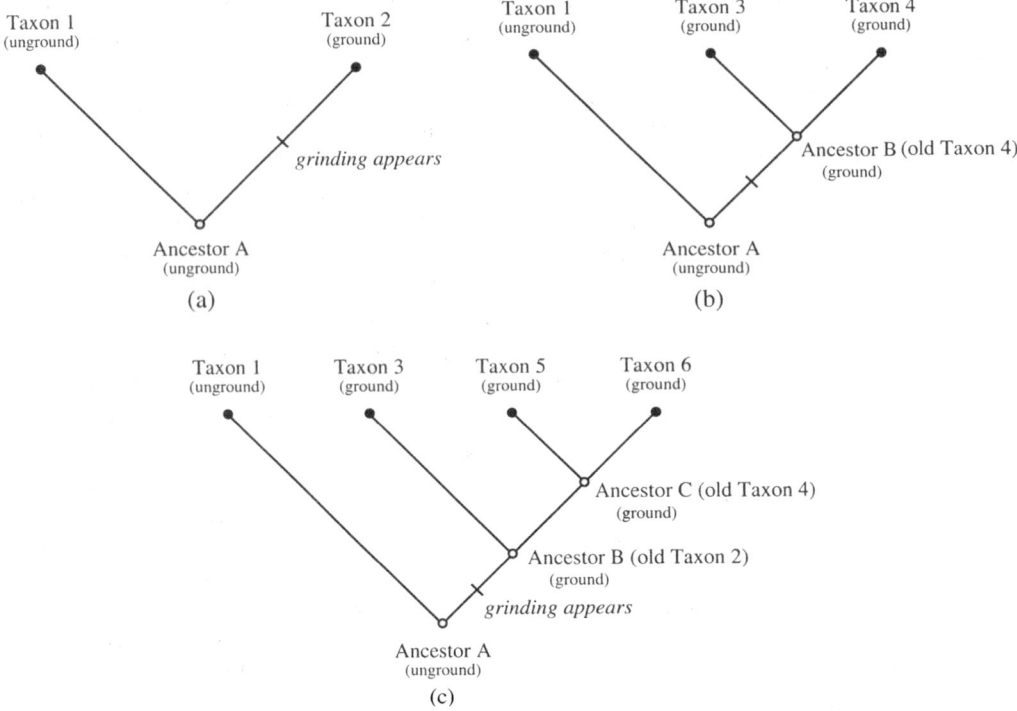

Figure 9.3. Phylogenetic trees showing the evolution of projectile-point taxa. In (a), basal grinding appears during the evolution of Taxon 2 out of its ancestral taxon. Its appearance in Taxon 2 is as an apomorphy, or derived character state. In (b), Taxon 2 has produced two taxa, 3 and 4, both of which contain basally ground specimens. The presence of grinding in those sister taxa and in their common ancestor makes grinding a synapomorphy, or *shared* derived character state. In (c), one of the taxa that appeared in the previous generation gives rise to two new taxa, 5 and 6, both of which contain ground specimens. If we focus attention *only* on those two new taxa, grinding is now a simple symplesiomorphy or *shared* ancestral (primitive) character state, because it is shared by more taxa than just sister taxa 5 and 6 and their immediate common ancestor. But if we include Taxon 3 in our focus, grinding is a synapomorphy because, following the definition, it occurs only in sister taxa, which in this case 3, 5, and 6 are, and in their immediate common ancestor, which is B (old Taxon 2).

and symplesiomorphies (Harmon et al. 2000; O'Brien and Lyman 2000b; O'Brien et al. 2001).

Identifying homologous traits is a significant analytical hurdle because a trait that is shared by two phenomena may be analogous —the result of convergence. Kroeber (1931: 151) suggested that "Where similarities are specific and structural and not merely superficial...has long been the accepted method in evolutionary and systematic biology." He was correct, for this was, and is, precisely how biologists distinguish between homologs and analogs, although such a simple statement belies the difficulties in so doing (Fisher 1994; Smith 1994; Szalay and Bock 1991). Kroeber (1931:151) pointed out that the "fundamentally different evidential value of homologous and analogous similarities for determination of historical relationship, that is, genuine systematic or genetic relationship, has long been an axiom in biological science. The distinction has been much less clearly made in anthropology, and rarely explicitly, but holds with equal force." He went on to imply that a "true homology" denoted "genetic unity," and he argued that "few biologists would doubt that sufficiently intensive

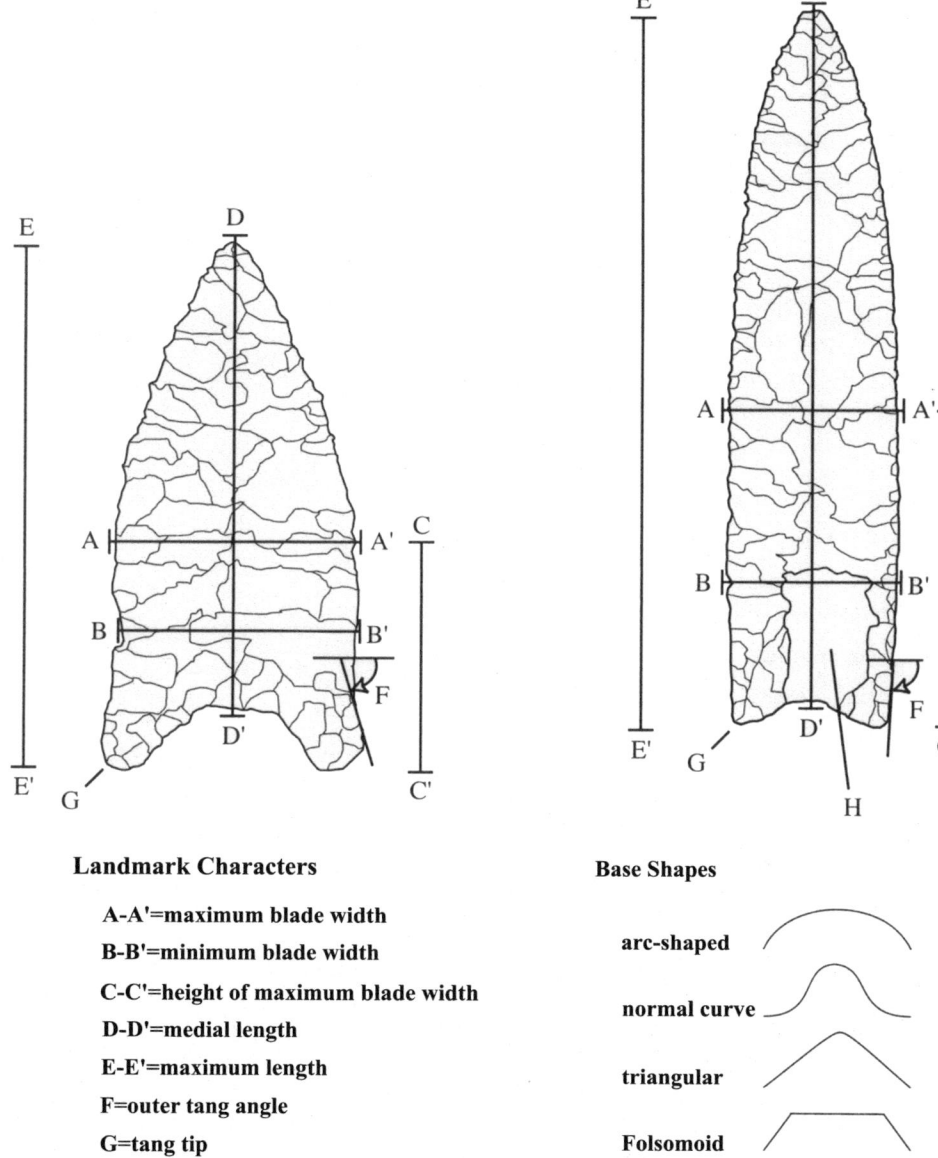

Landmark Characters

A-A'=maximum blade width
B-B'=minimum blade width
C-C'=height of maximum blade width
D-D'=medial length
E-E'=maximum length
F=outer tang angle
G=tang tip
H=flute

Base Shapes

arc-shaped
normal curve
triangular
Folsomoid

Figure 9.4. Locations of landmark characters used in the cladistical analysis of projectile points (see Table 9.4 for character states). Character states for base shape are shown at the lower right.

analysis of structure will ultimately solve such problems of descent.... There seems no reason why on the whole the same cautious optimism should not prevail in the field of culture" (Kroeber 1931:151).

Instead of implementing Kroeber's suggestions, archaeologists adopted the easily un-

derstood dictum "typological similarity is [an] indicator of cultural relatedness" (Willey 1953:363). This dictum was in fact central to the morphological-species concept of early twentieth-century biologists: Morphologically similar species were deemed members of the same taxon and thus seen as being

Table 9.4. System Used to Classify Projectile Points from the Southeastern United States

Character and Character State		Character and Character State	
I	Location of Maximum Blade Width	V.	Outer Tang Angle
1.	proximal quarter	1.	93°–115°
2.	secondmost proximal quarter	2.	88°–92°
3.	secondmost distal quarter	3.	81°–87°
4.	distal quarter	4.	66°–80°
		5.	51°–65°
		6.	≤ 50°
II.	Base Shape	VI.	Tang-Tip Shape
1.	arc-shaped	1.	pointed
2.	normal curve	2.	round
3.	triangular	3.	blunt
4.	folsomoid		
III.	Basal Indentation Ratio[a]	VII.	Fluting
1.	no basal indentation	1.	absent
2.	0.90–0.99 (shallow)	2.	present
3.	0.80–0.89 (deep)		
IV.	Constriction Ratio[b]	VIII.	Length/Width Ratio
1.	1.00	1.	1.00–1.99
2.	0.90–0.99	2.	2.00–2.99
3.	0.80–0.89	3.	3.00–3.99
4.	0.70–0.79	4.	4.00–4.99
5.	0.60–0.69	5.	5.00–5.99
6.	0.50–0.59	6.	≥ 6.00

[a] The ratio between the medial length of a specimen and its total length; the smaller the ratio, the deeper the indentation.

[b] The ratio between the minimum blade width (proximal to the point of maximum blade width) and the maximum blade width as a measure of "waistedness"; the smaller the ratio, the higher the amount of constriction.

phylogenetically related. This dictum was also axiomatic in culture history, and in both contexts it put the cart before the horse. It began to die in biology shortly after the Synthesis, and Simpson (1961:69) penned the obituary when he noted that individuals do not belong in the same taxon because they are similar; rather, they are similar *because they belong to the same taxon.* The dictum is,

however, still very much alive among many modern archaeologists. They note similarities between artifact types, assemblages of artifacts, and the like, and then *assume* that those similarities are the result of cultural transmission among the individuals who created the artifacts, thus making the latter homologs. But such similarities might not be of the homologous sort required to determine phylogenetic relations and write phylogenetic histories. That is, they might be symplesiomorphies instead of synapomorphies.

Cladistics, which uses only synapomorphies in making ancestor-descendant determinations, is a powerful method, although certainly not the only one, for constructing phylogenetic histories of anything that evolves over time, including material remains found in the archaeological record. It contrasts with phenetics and other grouping methods that use any character, regardless of origin, to make determinations of affinity. To date, the major use of cladistics has been in the biological realm, but the approach is identical in logic and similar in method to tracing historical patterns of descent in languages (Platnick and Cameron 1977; Ross 1997). Recently, archaeologists have begun to explore the use of cladistics in creating phylogenetic histories of artifacts (Harmon et al. 2000; O'Brien et al. 2001). The logical basis for extending cladistics into archaeology is the same as it is in biology: Artifacts are complex systems, comprising any number of replicators, units analogous to genes (Hull 1988a, 1988b; Lyman and O'Brien 1998). The kinds of changes that occur over generations of tool production are constrained, meaning that new structures and functions almost always arise through modification of existing structures and functions as opposed to arising de novo. The history of these changes, which include additions, losses, and transformations, is recorded in the similarities and differences in the complex characteristics of related objects—that is, in objects that have common ancestors (Hennig 1950).

We used cladistics to create a phylogenetic ordering of projectile points from the southeastern United States that date roughly 9250–8500 B.C. (O'Brien et al. 2001). Projectile point form varied considerably during that period, and although much of the variation undoubtedly is temporally related, there is no agreed-on historical ordering of traditional point types. There undoubtedly was heritable continuity between at least some sequent forms, but this has never been documented.

2	1	2	2	(5)	2	1	2	Class 1
2	1	2	2	4	(2)	1	2	Class 5
2	1	2	(2)	4	3	1	2	Class 4
(2)	1	2	1	4	3	1	2	Class 3
(1)	1	2	1	(4)	3	1	2	Class 16
2	1	2	(1)	5	3	1	2	Class 17
(2)	1	2	3	(5)	3	(1)	2	Class 15
(3)	1	2	(3)	4	3	2	2	Class 8
2	1	2	1	4	(3)	2	2	Class 2
2	1	2	1	(4)	2	2	2	Class 6
(2)	1	2	1	2	(2)	2	2	Class 14
(1)	1	2	(1)	2	1	2	2	Class 13
(3)	1	2	2	(2)	1	2	2	Class 12
2	1	2	2	(1)(1)		2	2	Class 9
2	1	2	2	3	(3)	2	(2)	Class 11
(2)(1)		2	(2)(3)		2	2	3	Class 7
1	2	2	1	2	2	2	3	Class 10

Time (vertical axis, upward arrow)

Figure 9.5. Arrangement of the 17 projectile-point classes ordered by the least number of character changes needed to create the ordering (28 steps). In effect, this is an occurrence seriation of the classes. If we have the classes in correct order, we can determine the evolution of characters through time, with each circled character state denoting a change from the immediately earlier state. Evolution, of course, is primarily a branching process as opposed to an anagenetic one; thus our interest is in knowing not only which character state is ancestral to another but also the pattern of evolving characters. Cladistics offers a solution to this problem.

Instead, common archaeological practice is to tie changes in form to mechanisms such as diffusion and population movement. We used paradigmatic classification to create our taxa, or classes, as shown in Figure 9.4 and Table 9.4.

Classes circumvent a problem that cladistics has faced since its inception—the use of

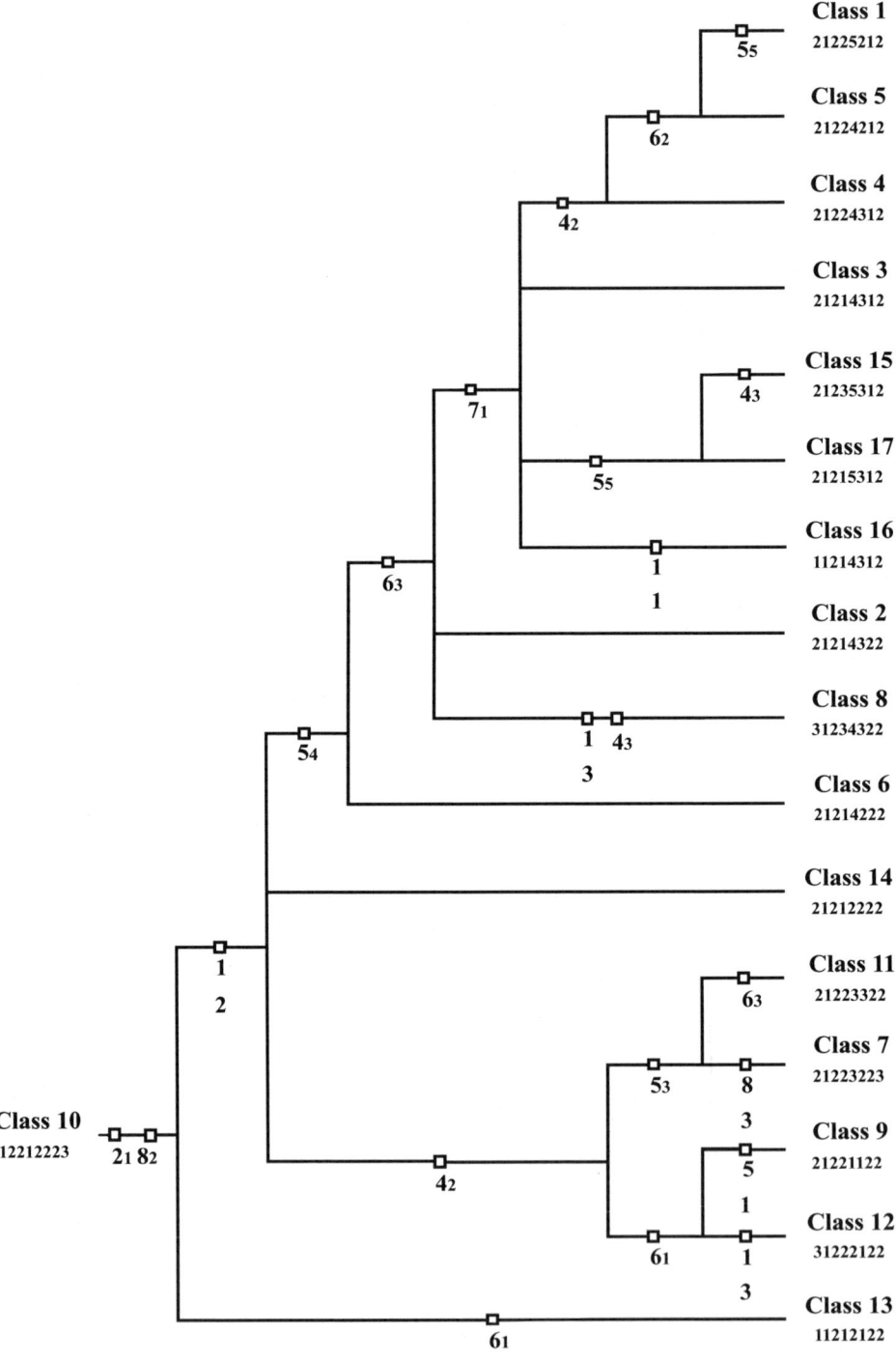

Figure 9.6. Phylogenetic tree of 17 projectile-point classes. The tree has been slightly simplified from the original (see O'Brien et al. [2001] for details). Class 10, shown here as an ancestor to all other classes, is the outgroup against which all other classes were compared. In a strict cladogram, it would be shown as a terminal taxon (located at branch tips), as are all the other taxa.

the term *transformation* or *transformation series*. Rarely is consideration given to the fact that characters do not transform from one state to another. Rather, the frequency of a particular state of a given character changes within a population relative to the frequencies of other states of that character, as shown in Table 9.3. Plotting such changes at the level of individual character offers a means of monitoring changes in character states throughout a lineage. In Figure 9.5, the 17 projectile point classes we used in the cladistical analysis are arranged in an order determined by the least number of character changes needed to create the ordering (28 steps). In effect, this is an occurrence seriation (O'Brien and Lyman 1999b, 2000b). If we have the classes in correct order, we can determine the evolution of characters through time, with each circled character state denoting a change from the immediately earlier state. But biological evolution is primarily a cladogenetic (branching) process as opposed to an anagenetic (linear) one; thus our interest is in knowing not only which character state is possibly ancestral to another but also the pattern of diversification. Cladistics, through its use of only shared *derived* characters (synapomorphies) as opposed to both shared derived and shared ancestral characters (symplesiomorphies), offers a solution to this problem.

The computer program PAUP* (version 4) (Swofford 1998) was used to generate the tree shown in Figure 9.6. That program, like other algorithms used in cladistics, uses a search routine to cull through the myriad possible trees, of which there may be thousands or even millions, to find those that require the fewest number of steps to produce, with steps defined as character-state changes. Depending on the number of classes and the number of characters, the program can produce multiple trees with the same tree length (number of steps), and it is up to the analyst to make the case for one tree over another. Most programs will also produce consensus trees in an attempt to resolve some of the disparity among the multiple trees. With respect to the 17 classes of projectile points, however,

only a single tree was produced. Notice that it contains several polytomies, or points at which the program cannot make a simple dichotomous split—for example, a trichotomous branching that produces classes 8, 2, and the clade comprising classes 1 + 5 + 4 + 3 + 15 + 17 + 16. The first characters in the ancestral taxon (class 10, defined as 12212223)[1] to change were (1) character II—base shape—which changed from state 2 (normal curve) to state 1 (arc-shaped), and (2) character VIII—length/width ratio—which changed from state 3 (3.00–3.99) to state 2 (2.00–2.99). This produced (1) an ancestor (11212222) that in turn produced class 13 after an additional change in character VI from state 2 to state 1 and (2) an ancestor to all the other taxa. The latter ancestor underwent a change in character I—location of maximum blade width—from state 1 (0–0.25) to state 2 (0.26–0.50) and produced an ancestor (21212222) that in turn produced (1) class 14 (with no modification), (2) the clade comprising classes 11 + 7 + 9 + 12, and (3) the clade comprising all remaining taxa.

Homoplasy, including functional convergence, is as problematic in reconstructing phylogenetic histories of artifacts as it is in reconstructing the histories of organisms. The tree shown in Figure 9.6 has a retention index of 0.7000 and a consistency index of 0.5909 —the latter much higher than we expected based on our review of cladistical analyses in biology and paleobiology, but still low enough to indicate that considerable homoplasy is present. Homoplasy obviously is present in the occurrence seriation as well (Fig. 9.5). For example, reading from bottom to top for character I, notice the reappearance of character states 1, 2, and 3 at different points in time. The phylogenetic tree, which has a length of 22, in essence requires six fewer steps to create than the 28 required for the occurrence seriation, suggesting that cladogenesis is as important a process in artifact evolution as it is in organismic evolution.

As pointed out in more detail elsewhere (O'Brien et al. 2001), we expect several objections to the use of cladistics in archaeology. First, it might be argued that artifacts do not breed—akin to Brew's (1946:53) statement quoted above that "phylogenetic relationships do not exist between inanimate objects." This statement is false. Tools (interactors) certainly do not breed, but neither do the teeth and bones (interactors) studied by paleobiologists. But tool makers *do* breed, and they *do* pass on information (replicators) to other tool makers. Cultural transmission, both vertical and horizontal (Boyd and Richerson 1982, 1983, 1985), creates *tool traditions,* or *lineages.* Second, it might be argued that although there are tool lineages, they are impossible to discover archaeologically because of the rapidity with which cultural evolution produces variation. The tempo of cultural evolution most certainly *is* much faster than that of biological evolution, but this hardly means that we cannot see change and track its manifestations. It might also be argued that the mode of cultural evolution can be different than the modes of biological evolution—reticulate and branching, respectively—although we note that a growing body of evidence indicates reticulate evolution occurs with some regularity in the biological realm (Arnold 1997; Doolittle 1999; Endler 1998).

The claim has been made (Dewar 1995; Moore 1994a, 1994b; Terrell 1988, 2001; Terrell and Stewart 1996; Terrell et al. 1997; Welsch and Terrell 1994; Welsch et al. 1992) that diffusion results in reticulation, thus swamping all traces of phylogenetic history and reducing the cultural landscape to little more than a blur of hybrid forms. This line of reasoning is not new (e.g., Kroeber 1948; Steward 1944), and it is just as incorrect today as it was over half a century ago. We agree that some cultural evolution is reticulate, but we do not view that as being particularly problematic to archaeological analysis. It again is a matter of scale, and the same principles apply regardless of whether one is studying the phylogenetic history of fossils, of cultural practices (Mace and Pagel 1994), or of languages (Platnick and Cameron 1977). Goodenough (1997:178) makes an

excellent point with respect to language: "Contact between Japan and the United States has resulted in considerable borrowing in language and culture by Japan and some reverse borrowing by the United States, but their languages and cultures retain their respectively distinct phylogenetic identities." Linguists do not guess as to whether two or more languages share a phylogenetic history. Innumerable case studies have provided the basis for deciding which linguistic characters might be apomorphic—bound morphemes and vocabulary, for example—and which might be homoplasious—syntax, for example (Nichols 1996). Thus the comparative method groups languages not on the basis of shared similarities but according to the distribution of shared innovations relative to a reconstructed protolanguage ancestral to the whole family (Ross 1997). This is nothing more than separating apomorphic from plesiomorphic characters and using the former to construct a phylogeny. The same principle applies in archaeology.

CONCLUDING REMARKS

Darwinian evolutionism is a theory about history—specifically, how and why genealogically connected things change over time. Evolutionists write historical narratives and then attempt to explain why those narratives look the way they do (Lyman and O'Brien 1998). Both steps employ concepts deeply embedded within Darwinian evolutionary theory, such as (1) lineage, which is a line of development owing its existence to heritability; (2) natural selection, which is a mechanism of change; (3) innovation, which is another source of new variants; (4) a transmission mechanism, which itself is a source of new variants; and (5) heritability. The fourth produces the fifth, and both ensure that we are examining change within a lineage rather than an instance of convergence.

Not surprisingly, evolutionary archaeology has numerous parallels to modern paleobiology. It is geared toward providing Darwinian-like explanations of the archaeological record, just as paleobiologists explain the paleontological record. Perhaps of more surprise is the fact that evolutionary archaeology is not really so different from a lot of what the discipline has been doing throughout the twentieth century (Lyman et al. 1997; O'Brien and Lyman 1998). Evolutionary archaeology *does* require a different perspective on how change is measured and on what the change means, but one does not have to proclaim an allegiance to Darwinian evolutionism in order to actually *do* evolutionary archaeology. All one need do is first, construct hereditarily based lineages of artifacts; second, monitor change over time in those lineages; and third, offer theoretically based explanations for the lineages looking the way they do. The key term is "theoretically based," meaning that the cause of change is lodged in theory as opposed to in the things being explained. Another way of looking at this is to say that cause is *external* to the things being examined.

Darwin did not understand inheritance the way we do today, but he understood the connection between inheritance and reproductive success. We prefer the term "replicative success" (Leonard and Jones 1987) rather than reproductive success, since it is portions of the human cultural phenotype—artifacts—that are evident in the archaeological record. The relation between the replicative success of artifacts, at least those that influence adaptive fitness, and the reproductive success of the organisms that bear them is clear: "The replicative success of artifact traits depends, at least in part, upon their contribution to the fitness of individuals possessing those traits as part of their phenotype but almost certainly also to the effectiveness of transmission mechanisms" (Jones et al. 1995:19).

If we define evolution as "any net directional change or any cumulative change in the characteristics of [genetically related] organisms or populations over many generations" (Endler 1986:5), then we are talking about descent with modification. There is a critical question here that must be addressed: If two things are similar in form and different in age, do they indicate that change has somehow taken place? From a modern Darwinian viewpoint, they represent change only if they are genetically—in a metaphorical sense with respect to artifacts—related, in which case the similarity of form and difference in age signify inheritance and thus continuity—an ancestor-descendant lineage. The issue of lineage construction must be explicitly considered if we ever hope to place archaeology on a sound scientific footing.

Notes

1. Technically, class 10 is referred to as *outgroup*—the taxon against which all other taxa are compared in order to determine which characters are ancestral and which are derived.

10

Does Americanist Archaeology Have a Future?

PATTY JO WATSON

In 1984, I was asked to contribute to a 50th Anniversary, Society for American Archaeology Plenary Session entitled "Current Trends and Future Prospects for American Archaeology." That session's papers were later published (Meltzer et al. 1986), and some were quite influential. The only part of my statement that anyone seems to remember, however, is a jingle ("The Very Model of a Modern Archaeologist") that I had modified slightly from Derek Roe's reworking of Gilbert and Sullivan's "The Very Model of a Modern Major General" (Roe 1984; Watson 1986). In the hope that something from my current contribution will also be remembered, I begin by evoking some themes of mid-1980s to mid-1990s Euroamerican archaeology in a second modification of that same venerable jingle.

The Very Model of a Post-Modern
  Archaeologist

I am the very model of a Post-Modern
  Archaeologist,
a structural.symbolic.hermeneutic.
  marxicologist.

I've twenty-two scenarios for one
  fifteen-item lithic lot;
My inspiration's from the Continent where
  social theory's always hot.

I intuit understandings from Foucault and
  Paul Ricoeur,
Creating heaps of *bricolage* without a single
  bricoleur.

If you're into *les Annales*, Fernand Braudel,
  and *longue durée*,
If you cogitate and contemplate the works of
  Godelier,

If you long to linger with La Durie, do-si-do
  with Pierre Bourdieu,
Then I'm the colleague to consult before you
  ditch that positivist paradigm,

I've hired Shanks and Tilley, and I've fired
  my ecologist:
I am the Very Model of a Post-Modern
  Archaeologist!

The jingle highlights various "postprocessualist" (postmodernist) approaches and critiques during the last two decades of the twentieth century (for a substantive treatment, see Pruecel and Hodder 1996). What else happened then, and what can we anticipate for the first decades of the 2000s?

Back in 1985—when I emerged from several years of obsession with my own research corner of west-central Kentucky—I was forcibly struck by two prominent features in the landscape of Americanist writings about archaeological theory.

First, there were several archaeologists who did not think a real past or the real past was accessible, and who were pursuing various alternative trajectories—sometimes radically so—to culture-historical and processualist ones. This group I called the archaeological minority. Among the archaeological minority were some postprocessualists (critical theorists), and some enthusiastic advocates of middle-range theory and ethnoarchaeology, who apparently believed that adequate archaeological interpretations could be secured only in the ethnographic present (Binford and Hodder). I also put Robert Dunnell into the archaeological minority category because of the very narrowly empiricist aims that characterized his evolutionary archaeological program as described by the mid-1980s.

The other striking feature of Americanist archaeology in the mid-1980s United States was the extent to which the whole enterprise had become a gigantic conservation and salvage operation.

In the following sections, I take up where I left off in 1985 to summarize what has happened since then regarding certain developments in archaeological theory and method, how they relate to postprocessualist ones, and whether Americanist archaeology as we know it now has a future in the twenty-first century.

INDIGENIST POLITICAL ACTION

The most significant event relevant to archaeology in the United States between 1985 and now was the passage of the Native American Graves Protection and Repatriation Act by Congress in November 1990. Similar political action had been taken previously, and was taken subsequently, in many other countries in response to the concerns of indigenous groups. Every archaeologist in every world area where such political actions occurred is now continuously affected by them. In the United States, NAGPRA forced a radical restructuring of archaeological practice that is more profound and more comprehensive than even the most powerful impacts of the

1974 Archaeological Conservation Act. Every major institution and hundreds of smaller ones housing Native American cultural property are striving to achieve compliance with the regulations implementing NAGPRA. Results so far cover a wide spectrum—from sharply adversarial (e.g., the Kennewick Man case, still under litigation several years following the initial discovery) to strongly collaborative (e.g., the Florida Natural History Museum's Calusa Project, whose director [William Marquardt] has established excellent working relations with the indigenous people of south Florida). Archaeologists, Indian people, and archaeopoliticians of all kinds are negotiating their way to viable or at least endurable compromises. The realm of NAGPRA provides a forum for archaeologists inclined toward the ideational or cognitive aspects of postprocessual approaches, as well as those committed to critical theory, and hence concerned with such themes as hegemony, resistance, class struggle, social agency, and social responsibility.

Intersection of these multiple sociopolitical vectors makes this arena complex and difficult to track. Nevertheless, there is considerable potential for breakthroughs that will permanently expand the boundaries of archaeological inference.

THE GROWTH OF CRM (RESCUE, SALVAGE, COMMERCIAL) ARCHAEOLOGY

Elsewhere in the CRM world, the multimillion dollar contracts of the 1980s (e.g., FAI 270 in the American Bottom, Black Mesa and Dolores in the Southwest), many of which went to university-based programs, did not characterize the 1990s. The action now seems to be primarily in the hands of small, medium, and large private firms, many of which specialize in an array of environmental impact assessment arenas, archaeology being only one among numerous others. Developments in private-sector firms are now directly and indirectly affecting academia, even though most of the academically based CRM operations themselves are shrinking or being closed down. According to the SAA's recent self-study (Zeder 1997), there is a discernible trend of men (often leaving universities at the M.A. level) preferring private sector employment to the fewer and slimmer options within academia, which are being increasingly taken by women with Ph.D.s. Indeed, the questionnaire data indicate that job satisfaction in both private and public sectors is higher than in academe (Zeder 1997:119–120), in spite of the fact that many public and private sector archaeologists expressed preferences for positions in graduate universities (Zeder 1997:60–65).

Another significant finding of the SAA study is the big difference between non-CRM and CRM funding for U.S. archaeology. Respondents reported obtaining a total of some 30 million federal dollars between 1989 and 1993 (mostly from NSF and NEH) for non-CRM archaeology, whereas federal sources for CRM archaeology totaled 90 million dollars (Zeder 1997:200). For 1989 to 1993, a total of somewhat more than 300 million dollars came from federal plus non-federal sources for CRM work: that sum was awarded to only 63 individuals over this five-year period. Extrapolating these numbers through the 25 years (1974–1999) since the Archaeological Conservation Act took effect gives a sum approaching and probably exceeding one billion dollars for CRM support of archaeology. This puts a rather impressive price tag on the conservation-salvage operation referred to earlier as characterizing U.S. archaeology at the end of the twentieth century. Will the government and the public continue to pay this bill? Perhaps, but it certainly seems important for archaeologists involved in the CRM system to evaluate the results continuously, and to intensify their public education, outreach, and advocacy activities.

NON-CRM ARCHAEOLOGY IN THE 1990S AND BEYOND

As government funding for non-CRM archaeology declined in the early 1990s (death of NEA, near-death of NEH, steady state—which means decline with reference to earlier funding levels—of NSF), some archaeologists did not turn to CRM, but instead increased their attention to a traditional support source: private backers (on the model of Lord Carnarvon and Howard Carter). For example, a classical archaeologist of my acquaintance has recently been assured of sums in excess of 25 million dollars for two field projects in Greece. The research of another colleague on early and middle Holocene prehistory in the western United States has been supported quite generously by a private patron for the past several years, and that arrangement is continuing.

The apogee of funding for archaeology at the moment, however, and probably for the near future is in the realm of cultural remains on the ocean floor. A melange of private entrepreneurial activity and military-scholarly-scientific collaborations is now deploying the latest high-tech means to reach shipwrecks lying 2 to 3 miles beneath the ocean's surface (Broad 1998; Goodheart 1999; "Technology and Archaeology in the Deep Sea" 1999). According to experts, 97 percent of the global ocean floor is now accessible to any group or any institution that can afford to hire the technology. Although discussions of a UN treaty have begun, at the moment, ocean-floor exploration and salvage are completely laissez-faire. There are precedents for unrestricted, entrepreneurial looting (RMS Titanic, Inc.), as well as for somewhat more restricted entrepreneurial raising of artifacts (Goodheart 1999). There are also carefully crafted, precariously balanced collaborations among private salvors, archaeologists, universities, museums, nonprofit research organizations, and/or the U.S. Navy, especially its nuclear submarines ("Technology and Archaeology in the Deep Sea" 1999). These projects have budgets in the multimillions of dollars (many of them would singly exceed the entire yearly amount NSF dispenses for archaeology), and are proliferating quite rapidly considering how complex and difficult their logistical arrangements have to be.

Meanwhile, what of the archaeological

minority, other than those postprocessualists engaged with the ramifications of NAGPRA?

THE ARCHAEOLOGICAL MINORITY TODAY

Postprocessualist themes of various kinds are central globally in the late 1990s as they were in the 1980s, and are certainly present in Americanist archaeology (e.g., Duke and Wilson 1995), but not so prominently as in many other world areas. For example, only about 23 sessions (this is a generous estimate) of the total 576 at the last three annual meetings of the Society for American Archaeology (1999, 2000, and 2001) were devoted to postprocessualist themes. Elsewhere within the group designated the archaeological minority in 1985, evolutionary archaeology (selectionist archaeology, plus evolutionary ecology; e.g., Boone and Smith 1998, Broughton and O'Connell 1989, Lyman and O'Brien 1998) accounts for approximately 11 of the 576 total sessions at the 1999, 2000, and 2001 annual meetings of the SAA.

Ethnoarchaeological research (a new and comprehensive account is provided by David and Kramer 2001), investigation of site formation processes, as well as other previously established culture-historical and processualist foci are still very much a central part of Americanist archaeology (see Chamblee and Mills 2001 for a characterization of current research concerns as expressed in the program of the SAA's 2001 annual meeting). Finally, it is encouraging that there are persistent efforts at dialogue among advocates of various alternative theoretical-methodological approaches (e.g., Lyman and O'Brien 1998; Schiffer 1999c; VanPool and VanPool 1999). Moreover, as regards CRM vis-à-vis non-CRM archaeology—at least one authoritative observer thinks that "the days when these employment sectors divided archaeology are passing" (Kelly 2002). At any rate, it is clear that the future of Americanist archaeology is significantly and permanently pluralistic, much more so than was the case at any time in the twentieth century.

SUMMARY AND CONCLUSIONS

So where exactly are we headed in the early twenty-first century? Debates and discussions about theoretical and meta-archaeological issues will continue, but—as at present—only a very small percentage of professional archaeologists will be persistently and centrally involved in these debates. Actual digging by professional archaeologists will be extremely limited, closely controlled, and 99 percent of it will be CRM activity of some sort. Micromorphological (e.g., Matthews et al. 1996) and geophysical (resistivity, conductivity, fluxgate radiometry, etc.) approaches as well as biochemical techniques (e.g., isotopic and DNA analyses) will be featured methodologically. Processual, postprocessual, and evolutionary approaches will all be readily detectable theoretically. Archival, curatorial, laboratory, and deskchair archaeologists will far outnumber leaders of major field projects. Collections, curation (with a heavy emphasis on administrative activity such as inventorying and tracking collections), nondestructive collections-based research, and interpretive-outreach programs for nonprofessionals will be the major foci for public sector and academic archaeologists, who will collaborate intensively and extensively with each other. The Archaeological Conservancy in the U.S., and other site-preservation initiatives here and elsewhere will become even more important than they are now. Private sector archaeology in the U.S.—including CRM and various forms of consulting archaeology—will function primarily in the corporate world, where lobbying Congress, and creating mergers (as well as buyouts or takeovers of other firms), will be frequent. Remote archaeology (i.e., archaeology by remotely controlled vehicles) with elaborate unmanned sensing devices and robotic capabilities, deployed on the ocean floor, and perhaps extraterrestrially on other planets or the moons of Jupiter, will be the new fieldwork frontier as more and more terrestrial sites are destroyed or sealed over by development, or become increasingly inaccessible for political reasons.

Does Americanist archaeology have a future in the twenty-first century? Yes, of course it does, but it will be so different from its traditional configuration that practitioners whose careers spanned a major portion of the twentieth century might have some difficulty recognizing it as their own discipline.

11

Essential Tensions

ROBERT D. LEONARD

The purpose of this final chapter is to provide comments on the previous chapters in the volume. So, where to begin? You might be thinking that I should begin with a consideration of the first chapter, but I mean before that. Before putting fingers to keyboard a writer establishes a perspective from which to proceed as well as chooses a voice. Judging from other chapters like this I have read, seeking intellectual (and if necessary, moral) high ground certainly has precedence, and donning at times respective cloaks of wisdom, authority, and importantly, objectivity are time-honored traditions in this genre. Of course, precedent also dictates that it is well to proceed without seeming pompous, arrogant, or ungenerous, and to be sure to give praise wherever praise is due, however faint. Of particular importance is that one must offer the appearance of balance and lack of bias.

These precedents, however, seem disingenuous to me, despite the fact that virtually every piece such as this ever written has done exactly this. I originally tried to do exactly as precedents indicated—especially the objective and unbiased part, but couldn't do it. Disingenuous is a good word. Not to appear pedantic (another good word), but my dictionary defines *disingenuous* as "lacking in frankness, candor, or sincerity; falsely or hypocritically ingenuous; insincere." Dishonest and misleading also come to mind here, but that may be overly critical of the genre, so let me simply state that the models I have to work from are simply not reflexive. And reflexive I must be, as my biases in the following endeavor will be very apparent to anyone who knows me and my work. Among the authors contributing these papers are friends, students, acquaintances, people I went to grad school with, individuals whose work I admire, whose theoretical perspectives I share and those I don't. There is also one person whom I have never met. Presuming that I (or anyone else, for that matter) can stand above all of this from a position of wisdom, authority, and objectivity is, well, disingenuous. So, I'll attempt to be reflexive, and contextual in my analysis. As such, this will be a very different chapter than you have ever read before.

While I will be reflexive, I will not abandon all precedents. The genre demands that one in my position consider the contributions of the volume as a whole, with thoughtful comments on individual chapters. Of course, ideally the positive comments should outweigh the negative, and never should one be too harsh—particularly on more junior authors. A general rumor circulates that the old birds (intellectually, that is) have a thick skin, can take the heat as they say, and probably don't care what the concluding chapter says anyway, while the newly minted intellectuals might crumble under criticism. I suspect that quite the opposite may indeed be true, that some old birds will get really pissed off and dream of the next peer review opportunity when they can have their revenge, while criticism may not bother the young intellectuals at all—they may profit or even learn from it, however accurate or misplaced your comments. They may even appreciate your efforts.

I also have noticed that some authors in my position choose to offer simple praise for the entire effort. This is the easy way out, and it is often taken. This is tempting, as one makes no enemies, and invites positive reciprocity at a future date—particularly at peer review time. While this tactic has the appearance of wisdom, objectivity and generosity, it is nothing of the sort. At a more innocuous extreme, it is simply intellectually lazy. At the other extreme, it is self-serving and destructive. No errors of fact or logic are corrected to serve the needs of the author as he or she socially positions his or herself for reciprocity that may be as personal as a thank you, or as public as awards, publication, and other career enhancements. And all of this time the author(s) can pat themselves on the back for being so magnanimous.

At the opposite extreme, other authors vilify or angrily dismiss many if not all of the contributions. This position works if your ego is very large and your position in the field secure—or at least you believe it to be. These authors either act or actually believe that they are simply being objective and honest—of course, nothing could be further from the truth, as they treat their grad school buddies with kid gloves, and few works deserve the total condemnation they suggest.

Neither extreme is intellectually honest, particularly since all works such as those in this volume have both their strengths and weaknesses, and it is best to point them out, politics be damned.

So, with a bit of reflexivity, let me first state that as a reviewer of a book on theory, my theoretical perspective is Darwinian, as interpreted by a framework called Selectionist or Evolutionary Archaeology. I also find Marxist analyses intriguing and valuable, and processual archaeology for the most part useful but often albeit a bit *passé* and more

dull than necessary. The only part of the prehistoric world that I know a bit about is the American Southwest and northern Mexico.

Those biases expressed up front, I will now reflexively consider the individual papers.

HODDER

I first met Ian Hodder when he agreed to visit a graduate theory seminar at the University of New Mexico in the late 1980s. The seminar was team-taught by Lew Binford and myself, and the opportunity to have the man whose work constituted the core of the New Archaeology and the man who sought to destroy it in the same room was a rare opportunity, both for me and for students.

I was a new untenured faculty member at the time, and team-teaching with Binford was, well, let us say, difficult if one did not always share his views on how archaeology should be done. While I do not remember much of what transpired that day, I do remember that Hodder held his own in the debate and Binford was not ungracious if occasionally red-faced. I am sure that I spoke that day, but I am not sure of what.

Of course, the general theme of discussion was the respective merits of processual and postprocessual archaeology. While I did not recognize it at the time, what Hodder and similar thinkers brought us was freedom. Yes, freedom. Freedom to address questions or issues that would have been met with ridicule in the 1970s and early 1980s are easily addressed now. Ideology and ritual behavior come to mind as two examples. It is very likely that a student wanting to pursue questions related to ideology or ritual would have been laughed out of the halls of the anthropology department at UNM during that time period, if not by the faculty, then by other graduate students. The irony was that science was everything, yet we were not always very good at it. Students and faculty were writing dissertations and articles about "systems" and "processes" with system components undefined or even immeasurable, and process nothing but a magic word—a bit of misdirection and sleight of hand and the recitation of appropriate utterances was called theory building. Of course good, even excellent, work was produced, but at the same time that we were rejecting research into ideology and ritual we were signing dissertations and writing papers that were more performance art using vague concepts and slippery narrative incantations than good science. And this was happening across the land, not just at UNM.

Now we do a lot of things at UNM, and elsewhere as well, thanks to Ian Hodder and those other brave intellectuals. Archaeologists are freer to pursue any intellectual endeavor than they ever have been, although a few who still identify with the "processual" label may be lying a bit low, though Pauketat's and especially Arnold's papers in this volume suggest otherwise.

At the same time that Hodder set us free, and many were creating wonderful new perspectives on the past, he also had us creating a bunch of crap. Yes, crap. Half-baked ideas, assertions, politics, and poor logic simmered in an interpretive stew peppered with the ridiculous. While the new archaeologists had to gather abundant data not only on material culture but the environment as well, all an archaeologist has to do today for a journal article or dissertation is to look at a pot and emote. Sure, that person has to socially contextualize themselves in that endeavor as they construct the narrative of the emotive event or series of events, but the data requirements are minimal. Let me simply say here that the standard of what constitutes good research is in a state of change, and perhaps not for the better.

But I would rather have it this way than it was before.

And so what has Hodder given us here in this volume? Not much new I'm afraid, and I'm disappointed. This paper reads as if it were tossed off with an hour or two of thought. While it worked at the symposium, it doesn't really work here. Regardless, let me speak to what he has to say. First Hodder tells us that he is attending psychology seminars among others, and that he is pleased that everyone across disciplines is reading "Foucault, Bourdieu, Douglas, Geertz, Rorty,

Habermas, Butler, and so on." He thinks that this is a good thing. But then he worries a bit about this, as it may be homogenizing and result in less intellectual diversity.

In the interest of assuaging his concern, I must admit that I have only read a bit of Foucault, less of Bourdieu, one interesting but largely irrelevant to archaeology book by Douglas, quit reading Geertz when he wrote about his dismay of returning to a village 30 years after he conducted his research only to be astounded that things had changed since he first visited it (duh!), and wouldn't know Rorty unless he or she and I had a fender bender, if he or she is still alive.

What I see everyone across disciplines reading is the work of Gould, Buss, Mayr, Sober, and Vrba, among others. The disciplines I am referring to are anthropology, sociology, economics, psychology, biology, and medicine, as general evolutionary principles are being seen as increasingly important in today's world.

Hodder then goes on and says that we should break down four main boundaries. First, he seeks to break down boundaries between what is fringe—popular pasts—and make it center. This sounds good to me, and who could argue that popularization of the past is not needed? Now, if we could only get the academic establishment to actually reward those who seek to popularize the past. Most departments (and the SAA and AAA) pay grand lip service to public outreach but seldom reward those who actually do it.

And with respect to what the public actually thinks about archaeology, *we* are the fringe. I recently read that 56 percent of the U.S. populace believes that dinosaurs and people walked the earth at the same time. While most of us sleep, 15 million people listen to fringe science, much of it related to archaeology, on Art Bell's widely syndicated radio show. In August 2002 while I write this, the most popular book with archaeology in the title on amazon.com is *Forbidden Archaeology: The Hidden History of the Human Race* by Michael Cremo and Richard Thompson. Most professional archaeologists who have read this book view it with disdain as fiction masquerading as fact. Yet, the public loves it. Our public is largely ignorant, and likely to remain so despite all of our best efforts, as the stories we tell are not quite as interesting as the fiction that people like Cremo and Thompson write (or Jean Auel for that matter).

Second, Hodder wants to break down the boundary between archaeology as science and as humanity. I doubt the boundary will ever be broken, as different worldviews drive these perspectives. However, each camp can learn to value the other, which would be highly productive. But more about this in my concluding remarks.

Third, Hodder wishes to break down the boundary between CRM and academic archaeology. In many areas this has already happened. As an academic whose dissertation was based on CRM research, and who has worked doing CRM for many years in the past I can speak to this personally. The collaboration can be very fruitful. It could be even more fruitful if more CRM archaeologists shared their results in traditional publication venues. Those that do so offer major contributions to our field, but they are unfortunately few and far between.

Fourth, Hodder wants archaeology out of the "sub-cultural ghetto of anthropology," and wants more than four fields. I could be the last to know, but I didn't realize we were in a sub-cultural ghetto (maybe when I wasn't looking ethnopoetics took over the field). More than four fields sounds good, but will be difficult to implement, especially since we will not be able to agree on what other fields are important. It would make for a very interesting and likely unproductive meeting in our department, should we choose to follow his recommendation and restructure our graduate program along these lines.

In general, Hodder has some good ideas, if not new ones. They are, however, very much underdeveloped, which is unusual.

SAITTA

Dean Saitta is a friend of mine. We both worked near Zuni, New Mexico, for many years, and have had long and interesting conversations at numerous conferences. We also spent a long weekend together with a geologist, a biologist, and a soils scientist at a retreat atop Mt. Evans, Colorado, in the dead of winter, sharing conversation and a bottle of fine cognac at 11,000 ft. A good time was had by all.

One time Dean was riding shotgun in the big Chevy Suburban we were riding around in, and everyone knows when you ride shotgun in the West, you are the person who opens and closes any gate encountered. Everyone also knows that if you encounter a gate that is difficult to handle—or even worse, close yourself on the wrong side of it, well, a little good-natured ribbing may well occur. So, Dean went to this particular gate and the rest of us watched him. I'll admit it looked like a difficult gate, and Dean began to wrestle with it, showing just a bit of frustration. The rest of us in the Suburban began to shout encouragement, saying things like— "Dean, remember that it's not a gate, it's only a social construct of a gate!" And, "Dean, how do you *feel* about your relationship between yourself and the gate technology? And what do you *feel* about the oppressive regime that placed that gate between yourself and your destination?"

Dean eventually conquered the gate with our encouragements, and came back to the vehicle, scowled, and put us in our place, calling us something like "fucking vulgar materialists" before we went our merry way.

I tell this story for a couple of reasons. First, the science/humanism dichotomy obvious in this book and our discipline is aptly illustrated by the story. Second, it also illustrates the nature of our relationship—at least in part. As such, I enter this section of my work with the bias of friendship and camaraderie biasing my efforts. I think that I will counter that bias with a shift from the familiar "Dean" to the more distant "Saitta" for at least the appearance of objectivity. Perhaps it is because of this friendship that I will find the courage to disagree with most if not all he has to say.

Saitta wants us to be pragmatists and turn to the problems of men (and women).

On the surface this sounds like a mom and apple pie kind of issue, and not much to disagree with. However, be certain here that Saitta's use of pragmatism is in the terms of the philosophical movement, not the common dictionary sense of the word. Like most labels, it is misleading, in much the same way that missiles in the Reagan administration were called "peacekeepers." The basic premise of pragmatism is that there are no fixed stable grounds on which knowledge claims can be based. Does this mean that the earth does not orbit the sun, aspirin does not thin the blood, and that Elvis is alive? If so, astrologers, faith healers, and Elvis fans will be elated. Of course, the earth orbits the sun, aspirin does thin the blood, and sadly the death of Elvis is well documented. These are stable claims to knowledge and are subject to continual evaluation. Furthermore, this knowledge, for at least the first two examples anyway, has been determined through the application of science, a system of knowledge generation that Saitta has problems with, to which I will return to below. While we know that sometimes there are indeed no fixed and stable grounds on which knowledge is based, the goal of humanity has long been to find those grounds from which we can indeed make sure statements.

Saitta states that "for the pragmatist truth is what is good to believe; truth is belief justified by social need, rather than by the way things are in nature (Posner 1990)." This would indeed be very convenient, if true. Infinite examples of how wonderful this would be come to mind—for instance, it would be welcome in the U.S. for the 2000 presidential election to have been legitimate whatever the outcome, the entire world hopes for peace in the Middle East, and why not a cure for cancer and fat bank accounts for all of us while we are at it? Unfortunately, we simply cannot believe something into reality no matter how hard we wish it to be true. Certainly political and social entities as well as individuals create pasts to serve their purposes—or as Saitta might put it—believe them into existence, but that does not make them correct, no matter

how many people believe it or to what ends the created pasts are put.

But, we can still solve the problems of men with more than good wishes. Archaeology has long helped to solve the problems of men. The mound builder controversy in eastern North America is one of the first examples that comes to mind and they are countless, including land claim and water rights cases for Native American groups in North America and people in numerous other places around the world. In general, ALL of cultural resource management helps solve problems in bringing power, water, and land, among other resources, to people with as limited destruction of cultural resources as possible. The earth's population has now exceeded 6 billion, and they need places to live comfortably and CRM archaeology helps make this happen. To my knowledge, most CRM is a strong voice toward reasonable development, if such a thing is indeed possible in many parts of the world. Most archaeologists that I know appreciate nature, and value the contributions of diverse cultures. They rank among the best, if not most powerful, voices of good stewardship that one can encounter. This does not mean that the role of CRM shouldn't be evaluated as one considers the diminishing natural and cultural resources of the earth in the context of globalization. It must be, and those efforts are continuing. Of course, CRM exists only within local regulatory environments, and the real strength lies with those who make the laws. Archaeology and anthropology must play a more prominent role in this realm as well, a fact that I am sure Saitta would agree.

So does this mean that so-called pure research shouldn't be done? I think not. Researchers should pursue any topic they wish, as they always have, and for good reasons. What may seem non-pragmatic today may be extremely valuable tomorrow. For example, for years researchers at the University of New Mexico pursued research on the field mouse genus *Peromyscus*. Of what value could that possibly be to human affairs? Recently, these researchers and medical personnel discovered that this field mouse was the primary vector for the hantavirus, which eventually led to the successful treatment of the disease for many. Likewise, no one knew the "pure research" done by Leslie Spier at Zuni Pueblo in the early twentieth century would provide a baseline for successful mitigation by the tribe regarding land claims nearly a century later.

So should we turn to the problems of men? Of course. It will be good science, however, not pragmatism, that will solve them. Regardless, the world will be a better place if Dean succeeds in his efforts, and I wish him luck.

LEONE

I don't really know Mark Leone. We have spoken a few times, but of nothing of substance. Now that I think about it, I believe that our conversations have been limited to basic life pleasantries as in hello, how are you, good to see you, and other mundane matters of human interaction. He does, however, remind me of an actor who played in numerous 1940s and 1950s American melodramas, but that will not likely influence my observations on his work.

Marxism, as done by Leone, has resulted in some of the most interesting archaeological analyses I have ever read. Perhaps a better way to put it is that he is a splendid storyteller. His strength as a storyteller is profound: he can make broken dishes among other bits of material culture tell tales of class struggle and oppression. And that is what he is encouraging all of us to do in this programmatic piece. He is advising us to do archaeology for the oppressed.

Of course, this is a good idea, and I think that this is exactly what Dean Saitta is arguing for as well. Leone skips the discussion of pragmatism to come to the same conclusion as Saitta, so maybe Saitta's program can proceed profitably without the burden of pragmatism. As I noted above however, their perspective however fruitful it can be at times, is not without peril. The oppressed may not give a damn what we think about their past (personal experience with one past tribal council at Zuni Pueblo while I was employed

there allows me to state this quite unequivocally).

Not only does Leone want us to do research for the oppressed, he is damn urgent about it and I suspect that he is downright puzzled that most of us continue to work on problems of our own interest without recognizing, or even denying the politics that accompany it, albeit subconsciously perhaps. To Leone, not only are we fiddling while Rome burns, we are doing so from the seat of a fire truck that could be put to good use.

Leone also recognizes that sometimes the concepts that we use—like Culture—if viewed statically, don't help us at all. Societies that are greatly impacted by other societies do not result in people without Culture, although Leone is a bit confusing on this—of course all individuals have culture.

Leone has another mission here. He likes the work of Carmel Shrire and Christopher Tilley among others, and thinks we should be paying more attention to it. If this work is as interesting as Leone's, we would all profit by reading it (perhaps after I finish Hodder's reading list, I can start with Leone's).

So, in sum, I liked this piece, but I am a bit set in my ways and will probably not do as Leone suggests despite the coherency of his logic. Neither will most of you. It will be a loss for archaeology and humanity, and especially for those who have suffered at the hands of colonial powers. But sadly, we don't care.

I also feel obligated to state while I profited from reading this piece and that it deserves not only publication but a wide reading, it probably wouldn't have been published in a refereed journal format. It contained no new analyses and no data. Of course, programmatic statements without data are occasionally published in a refereed journal, but only if you went to grad school with the editor or are really old and did something important long ago and are near death. We should probably change this.

CUNNINGHAM
My First Draft

To the best of my knowledge I have not had the pleasure of meeting Cunningham and

have read nothing of his work. I look for-
ward to meeting him someday, and sincerely
hope that he will be kind enough to tell me
what he has accomplished with this chapter.
He begins with what he calls Childe's para-
dox, which to me is not a paradox at all. Of
course we get our ideas from the real world
(most of them anyway—I'm thinking pure
mathematics and science fiction are excep-
tions), but it is not a paradox that we cannot
create exact reflections of that real world. I
realize that Childe's "paradox" was not criti-
cal to his (Cunningham's) arguments, but I
found the logic of the rest of the paper consis-
tent with his opening discussion. I am sure
the paper contributes to the literature on style
and function, otherwise the editors of the vol-
ume and its reviewers would not have recom-
mended that it be included in the book. There
are other things I would like to say here but
do not feel comfortable doing so without dis-
cussing this paper with the author.

That is what I first had to say about the
Cunningham paper. Then the editors of this
volume passed by my office door and I told
them a paraphrased version of the above.
They looked at me with good humor and pa-
tience (if they were teenagers they would
have rolled their eyes) and said I must have
missed something, as they liked the paper a
lot, and that Cunningham had much to say of
significance. Furthermore, one reviewer of
the volume thought it was among the best
pieces in the volume. With professorial indig-
nity I harrumphed for a bit and said that that
is all well and good, but too bad. I didn't like
it.

Then they told me that Jane Kelley liked
the paper. *Shit,* I thought. Jane Kelley is a
friend of mine and a smart lady. I better read
it again, and be more thoughtful this time.
So, I did.

I still didn't like it.

While the materialist-idealist dichotomy
and discussions of style were a bit more interesting this time, the dichotomy, like "Childe's
paradox" didn't work for me a second and
third time through. So, read it and judge
for yourself. I may be missing the point. It
wouldn't be the first time.

PAUKETAT

I first met Tim Pauketat almost 20 years ago
in Carbondale, Illinois, where he was getting
his M.A. at Southern Illinois University and I
was working for the Black Mesa Archaeological Project at SIU. While most of my time
was spent talking Southwestern archaeology
with the many fine scholars employed by
BMAP, I also remember fondly discussions
with Pauketat, Charles Cobb, and Paul Webb.
It seemed to me that these guys knew *everything* there was to know about the archaeology of the Midwestern and Eastern United
States, and I learned a lot from them in a dark
establishment where the beer was cold and
peanut shells were thrown on the floor. They
talked about archaeology in a different way
than I knew how, and I found our discussions
stimulating. I have followed Tim's writings
with interest since that time, and am in-
trigued by what he and his colleagues have
been writing about Cahokia and the surrounding environs for some time. So, it is
tough for me to be unbiased in my assessment
here. Minimally I have read this paper *harder*
than I may have other papers, a bias to be
sure.

Here Pauketat outlines his intriguing view
of the archaeological world, offering what
some may call a new paradigm, Historical
Processualism (Tim was too modest to capi-
talize the label for the incipient movement, so
let me be the first to do it here). Impressively,
he illustrates how Historical Processualism
will change how we look at the major archaeological phenomena of Cahokia, Poverty
Point, and Chaco if we operationalize it.
Unlike many influenced by the writings of
Marxists and many postmodernists, Tim isn't
ready to abandon Processualism. He simply
wants to make it better. I find this attitude re-
freshing, as Processualism had lots to offer us
for much of the last half of the past century.
However, the label Processualism, if not some
of its intellectual content, may have been so
tainted by critics in the 80s and 90s such that
it will not be easily redeemed. Regardless,
Pauketat's ideas are clever enough to have
made me think of the largest phenomenon of
my research area—Paquimé—in new ways.

He didn't come to many conclusions, and neither did I, but it is an interesting way to think. I hope scholars take this work seriously, and that his ideas stand the test of practice.

ARNOLD

What Pauketat and others (e.g., VanPool and VanPool 1999) seek to bring together, Arnold seeks to tear asunder. Arnold is clearly peeved at the attempts to bring together the processual and the postprocessual, and writes an engaging piece outlining why the differences between the two perspectives are too great to bridge. This is the most interestingly written chapter in the volume, despite Arnold's propensity to extend his metaphors beyond distraction.

Arnold also offers a thoughtful discussion of the Middle-Range Program and how "poorly it has been served over the last 25 years." I didn't really *read* this chapter as much as *imagined* Arnold speaking it to an enthusiastic audience. This was easy for me to do because it was so engagingly written and I am aware of his excellent speaking abilities. I also know of his passion for processual archaeology. I first met Arnold in 1987 when I was hired at the University of New Mexico, and he was an advanced graduate student in the throes of finishing his dissertation. He was, and still is, a true believer—and having learned processual archaeology at the feet of the master, he has little respect for intellectual pretenders who didn't follow the "true path." He and I share much in common here, although our "true paths" diverge.

Regardless, not only is this the most engagingly written paper in the volume, it is also one of the most valuable. This chapter's only failing is that the example illustrating the application of the Middle-Range Program is surprisingly underelaborated and unconvincing.

Anyone interested in the relationship between processual and postprocessual archaeology should read it, as should anyone interested in the logic and intellectual history of processual archaeology. This is not to say that his history or even his logic is correct, but that it should be taken seriously, albeit with a caveat. Here the words of the historian Herbert Butterfield should be kept in mind as Arnold is not only wordsmith, but warrior. Butterfield (1981) states:

> It has been said that the historian is the avenger, and that standing as a judge between the parties and rivalries and causes of bygone generations he can lift up the fallen and beat down the proud, and by his exposures and his verdicts, his satire and his moral indignation, can punish unrighteousness, avenge the injured or reward the innocent.

Arnold had done a bit of this and more. Good for him. And us.

KANTNER

I have followed John Kantner's research for several years now, and find much of his work intriguing. We share a common research area, the American Southwest, and an interest in evolutionary theory. I first met him at the SAAs at a dinner party for the participants in the symposium session on which this book is based. My review of his piece here is thereby biased by our pleasant conversations of that evening both with him and my other dinner companions.

In this piece Kantner evaluates a number of evolutionary programs, and not surprisingly concludes that the one he employs, behavioral ecology, is the most useful. Evolutionary archaeology or selectionism, the evolutionary perspective I find valuable, comes under strong criticism. While I disagree with most of what he has to say, he has demonstrated his knowledge of evolutionary theory, and he has actually read and understands much of the evolutionary archaeological literature, unlike several of its other critics. For this I give him credit. I do wonder, however, how much of this criticism was necessary for him to get to his point, the value of behavioral ecology.

Kantner comes up with two interesting examples of the application of behavioral ecology to the prehistoric Southwest, but I do not believe that he actually needed behavioral ecology to come to the conclusions he did. As a consequence, he really didn't illustrate that Behavioral Ecology is actually the superior intellectual program as he asserts. Perhaps in the future he will.

VANPOOL AND VANPOOL

If ever a bias must be admitted in a review like this, it is mine with the VanPools's paper. As I write this, they are hard at work at an office not 20 ft away from me. We have just returned from lunch, a routine we practice nearly every day, and have so for years. We often talk archaeology, and more often archaeological theory. Furthermore, we have spent months together in the field in both New Mexico and Mexico. We have also published together, and I sit on both of their dissertation committees. Our interactions have been most productive, and I honestly feel that I am now learning more from them than they from me. Given this obvious set of biases, I will be brief.

Not surprisingly, I enjoyed reading their paper. It is in their nature to find common ground, and they have done it here, between those who seek to apply agency approaches, and those that use evolutionary theory as they seek to understand the archaeological record. While that is ostensibly the purpose and result of their paper, there are deeper and more profound issues at hand here. What the VanPools have done here and in their earlier paper that sought common ground between processual and postprocessual archaeology (VanPool and VanPool 1999) is to address a more than century-old debate whether or not anthropology should be general or particular, nomothetic or idiographic, science or humanity. Historic debates between the nineteenth-century evolutionists and Boas, in the twentieth century between the Culture Historians and the Processual Archaeologists, and the Processualists and the Postprocessualists have been this same debate played over and over again in different time periods. Perhaps at last we can agree with the VanPools and consider that anthropology can and should be both scientific and humanistic and finally this debate can come to an end.

O'BRIEN AND LYMAN

Suppose that someone proposed a methodology that allowed us to generate hypothesis about intellectual lineages or learning traditions in the past? A methodology that would allow us to know, say, which painter influenced another painter, one author another, or what piece of technology or art were intellectually part of the same learning tradition with great precision? And that we could apply this methodology to the archaeological record?

Art historians and archaeologists in particular have dreamed of having such a methodology for years. Well, we now have it. It is the phylogenetic analysis that O'Brien and Lyman present here. Will the archaeological and historical world beat a path to their door as they should? Probably not, and for several reasons. First, it is evolutionary, and most scholars in the social sciences shy away from evolutionary approaches if they are not openly hostile to them. Second, understanding what O'Brien and Lyman have to say is difficult, and sadly, most archaeologists will not go to the work that is necessary to learn how to do what they do. A few graduate students will, unless they have already been put off evolutionary theory by faculty who have dismissed evolutionary theory without really knowing anything about it. It is most unfortunate that despite the importance of what O'Brien and Lyman have done, most archaeologists will not read it. Most who start reading it will not understand it because they haven't had the requisite intellectual training to do so. Those that do understand it may not actually seek to operationalize it because it is time-consuming and difficult to do so. It is simpler to continue doing what they are already doing. Regardless, if this program is operationalized widely, it will revolutionize archaeology and our understanding of the prehistoric world.

Do I have any biases here? Of course. First and foremost, I have gone to the trouble to understand what they are doing, and it wasn't easy. Furthermore, my students and I are building phylogenies, and helping operationalize their program. O'Brien, Lyman, and I also share a theoretical perspective, and published together and have plans to do so in the future. Lyman and I went to graduate school together and shared an office. The three of us wander the halls of the hotels at the SAAs discussing these issues endlessly, and cracking jokes that others would probably not understand, or if they understood, not appreciate. These guys are my pals.

WATSON

Patty Jo Watson co-authored with Steve LeBlanc and Chuck Redman the first book on archaeology that I ever read all the way through—*Explanation in Archaeology: An Explicitly Scientific Approach*. I suspect that most readers of this book have also read that one, but if you have not, I encourage you to do so. It was published in 1971, and everyone who went to graduate school in the 70s and 80s read it. I hope it, or its 1984 successor—*Archaeological Explanation: The Scientific Method in Archaeology*, by the same authors, is still widely read.

So, Watson's ideas have been influencing me since I started in this field, and I still read nearly everything she writes. We have met, speak cordially at meetings, but we have had no opportunity to work together or have extended discussions. The only bias that comes to mind here is my respect for her formidable body of work and her influence on my ideas at an early stage of my career.

This article is worth reading if only because of her "jingle." More substantively, she assesses the current state of archaeology and our prospects for the future. There is much food for thought here, and little to disagree with. As a time capsule, this article works well.

Here, I must admit after writing the above paragraphs, I read the chapter once more in an attempt to find something to quibble about, but failed.

CONCLUSIONS

So what did I think of the book as a whole? Most of it was interesting, some of it intriguing, and all of it is worth reading. It certainly is a major contribution to the current state of theory as we enter the millennium. Are there gaps? Sure. It would be nice if there were chapters on behavioral archaeology, gender, structuralist and poststructuralist theory as well as a variety of other theoretical endeavors. The editors assure me that contributions were solicited on these topics, but were not forthcoming.

Each contributor to the volume was asked to identify and attempt to resolve an open theoretical or methodological issue. While they have succeeded to varying degrees with respect to the specific issues they raised, more generally they have also provided us with an evaluation of contemporary archaeological method and theory. As such, this book is an unqualified success.

Sometimes I wonder what the archaeological world would be like if we had an integrated body of theory rather than diverse theories that we now employ as illustrated by this volume. An integrated body of theory helps most disciplines—biology, physics, and chemistry come to mind here. It might help ours, too. Yet, serving the twin masters of science and the humanities may not allow a common body of theory, as each demands a unique world view that may never be reconciled. And I, for one, enjoy scientific and humanistic contributions *and* hope that archaeology will continue to employ both.

With this in mind, may we continue to learn and grow from both the sciences and the humanities, as did Jonathan Swift's Gulliver though his exposure to the very different worlds of Lilliput and Brobdingnag. I certainly have profited by reading the contributions graciously offered by the authors of this volume, quibbles and quakes aside.

References Cited

Adler, M. A.
1994   Population Aggregation and the Anasazi Social Landscape: A View from the Four Corners. In *The Ancient Southwestern Community: Models and Methods for the Study of Prehistoric Social Organization,* edited by W. H. Wills and R. D. Leonard, pp. 85–102. University of New Mexico Press, Albuquerque.
1996   (ed.) *The Prehistoric Pueblo World A.D. 1150–1350.* University of Arizona Press, Tucson.

Adler, M. A., T. L. VanPool, and R. D. Leonard
1996   Ancestral Pueblo Population and Abandonment in the North American Southwest. *Journal of World Prehistory* 10:375–438.

Alland, A., Jr.
1973   *Evolution and Human Behavior.* 2nd ed. Anchor, Doubleday, Garden City, New York.

Allen, M. S.
1996   Style and Function in East Polynesian Fish-Hooks. *Antiquity* 70:97–116.

Alt, S.
2001   Cahokian Change and the Authority of Tradition. In *The Archaeology of Traditions: History and Agency before and after Columbus,* edited by T. R. Pauketat, pp. 141–156. University Press of Florida, Gainesville.

Anderson, B.
1991   *Imagined Communities: Reflections on the Origin and Spread of Nation-alism.* Verso Publishing, London, New York.

Anschuetz, K. F., R. H. Wilshusen, and C. L. Scheick
2001   An Archaeology of Landscapes: Perspectives and Directions. *Journal of Archaeological Research* 9:157–211.

Anyon, R., T. J. Ferguson, L. Jackson, L. Lane, and P. Vicenti
1997   Native American Oral Tradition and Archaeology: Issues of Structure, Relevance, and Respect. In *Native Americans and Archaeologists,* edited by N. Swidler, K. Dongoske, R. Anyon, and A. Downer, pp. 77–87. Altamira Press, Walnut Creek, California.

Appadurai, A.
1986   Introduction: Commodities and the Politics of Value. In *The Social Life of Things: Commodities in Cultural Perspective,* edited by A. Appadurai, pp. 3–63. Cambridge University Press, Cambridge.

Appleby, J., L. Hunt, and M. Jacob
1994   The Future of History. In *Telling the Truth About History,* by J. Appleby, L. Hunt, and M. Jacob, pp. 271–309. W. W. Norton, New York.

Aranyosi, E. F.
1999   Wasteful Advertising and Variance Reduction: Darwinian Models for the Significance of Nonutilitarian Architecture. *Journal of Anthropological Archaeology* 18:356–375.

Armelagos, G. J.
1990   Health and Disease in Prehistoric

Populations in Transition. In *Disease in Populations in Transition: Anthropological and Epidemiological Perspectives,* edited by A. C. Swedlund, and G. J. Armelagos, pp. 127–144. Bergin and Garvey, New York.

Arnold, M. L.

1997   *Natural Hybridization and Evolution.* Oxford University Press, New York.

Arnold, P. J., III

1990   The Organization of Refuse Disposal and Ceramic Production within Contemporary Mexican Houselots. *American Anthropologist* 92:915–932.

1991   *Domestic Ceramic Production and Spatial Organization: A Mexican Case Study in Ethnoarchaeology.* Cambridge University Press, Cambridge.

1999   On Typologies, Selection, and Ethnoarchaeology in Ceramic Production Studies. In *Material Meanings: Critical Approaches to the Interpretation of Material Culture,* edited by E. S. Chilton, pp. 103–117. University of Utah Press, Salt Lake City.

2000   Working Without a Net: Recent Trends in Ceramic Ethnoarchaeology. *Journal of Archaeological Research* 8:105–133.

Arnold, P. J., III, C. A. Pool, R. R. Kneebone, and R. S. Santley

1993   Intensive Ceramic Production and Classic-Period Political Economy in the Sierra de los Tuxtlas, Mexico. *Ancient Mesoamerica* 4:175–191.

Arnold, P. J., III, and B. Wilkens

2001   On the VanPool's "Scientific Postprocessualism." *American Antiquity* 66:361–366.

Ascher, R.

1961   Analogy in Archaeological Interpretation. *Southwestern Journal of Anthropology* 17:317–325.

Ashmore, M., R. Wooffitt, and S. Harding

1994   Humans and Others, Agents and Things. *American Behavioral Scientist* 37:733–740.

Axelrod, R.

1984   *The Evolution of Cooperation.* Basic Books, New York.

Bapty, I., and T. Yates

1990a   (eds.) *Archaeology after Structuralism.* Routledge, London.

1990b   Introduction: Archaeology and Post-Structuralism. In *Archaeology after Structuralism,* edited by I. Bapty and T. Yates, pp. 1–32. Routledge, London.

Barham, A.

1995   *Archaeological Sediments and Soils: Analysis, Interpretation and Management.* Institute of Archaeology, London.

Barnes, E.

1994   *Developmental Defects of the Axial Skeleton in Paleopathology.* University of Colorado Press, Boulder.

Barrett, J.

1994   *Fragments from Antiquity.* Blackwell, Oxford.

Barrett, S. R.

1996   *Anthropology: A Student's Guide to Theory and Method.* University of Toronto Press, Toronto.

Bayard, D. T.

1969   Science, Theory, and Reality in the 'New Archaeology.' *American Antiquity* 34:376–384.

Beck, C.

1995a   Style, Function, Technology, and Chronological Units. Paper presented at the 60th annual meeting of the Society for American Archaeology, Minneapolis.

1995b   Functional Analysis and the Differential Persistence of Great Basin Dart Forms. *Journal of California and Great Basin Anthropology* 17:222–243.

1998   Projectile Point Types as Valid Chronological Units. In *Unit Issues in Archaeology: Measuring Time, Space, and Material,* edited by A. F. Ramenofsky and A. Steffen, pp. 21–40. University of Utah Press, Salt Lake City.

Behrensmeyer, A. K., and A. P. Hill

1980   (eds.) *Fossils in the Making: Vertebrate Taphonomy and Paleoecology.* University of Chicago Press, Chicago.

Bell, J.

1982   Archaeological Explanation: Progress through Criticism. In *The-*

ory and Explanation in Archaeology, edited by C. Renfrew, M. J. Rowlands, and B. A. Segraves, pp. 65–72. Academic Press, New York.

1992 On Capturing Agency in Theories about Prehistory. In *Representations in Archaeology,* edited by J.-C. Gardin and C. S. Peebles, pp. 30–55. Indiana University Press, Bloomington.

Bennett, J. W.

1998 *Classic Anthropology, Critical Essays: 1944–1996.* Transaction, New Brunswick, New Jersey.

Bentley, G.

1996 How Did Prehistoric Women Bear "Man the Hunter"?: Reconstructing Fertility from the Archaeological Record. In *Gender and Archaeology,* edited by R. A. Wright, pp. 23–51. University of Pennsylvania Press, Philadelphia.

Bentley, G. R., T. Goldberg, and G. Jasienska

1993 The Fertility of Agricultural and Non-Agricultural Traditional Societies. *Population Studies* 47:269–281.

Bernstein, R.

1988 Pragmatism, Pluralism, and the Healing of Wounds. In *The New Constellation,* by R. Bernstein, pp. 323–340. MIT Press, Cambridge, Massachusetts.

Bettinger, R. L., R. Boyd, and P. J. Richerson

1996 Style, Function, and Cultural Evolutionary Processes. In *Darwinian Archaeologies,* edited by H.D.G. Maschner, pp 133–164. Plenum, New York.

Bettinger, R. L., and J. Eerkens

1997 Evolutionary Implications of Metrical Variation in Great Basin Projectile Points. In *Rediscovering Darwin: Evolutionary Theory in Archeological Explanation,* edited by C. M. Barton and G. A. Clark, pp. 177–191. Archeological Papers no. 7, American Anthropological Association, Washington, D.C.

1999 Point Typologies, Cultural Transmission, and the Spread of Bow-and-Arrow Technology in the Prehistoric Great Basin. *American Antiquity* 64:231–242.

Bettinger, R. L., and P. J. Richerson

1996 The State of Evolutionary Archaeology: Evolutionary Correctness, or the Search for the Common Ground. In *Darwinian Archaeologies,* edited by H.D.G. Maschner, pp. 221–232. Plenum Press, New York.

Betzig, L. L.

1988 Redistribution: Equity or Exploitation? In *Human Reproductive Behavior: A Darwinian Perspective,* edited by L. L. Betzig, M. Borgerhoff Mulder, and P. Turke, pp. 49–64. Cambridge University Press, Cambridge.

Biersack, A.

1999 Introduction: From the "New Ecology" to the New Ecologies. *American Anthropologist* 101:5–18.

Binford, L. R.

1962 Archaeology as Anthropology. *American Antiquity* 28(2):217–225.

1963 "Red Ocher" Caches from the Michigan Area: A Possible Case of Cultural Drift. *Southwestern Journal of Anthropology* 19:89–108.

1965 Archaeological Systematics and the Study of Culture Process. *American Antiquity* 31(2):203–210.

1968a Some Comments on Historical versus Processual Archaeology. *Southwest Journal of Anthropology* 24:267–275.

1968b Archeological Perspectives. In *New Perspectives in Archeology,* edited by S. R. Binford and L. R. Binford, pp. 5–32. Aldine, New York.

1977 General Introduction. In *For Theory Building in Archaeology,* edited by L. R. Binford, pp. 1–10. Academic Press, New York.

1978 *Nunamiut Ethnoarchaeology.* Academic Press, New York.

1981 *Bones: Ancient Men and Modern Myths.* Academic Press, New York.

1982 Objectivity—Explanation—Archaeology 1981. In *Theory and Explanation in Archaeology: The Southampton Conference,* edited by C. Renfrew, M. J. Rowlands, and B. Seagraves-Whallon, pp. 125–138. Academic Press, New York.

1983a Working at Archaeology: The Late 1960s and Early 1970s. In *Working at Archaeology,* pp. 3–20. Academic Press, New York.

1983b   Working at Archaeology: The Mousterian Problem—Learning How to Learn. In *Working at Archaeology,* pp. 65–69. Academic Press, New York.

1983c   Working at Archaeology: Some Thoughts about the 1970s and Beyond. In *Working at Archaeology,* pp. 389–394. Academic Press, New York.

1983d   *In Pursuit of the Past: Decoding the Archaeological Record.* Thames and Hudson, London.

1985   "Brand X" Versus the Recommended Product. *American Antiquity* 50:580–590.

1987   Data, Relativism, and Archaeological Science. *Man* 22:391–404.

1989   Styles of Style. *Journal of Anthropological Archaeology* 8:51–67.

Binford, L. R., and J. A. Sabloff
1982   Paradigms, Systematics, and Archaeology. *Journal of Anthropological Research* 38:137–153.

Binford, S.
1968   Variability and Change in the Near Eastern Mousterian of Levallois Facies. In *New Perspectives in Archaeology,* edited by S. R. Binford and L. R. Binford, 49–60. Aldine Publishing Company, Chicago.

Binford, S. R., and L. R. Binford
1968   (eds.) *New Perspectives in Archaeology.* Aldine, Chicago.

Bird, D. W.
1997   Behavioral Ecology and the Archaeological Consequences of Central Place Foraging among the Meriam. In *Rediscovering Darwin: Evolutionary Theory and Archeological Explanation,* edited by C. M. Barton and G. A. Clark, pp. 291–308. Archeological Papers No. 7 American Anthropological Association, Arlington, Virginia.

Blackmore, S.
1999   *The Meme Machine.* Oxford University Press, New York.

Blanton, R. E.
1995   The Cultural Foundations of Inequity in Households. In *Founda-tions of Social Inequity,* edited by T. D. Price and G. M. Feiman, pp. 105–128. Plenum Press, New York.

Bliege Bird, R. L., and D. W. Bird
1997   Delayed Reciprocity and Tolerated Theft. *Current Anthropology* 38:49–78.

Blintiff, J.
1991   (ed.) *The Annales School and Archaeology.* Leicester University Press, Leicester.

Blintiff, J., and A. Snodgrass
1988   Off-Site Pottery Distributions: A Regional and Interregional Perspective. *Current Anthropology* 29:506–513.

Boast, R.
1997   A Small Company of Actors: A Critique of Style. *Journal of Material Culture* 2(2):173–198.

Bodnar, J.
1992   *Remaking America: Public Memory, Commemoration, and Patriotism in the Twentieth Century.* Princeton University Press, New Jersey.

Boehm, C.
1996   Emergency Decisions, Cultural-Selection Mechanics, and Group Selection. *Current Anthropology* 37:763–793.

Bohman, J.
1991   *New Philosophy of Social Science: Problems of Indeterminacy.* MIT Press, Cambridge.

Bongaarts, J., and R. G. Potter
1983   *Fertility, Biology, and Behavior: An Analysis of the Proximate Determinants.* Academic Press, New York.

Boone, J. L.
1992   Competition, Conflict, and the Development of Social Hierarchies. In *Evolutionary Ecology and Human Behavior,* edited by E. A. Smith and B. Winterhalder, pp. 301–337. Aldine de Gruyter, New York.

Boone, J. L., and E. A. Smith
1998   Is it Evolution Yet? A Critique of Evolutionary Archaeology. *Current Anthropology* 39:S141–S173.

Bourdieu, P.
1977   *Outline of a Theory of Practice.* Translated by R. Nice. Cambridge University Press, Cambridge.

Boyd, R., and P. J. Richerson
1982   Cultural Transmission and the

Evolution of Cooperative Behavior. *Human Ecology* 10:325–351.

1983   The Cultural Transmission of Acquired Variation: Effects on Genetic Fitness. *Journal of Theoretical Biology* 100:567–596.

1985   *Culture and the Evolutionary Process.* University of Chicago Press, Chicago.

Bradley, R.

1996   Long Houses, Long Mounds and Neolithic Enclosures. *Journal of Material Culture* 1:239–256.

1999   Shell Exchange within the Southwest: The Casas Grandes Interaction Sphere. In *The Casas Grandes World*, edited by C. F. Schaafsma and C. L. Riley, pp. 213–228. University of Utah Press, Salt Lake City.

Brain, C. K.

1969   The Contribution of Namib Desert Hottentots to an Understanding of Australopithecine Bone Accumulations. *Scientific Papers of the Namib Desert Research Station* 39:13–22.

Braithwaite, M.

1982   Decoration as Ritual Symbol: A Theoretical Proposal and an Ethnographic Study in Southern Sudan. In *Symbolic and Structural Archaeology*, edited by I. Hodder, pp. 80–88. Cambridge University Press, Cambridge.

1984   Ritual and Prestige in the Prehistory of Wessex, 2200–1400 B.C.: A New Dimension to the Archaeological Evidence. In *Ideology, Power, and Prehistory*, edited by D. Miller and C. Tilley, pp. 93–110. Cambridge University Press, Cambridge.

Brand, D. D.

1933   The Historical Geography of Northwestern Chihuahua. Ph.D. diss., University of California, Berkeley.

Brandon, R. N.

1990   *Adaptation and Environment.* Princeton University Press, Princeton, New Jersey.

Braniff, B. C.

1994   Norte de México: La Gran Chichimeca. *Arqueología Mexicana* 1(6):12–21.

Braudel, F.

1976   *The Mediterranean and the Mediter-ranean World in the Age of Philip II*, 2 vols., translated by S. Reynolds. Harper and Row, New York.

Braun, D. P.

1990   Selection and Evolution in Nonhierarchical Organization. In *The Evolution of Political Systems*, edited by S. Upham, pp. 62–86. Cambridge University Press, Cambridge.

1991   Are there Cross-Cultural Regularities in Tribal Social Practices? In *Between Bands and States*, edited by S. A. Gregg, pp. 423–444. Occasional Paper No. 9. Center for Archaeological Investigations, Southern Illinois University, Carbondale.

1995   Style, Selection, and Historicity. In *Style, Society and Person: Archaeological and Ethnological Perspectives*, edited by C. Carr and J. E. Neitzel, pp. 123–141. Plenum, New York.

Breitburg, E.

1993   The Evolution of Turkey Domestication in the Greater Southwest and Mesoamerica. In *Culture and Contact: Charles C. Di Peso's Gran Chichimeca*, edited by A. I. Woosley and J. C. Ravesloot, pp. 153–172. Amerind Foundation and the University of New Mexico, Albuquerque.

Brew, J. O.

1946   *Archaeology of Alkali Ridge, Southeastern Utah.* Papers, vol. 21, Peabody Museum of American Archaeology and Ethnology, Harvard University, Cambridge, Massachusetts.

Broad, W. J.

1998   Deep-Sea Clues to an Ancient Culture. *New York Times*, Monday, October 12, 1998:A9.

Brooks, P.

1973   An Analysis of Painted Pottery Designs of the Casas Grandes Culture. *Awanyu* 1(2):11–33.

Broughton, J. M., and J. F. O'Connell

1999   On Evolutionary Ecology, Selectionist Archaeology, and Behavioral Archaeology. *American Antiquity* 64: 153–165.

Brown, D. E.

1994   (ed.) *Biotic Communities: South-*

western United States and North-western Mexico. University of Utah Press, Salt Lake City.

Brumfiel, E. M.

1992   Distinguished Lecture in Archaeology: Breaking and Entering the Ecosystem—Gender, Class, and Faction Steal the Show. *American Anthropologist* 94:551–567.

1994   Factional Competition and Political Development in the New World: An Introduction. In *Factional Competition and Political Development in the New World*, edited by E. M. Brumfiel and J. W. Fox, pp. 3–13. Cambridge University Press, Cambridge.

Buikstra, J. E., L. Konigsberg, and J. Bullington

1986   Fertility and the Development of Agriculture in the Prehistoric Midwest. *American Antiquity* 51:528–546.

Butterfield, H.

1931   *The Whig Interpretation of History*. G. Bell, London. Republished electronically at http://www.eliohs. unifi.it/testi/900/butterfield/introduction.html.

Cameron, C.

1998   Coursed Adobe Architecture, Style, and Social Boundaries in the American Southwest. In *The Archaeology of Social Boundaries*, edited by M. T. Stark, pp. 183–207. Smithsonian Institution Press, Washington, D.C.

Campbell, D. T.

1970   Natural Selection as an Epistemological Model. In *A Handbook of Method in Cultural Anthropology*, edited by R. Naroll and R. Cohen, pp. 51–85. Natural History Press, New York.

Campbell, K. L., and J. W. Wood

1988   Fertility in Traditional Societies. In *Natural Human Fertility: Social and Biological Mechanisms*, edited by P. Diggory, S. Teper, and M. Potts, pp. 39–69. Macmillan, London.

Carr, C.

1995a   Building a Unified Middle-Range Theory of Artifact Design: Historical Perspectives and Tactics. In *Style, Society and Person: Archaeological*

and Ethnological Perspectives, edited by C. Carr and J. E. Neitzel, pp. 151–170. Plenum, New York.

1995b   A Unified Middle-Range Theory of Artifact Design. In *Style, Society and Person: Archaeological and Ethnological Perspectives*, edited by C. Carr and J. E. Neitzel, pp. 171–258. Plenum, New York.

Carr, C., and J. E. Neitzel

1995a   (eds.) *Style, Society and Person: Archaeological and Ethnological Perspectives*. Plenum, New York.

1995b   Integrating Approaches to Material Style in Theory and Philosophy. In *Style, Society and Person: Archaeological and Ethnological Perspectives*, edited by C. Carr and J. E. Neitzel, pp. 393–417. Plenum, New York.

Cashdan, Elizabeth

1992   Spatial Organization and Habitat Use. In *Evolutionary Ecology and Human Behavior*, edited by E. A. Smith and B. Winterhalder, pp. 237–268. Aldine de Gruyter, New York.

Castañeda, Q. E.

1996   *In the Museum of Maya Culture*. University of Minnesota Press, Minneapolis.

Cavalli-Sforza, L. L., and M. W. Feldman

1981   *Cultural Transmission and Evolution: A Quantitative Approach*. Princeton University Press, Princeton, New Jersey.

Chamblee, J. F., and B. J. Mills

2001   Archeology in 2001: Current Research Based on the SAA Annual Meeting Program. *The SAA Archaeological Record* 1(5):24–28.

Childe, V. G.

1949   *Social Worlds of Knowledge*. Oxford University Press, London.

1956   *Society and Knowledge*. Harper and Brothers Publishers, New York.

Clark, G. A.

1993   Paradigms in Science and Archaeology. *Journal of Archaeological Research* 1:203–234.

Clark, J. E.

1997   The Arts of Government in Early Mesoamerica. *Annual Review of Anthropology* 26:211–234.

1999   On "Stone Tools: Theoretical Insight

into Human Prehistory" by G. H. Odell. *Lithic Technology* 24:126–135.

2000 Towards a Better Explanation of Hereditary Inequity: A Critical Assessment of Natural and Historic Human Agents. In *Agency in Archaeology*, edited by M-A Dobres and J. Robb, pp. 92–112. Routledge, New York.

Clark, J. E., and W. J. Parry
1990 Craft Specialization and Cultural Complexity. *Research in Economic Anthropology* 12:289–346.

Clarke, D.
1968 *Analytical Archaeology*. Methuen, London.

Cobb, C. R.
1998 Social Reproduction and the *Longue Durée* in the Prehistory of the Midcontinental United States. In *Reader in Archaeological Theory: Post-Processual and Cognitive Approaches*, edited by D. S. Whitley, pp. 199–218. Routledge, New York.

Cochrane, E. E.
2001 Style, Function, and Systematic Empiricism: The Conflation of Process and Pattern. In *Style and Function in Archaeology*, edited by T. D. Hurt and G.F.M. Rakita, pp. 183–202. Bergin and Garvey, Westport, Connecticut.

Cohen, I.
1987 Structuration Theory and Social Praxis. In *Social Theory Today*, edited by A. Giddens and J. H. Turner, pp. 273–308. Stanford University Press, Stanford.

Colton, H. S., and L. L. Hargrave
1937 *Handbook of Northern Arizona Pottery Wares*. Bulletin, no. 11, Museum of Northern Arizona, Flagstaff.

Comaroff, J.
1982 Dialectical Systems, History and Anthropology: Units of Study and Questions of Theory. *Journal of South African Studies* 8:143–172.

Comaroff, J., and J. Comaroff
1991 *Of Revelation and Revolution: Christianity, Colonialism and Consciousness in South Africa*. University of Chicago Press, Chicago.

Conkey, M. W.
1978 Style and Information in Cultural Evolution: Toward a Predictive Model for the Paleolithic. In *Social Archaeology: Beyond Subsistence and Dating*, edited by C. Redman, M. Berman, E. Curtin, W. Langhorne, N, Versaggi, and J. Wanser, pp. 61–85. Academic Press, New York.

1982 Boundedness in Art and Society. In *Symbolic and Structural Archaeology*, edited by I. Hodder, pp. 115–128. Cambridge University Press, Cambridge.

1990 Experimenting with Style in Archaeology: Some Historical and Theoretical Issues. In *The Uses of Style in Archaeology*, edited by M. W. Conkey and C. A. Hastorf, pp. 5–17. Cambridge University Press, Cambridge.

1999 An End Note: Reframing Materiality for Archaeology. In *Material Meanings: Critical Approaches to the Interpretation of Material Culture*, edited by E. S. Chilton, pp. 133–141. University of Utah Press, Salt Lake City.

Conkey, M. W., and J. Gero
1997 Program to Practice: Gender and Feminism in Archaeology. *Annual Review of Anthropology* 26:411–437.

Conkey, M. W., and C. A. Hastorf
1990 Introduction. In *The Uses of Style in Archaeology*, edited by M. W. Conkey and C. A. Hastorf, pp. 1–4. Cambridge University Press, Cambridge.

Cordell, L.
1997 *Archaeology of the Southwest*. Academic Press, San Diego.

Costin, C. L., and R. P. Wright
1998 (eds.) *Craft and Social Identity*. Archeological Papers of the American Anthropological Association No. 8, Washington, D.C.

Cowgill, G. L.
1993 Distinguished Lecture in Archaeology: Beyond Criticizing New Archaeology. *American Anthropologist* 95:551–573.

2000 "Rationality" and Contexts in

Agency Theory. In *Agency in Archaeology,* edited by M. Dobres and J. Robb, pp. 51–60. Routledge Publishing, New York.

Cronk, Lee
1991   Human Behavioral Ecology. *Annual Review of Anthropology* 20:25–53.
1999   *That Complex Whole: Culture and the Evolution of Human Behavior.* Westview Press, Boulder, Colorado.

Crown, P. L., and W. H. Wills
1995   Origins of Southwestern Ceramic Containers. *Journal of Anthropological Research* 51:173–186.

Cruz Antillón, R., and T. Maxwell
1999   The Villa Ahumada Site: Archaeological Investigations East of Paquimé. In *The Casas Grandes World,* edited by C. F. Schaafsma and C. L. Riley, pp. 43–53. University of Utah Press, Salt Lake City.

Cullen, B.R.S.
1993   The Darwinian Resurgence and the Cultural Virus Critique. *Cambridge Archaeological Journal* 3:179–202.

Cunningham, J. J.
1999   Pots and Incoherent Culture: Recovering Borderlands at the Van Bree Site (AgHk-32). Unpublished Masters thesis, Department of Anthropology, University of Western Ontario, London.
2001   Ceramic Variation and Ethnic Holism: A Case Study from the "Younge-Early Ontario Iroquoian Border" in Southwestern Ontario. *Canadian Journal of Archaeology* 25(1–2):1–27.
n.d.   Essentializing Culture: Conceptual Hurdles to Pluralism in Archaeology. *Indigenous People and Archaeology, Proceedings of the 32nd Annual Chacmool Conference.* University of Calgary Press, Calgary. (In press)

Damuth, J., and I. L. Heisler
1988   Alternative Formulations of Multilevel Selection. *Biology and Philosophy* 3:407–430.

Dart, R.
1957   The Makapansgat Australopithecine Osteodontokeratic Culture. In *Third Pan-African Congress on Prehistory,* edited by J. D. Clark and S. Cole, pp. 161–171. Routledge, London.

David, N., and C. Kramer
2001   *Ethnoarchaeology in Action.* Cambridge University Press, Cambridge.

Davies, D.
1996   Explanatory Disunities and the Unity of Science. *International Studies in the Philosophy of Science* 10(1):5–21.

Dawkins, R.
1982   *The Extended Phenotype.* Oxford University Press, Oxford.
1987   *The Blind Watchmaker.* W. W. Norton and Company, New York.
1996   *Climbing Mount Improbable.* W. W. Norton and Company, New York.

Dean, J. S.
1996   Demography, Environment, and Subsistence Stress. In *Evolving Complexity and Environmental Risk in the Prehistoric Southwest: Proceedings of the Workshop "Resource Stress, Economic Uncertainty, and Human Response in the Prehistoric Southwest,"* edited by J. A. Tainter and B. B. Tainter, pp. 25–56. Proceedings No. 24, Santa Fe Institute Studies in the Sciences of Complexity, New Mexico. Addison-Wesley Publishing Company, Reading, Pennsylvania.

Dean, J. S., R. C. Euler, G. J. Gumerman, F. Plog, R. H. Hevly, and T.N.V. Karlstrom
1985   Human Behavior, Demography, and Paleoenvironment on the Colorado Plateaus. *American Antiquity* 50:537–554.

Deetz, J.
1965   *The Dynamics of Stylistic Change in Arikara Ceramics.* University of Illinois Studies in Anthropology 4. University of Illinois Press, Urbana.

DeMarrais, E., L. J. Castillo, and T. Earle
1996   Ideology, Materialization, and Power Strategies. *Current Anthropology* 37:15–31.

Dewar, R. E.
1995   Of Nets and Trees: Untangling the Reticulate and Dendritic in Madagascar Prehistory. *World Archaeology* 26:301–318.

Dewey, J.
1917   The Need for a Recovery of Philoso-
        phy. In *Creative Intelligence: Essays
        in the Pragmatic Attitude,* by J.
        Dewey and others, pp. 3–69. Henry
        Holt, New York.

Dietler, M., and I. Herbich
1989   Tich Matek: The Technology of Luo
        Pottery Production and the Defini-
        tion of Ceramic Style. *World Ar-
        chaeology* 21:148–164.

1998   *Habitus,* Techniques, Style: An Inte-
        grated Approach to the Social Un-
        derstanding of Material Culture and
        Boundaries. In *The Archaeology of
        Social Boundaries,* edited by M. T.
        Stark, pp. 232–263. Smithsonian In-
        stitution Press, Washington D.C.

Di Peso, C. C.
1974   *Casas Grandes: A Fallen Trading
        Center of the Gran Chichimeca,*
        vols. 1–3. The Amerind Foundation
        and Northland Press, Dragoon and
        Flagstaff, Arizona.

Di Peso, C. C., J. B. Rinaldo, and G. J. Fenner
1974   (eds.) *Casas Grandes: A Fallen Trad-
        ing Center of the Gran Chichimeca,*
        vols. 4–8. The Amerind Foundation
        and Northland Press, Dragoon and
        Flagstaff, Arizona.

Dobres, M.-A.
1995   Gender and Prehistoric Technology:
        On Social Agency of Technological
        Strategies. *World Archaeology* 27:
        25–49.

1999   Technologies, Links and Chains:
        The Processual Unfolding of Tech-
        nique and Technician. In *Making
        Culture: Essays on Technological
        Practice, Politics, and World Views,*
        edited by M.-A. Dobres and C.
        Hoffman, pp. 124–146. Smithsonian
        Institution Press, Washington D.C.

2000   *Technology and Social Agency.*
        Blackwell, Oxford.

Dobres, M.-A., and C. R. Hoffman
1994   Social Agency and the Dynamics of
        Prehistoric Technology. *Journal of
        Archaeological Method and Theory*
        1:211–258.

Dobres, M.-A., and J. Robb
2000a   Agency in Archaeology: Paradigm or
        Platitude? In *Agency in Archaeology,*
        edited by M. Dobres and J. Robb,
        pp. 3–17. Routledge Publishing,
        New York.

2000b   (eds.) *Agency in Archaeology.* Rout-
        ledge, London.

Doolittle, W.
1993   Canal Irrigation at Casas Grandes.
        In *Culture and Contact: Charles C.
        Di Peso's Gran Chichimeca,* edited
        by A. I. Woosley and J. C. Raves-
        loot, pp. 133–152. Amerind Founda-
        tion Publications, Dragoon, Arizona,
        and University of New Mexico
        Press, Albuquerque.

1999   Phylogenetic Classification and the
        Universal Tree. *Science* 284:2124–
        2128.

Driver, H. E., and W. C. Massey
1957   Comparative Studies of North
        American Indians. *Transactions of
        the American Philosophical Society*
        47:165–456.

Duke, P.
1999   (compiler) *Affiliation Conference on
        Ancestral Peoples of the Four Cor-
        ners Region.* Papers and Transcripts,
        vols. 1–3. Fort Lewis College and
        National Park Service, Colorado.

Duke, P., and D. Saitta
1998   An Emancipatory Archaeology for
        the Working Class. Assemblage 4.
        http://www.shef.ac.uk/~assem/
        44duk_sai.html.

Duke, P., and Michael Wilson
1995   (eds.) *Beyond Subsistence: Plains
        Archaeology and the Postprocessual
        Critique.* University of Alabama
        Press, Tuscaloosa.

Dunnell, R. C.
1971   *Systematics in Prehistory.* Free Press,
        New York.

1978a   Style and Function: A Fundamental
        Dichotomy. *American Antiquity*
        43:192–202.

1978b   Archaeological Potential of Anthro-
        pological and Scientific Models
        of Function. In *Archaeological
        Essays in Honor of Irving B. Rouse,*
        edited by R. C. Dunnell and E. S.
        Hall Jr., pp. 41–73. Mouton, The
        Hague.

1980   Evolutionary Theory and Archaeol-
        ogy. *Advances in Archaeological*

Method and Theory, vol. 3, edited by M. B. Schiffer, pp. 35–99. Academic Press, New York.

1986   Fifty Years of American Archaeology. In *American Archaeology, Past and Future,* edited by D. J. Meltzer, D. D. Fowler, and J. A. Sabloff, pp. 25–49. Smithsonian Institution Press, Washington, D.C.

1989   Aspects of the Application of Evolutionary Theory in Archaeology. In *Archaeological Thought in America,* edited by C. C. Lamberg-Karlovsky, pp. 35–49. Cambridge University Press, Cambridge.

1995   What Is it that Actually Evolves? In *Evolutionary Archaeology: Methodological Issues,* edited by P.A. Teltser, pp. 33–50. University of Arizona Press, Tucson.

Dunnell, R. C., and J. K. Feathers
1991   Late Woodland Manifestations of the Malden Plain, Southeast Missouri. In *Stability, Transformation, and Variation: The Late Woodland Southeast,* edited by M. S. Nassaney and C. R. Cobb, pp. 21–45. Plenum, New York.

Dupré, J.
1993   *The Disorder of Things: Metaphysical Foundations of the Disunity of Science.* Harvard University Press, Cambridge, Massachusetts.

Durham, William H.
1991   *Coevolution: Genes, Culture, and Human Diversity.* Stanford University Press, Stanford.

1992   Applications of Evolutionary Culture Theory. *Annual Review of Anthropology* 21:331–355.

Durkheim, E.
1964   [1895] *The Rules of the Sociological Method.* The Free Press, New York.

Earle, T.
1991   The Evolution of Chiefdoms. In *Chiefdoms: Power, Economy, and Ideology,* edited by T. K. Earle, pp. 1–15. Cambridge University Press, Cambridge.

1994   Positioning Exchange in the Evolution of Human Society. In *Prehistoric Exchange Systems in North America,* edited by T. G. Baugh and J. E. Ericson, pp. 419–437. Plenum Press, New York.

Echo-Hawk, R.
2000   Ancient History in the New World: Integrating Oral Traditions and the Archaeological Record in Deep Time. *American Antiquity* 65: 267–290.

Eldredge, N.
1971   The Allopatric Model and Phylogeny in Paleozoic Invertebrates. *Evolution* 25:156–167.

1985   *Unfinished Synthesis: Biological Hierarchies and Modern Evolutionary Thought.* Oxford University Press, Oxford.

1995   *Reinventing Darwin: The Great Debate at the High Table of Evolutionary Theory.* Wiley, New York.

Eldredge, N., and S. J. Gould
1972   Punctuated Equilibria: An Alternative to Phyletic Gradualism. In *Models in Paleobiology,* edited by T. J. M. Schopf, pp. 82–115. Freeman, Cooper, San Francisco.

Ellen, R.
1982   *Environment, Subsistence and System: The Ecology of Small-Scale Social Formations.* Cambridge University Press, Cambridge.

Ellison, P. T.
1991   Reproductive Ecology and Human Fertility. In *Biological Anthropology and Human Affairs,* edited by G. Lasker and N. Mascie-Taylor, pp. 14–54. Cambridge University Press, Cambridge.

Ember, M., and C. R. Ember
1995   Worldwide Cross-Cultural Studies and Their Relevance for Archaeology. *Journal of Archaeological Research* 3:87–111.

Emerson, T. E.
1997   *Cahokia and the Archaeology of Power.* University of Alabama Press, Tuscaloosa.

Emerson, T. E., and R. E. Hughes
2000   Figurines, Flint Clay Sourcing, the Ozark Highlands, and Cahokian Acquisition. *American Antiquity* 65:79–101.

Endler, J. A.
1986   *Natural Selection in the Wild.* Princeton University Press, Princeton, New Jersey.

1998   The Place of Hybridization in Evolution. *Evolution* 52:640–644.

Ereshefsky, M.

1995 Critical Notice: John Dupré, The Disorder of Things. *Canadian Journal of Philosophy* 25(1):143–158.

1998 Species Pluralism and Anti-Realism. *Philosophy of Science* 65:103–120.

Escobar, A.

1999 After Nature. *Current Anthropology* 40:1–16.

Farnell, B.

1999 Moving Bodies, Acting Selves. *Annual Review of Anthropology* 28:341–373.

Feinman, G. M.

1995 The Emergence of Inequality: A Focus on Strategies and Processes. In *Foundations of Social Inequality,* edited by T. D. Price and G. M. Feinman, pp. 255–280. Plenum Press, New York.

Ferguson, Cheryl

1980 Analysis of Skeletal Remains. In *Tijeras Canyon: Analyses of the Past,* edited by L. S. Cordell, pp. 121–148. Maxwell Museum of Anthropology and University of New Mexico Press, Albuquerque.

Ferguson, L.

1992 *Uncommon Ground: Archaeology and Early African America, 1650–1800.* Smithsonian Institution Press, Washington, D.C.

Feyerabend, P.

1975 *Against Method.* New Left Books, London.

Fish, P. R., and S. K. Fish

1999 Reflections on the Casas Grandes Regional System from the Northwestern Periphery. In *The Casas Grandes World,* edited by C. F. Schaafsma and C. L. Riley, pp. 27–42. University of Utah Press, Salt Lake City.

Fisher, D. C.

1994 Stratocladistics: Morphological and Temporal Patterns and Their Relation to Phylogenetic Process. In *Interpreting the Hierarchy of Nature,* edited by L. Grande and O. Rieppel, pp. 133–171. Academic Press, San Diego.

Fitzhugh, Ben

2001 Risk and Invention in Human Technological Evolution. *Journal of Anthropological Archaeology* 20:125–167.

Flannery, K. V.

1967 Culture History v. Culture Process: A Debate in American Archaeology. *Scientific American* 217:119–122.

Ford, J. A., P. Phillips, and W. G. Haag

1955 *The Jaketown Site in West-Central Mississippi.* Anthropological Papers of the American Museum of Natural History, vol. 45, pt. 1, New York.

Ford, J. A., and C. H. Webb

1956 *Poverty Point, a Late Archaic Site in Louisiana.* Anthropological Papers of the American Museum of Natural History, vol. 46, pt. 1, New York.

Ford, R.

1973 Archaeology Serving Humanity. In *Research and Theory in Current Archaeology,* edited by C. Redman, pp. 83–93. Wiley, New York.

Foster, L.

1991 *Women, Family, and Utopia: Communal Experiments of the Shakers, the Oneida Community, and the Mormons.* Syracuse University Press, Syracuse, New York.

Frazier, E. F.

1965 *Black Bourgeoisie.* Free Press, New York.

Fritz, J. M., and F. T. Plog

1970 The Nature of Archaeological Explanation. *American Antiquity* 35:405–412.

Fukuyama, F.

1992 *The End of History and the Last Man.* Free Press, Toronto.

Galison, P.

1997 *Image and Logic: A Material Culture of Microphysics.* University of Chicago Press, Chicago.

Gero, J. M.

2000 Troubled Travels in Agency and Feminism. In *Agency in Archaeology,* edited by M. Dobres and J. Robb, pp. 34–39. Routledge Publishing, New York.

Gibson, J. L.

1974 Poverty Point, the First North American Chiefdom. *Archaeology* 27:96–105.

1986 Earth Sitting: Architectural Masses at Poverty Point, Northeastern Louisiana. In *Recent Research at the Poverty Point Site,* edited by

K. M. Byrd. *Louisiana Archaeology* 13:201–248.

1994a   Empirical Characterization of Exchange Systems in Lower Mississippi Valley Prehistory. In *Prehistoric Exchange Systems in North America,* edited by T. G. Baugh and J. E. Ericson, pp. 127–175. Plenum Press, New York.

1994b   Before Their Time? Early Mounds in the Lower Mississippi Valley. *Southeastern Archaeology* 13:162–186.

1996   Poverty Point and Greater Southeastern Prehistory: The Culture That Did Not Fit. In *Archaeology of the Mid-Holocene Southeast,* edited by K. E. Sassaman and D. G. Anderson, pp. 288–305. University Press of Florida, Gainesville.

2000   *The Ancient Mounds of Poverty Point: Place of Rings.* University Press of Florida, Gainesville.

Giddens, A.

1979   *Central Problems in Social Theory: Action, Structure and Contradiction in Social Analysis.* University of California Press, Berkeley.

1984   *The Constitution of Society: Outline of the Theory of Structuration.* University of California Press, Berkeley.

Giles, K.

1999   The 'Familiar' Fraternity: The Appropriation and Consumption of Medieval Guildhalls in Early Modern York. In *The Familiar Past?,* edited by S. Tarlow and S. West, pp. 87–102. Routledge, New York.

Gillespie, S. D.

2001   Personhood, Agency, and Mortuary Ritual: A Case Study from the Ancient Maya. *Journal of Anthropological Archaeology* 20(1):73–112.

Gladwin, H. S.

1936   Editorials: Methodology in the Southwest. *American Antiquity* 1:256–259.

Gladwin, W., and H. S. Gladwin

1930   *A Method for the Designation of Southwestern Pottery Types.* Medallion Papers, no. 7, Gila Pueblo, Globe, Arizona.

1934   *A Method for the Designation of Cultures and Their Variations.* Medallion Papers, no. 15, Gila Pueblo, Globe, Arizona.

Godelier, M.

1982   Social Hierarchies among the Baruya of New Guinea. In *Inequality in New Guinea Highlands Society,* edited by A. Strathern, pp. 3–34. Cambridge University Press, Cambridge.

Goodenough, W. H.

1997   Comment on "The Dimensions of Social Life in the Pacific: Human Diversity and the Myth of the Primitive Isolate" by J. E. Terrell, T. L. Hunt, and C. Gosden. *Current Anthropology* 38:177–178.

Goodheart, A.

1999   Into the Depths of History. *Preservation* 51:36–45.

Gosden, C.

1989   Debt, Production, and Prehistory. *Journal of Anthropological Archaeology* 8:355–387.

Gould, R. A.

1978a   Beyond Analogy in Ethnoarchaeology. In *Explorations in Ethnoarchaeology,* edited by R. A Gould, pp. 249–293. University of New Mexico Press, Albuquerque.

1978b   (ed.) *Explorations in Ethnoarchaeology.* University of New Mexico Press, Albuquerque.

Gould, R. A., and P. J. Watson

1982   A Dialogue on the Meaning and Use of Analogy in Ethnoarchaeological Reasoning. *Journal of Anthropological Archaeology* 1:355–381.

Gould, S. J.

1986   Evolution and the Triumph of Homology, or Why History Matters. *American Scientist* 74:60–69.

1987   The Panda's Thumb of Technology. *Natural History* 96(1):14–23.

1991   The Disparity of the Burgess Shale Arthropod Fauna and the Limits of Cladistic Analysis: Why We Must Strive to Quantify Morphospace. *Paleobiology* 17:411–423.

1996   *Full House: The Spread of Excellence from Plato to Darwin.* Harmony Books, New York.

Gould, S. J., N. L. Gilinsky, and R. Z. German

1987   Asymmetry of Lineages and the Direction of Evolutionary Time. *Science* 236:1437–1441.

Graves, M. W.

1994   Community Boundaries in Late Prehistoric Puebloan Society: Kalinga

Ethnoarchaeology as a Model for the Southwestern Production and Exchange of Pottery. In *The Ancient Southwestern Community: Models and Methods for the Study of Prehistoric Social Organization,* edited by W. H. Wills and R. Leonard, pp. 149–170. University of New Mexico Press, Albuquerque.

Graves, M. W., and T. N. Ladefoged
1995   The Evolutionary Significance of Ceremonial Architecture. In *Evolutionary Archaeology: Methodological Issues,* edited by P. A. Teltser, pp. 149–174. University of Arizona Press, Tucson.

Green, L., P. C. Price, and M. E. Hamburger
1995   Prisoner's Dilemma and the Pigeon: Control by Immediate Consequences. *Journal of the Experimental Analysis of Behavior* 64:1–17.

Hamilton, F. E.
1999   Southeastern Archaic Mounds: Examples of Elaboration in a Temporally Fluctuating Environment. *Journal of Anthropological Archaeology* 18:344–355.

Hard, R. J., and J. R. Roney
1998   A Massive Terraced Village Complex in Chihuahua, Mexico, 3000 Years before Present. *Science* 279: 1661–1664.

Harmon, M. J., R. D. Leonard, C. S. VanPool, and T. L. VanPool
2000   Cultural Transmission: Shared Intellectual Traditions in Ceramics of the Prehistoric American Southwest and Northern Mexico. Paper presented at the 65th annual meeting of the Society for American Archaeology, Philadelphia.

Harris, E. C.
1989   *Zasady Stratigrafia Archeologica [Principles of Archaeological Stratigraphy].* 1st ed. Polish edition. Os rodck Dukumentacji Zabytkow, Warsaw.

Harris, M.
1966   The Cultural Ecology of India's Sacred Cattle. *Current Anthropology* 7:51–66.8
1968   Comments by Marvin Harris. In *New Perspectives in Archeology,* edited by S. R. Binford and L. R. Binford, pp. 359–361. Aldine, Chicago.

1974   *Cows, Pigs, Wars and Witches.* Random House, New York.

Hastorf, C. A.
1991   Gender, Space, and Food in Prehistory. In *Engendering Archaeology: Women and Prehistory,* edited by J. M. Gero and M. W. Conkey, pp. 132–159. Basil Blackwell, Oxford.

Hawkes, K.
1992   Sharing and Collective Action. In *Evolutionary Ecology and Human Behavior,* edited by E. A. Smith and B. Winterhalder, pp. 269–300. Aldine de Gruyter, New York.
1993   Why Hunter-Gatherers Work. *Current Anthropology* 34:341–361.

Hayden, B.
1995   Pathways to Power: Principles for Creating Socioeconomic Inequalities. In *Foundations of Social Inequality,* edited by T. D. Price and G. M. Feinman, pp. 15–86. Plenum Press, New York.

Hayden, B., and R. Gargett
1990   Big Man, Big Heart? A Mesoamerican View of the Emergence of Complex Society. *Ancient Mesoamerica* 1:3–20.

Headland, T. N.
1997   Revisionism in Ecological Anthropology. *Current Anthropology* 38: 605–630.

Hegmon, M.
1992   Archaeological Research on Style. *Annual Review of Anthropology* 21: 517–536.

Helms, M. W.
1988   *Ulysses' Sail: An Ethnographic Odyssey of Power, Knowledge, and Geographic Distance.* Princeton University Press, Princeton, New Jersey.
1994a   *Craft and the Kingly Ideal: Art, Trade, and Power.* University of Texas Press, Austin.
1994b   Chiefdom Rivalries, Control, and External Contacts in Lower Central America. In *Factional Competition and Political Development in the New World,* edited by E. M. Brumfiel and J. W. Fox, pp. 55–60. Cambridge University Press, Cambridge.
1999   Why Maya Lords Sat on Jaguar Thrones. In *Material Symbols: Culture and Economy in Prehistory,*

edited by J. Robb, pp. 56–69. Center for Archaeological Investigations, Occasional Papers no. 26, Southern Illinois University, Carbondale.

Hendon, J. A.
1996   Archaeological Approaches to the Organization of Domestic Labor: Household Practices and Domestic Relations. *Annual Review of Anthropology* 25:45–61.

Hendrickson, M.
2000   Design Analysis of Chihuahuan Polychrome Jars from North American Museum Collections. Master's thesis, University of Calgary, Alberta.
2001   Lost Pots and Untold Tales: Design Analysis of Chihuahuan Medio Period Polychrome Jars from Museum Collections. In *From Paquimé to Mata Ortiz: The Legacy of Ancient Casas Grandes,* edited by G. Johnson, pp. 37–54. San Diego Museum Papers 40, San Diego Museum of Man, California.

Hennig, W.
1950   *Grundzüge einer Theorie der phylogenetischen Systematik.* Deutscher Zentralverlag, Berlin.

Herold, L. C.
1965   *Trincheras and Physical Environment along the Rio Gavilan, Chihuahua, Mexico.* Publications in Geography, Technical Paper 65(1). University of Denver, Colorado.

Hewlett, B. S., A. de Silvestri, and C. R. Guglielmino
2002   Semes and Genes in Africa. *Current Anthropology* 43:313–321.

Hexter, J. H.
1972   Fernand Braudel and the Monde Braudellien. *Journal of Modern History* 44:480–539.

Hill, J. N.
1970   *Broken K Pueblo: Prehistoric Social Organization in the American Southwest.* Anthropological Papers University of Arizona No. 18. Tucson.
1985   Style: A Conceptual Evolutionary Framework. In *Decoding Prehistoric Ceramics,* edited by B. A. Nelson, pp. 362–385. Southern Illinois University Press, Carbondale.

Hill, W. D.
1992   Chronology of the El Zurdo Site, Chihuahua. Master's thesis, University of Calgary, Alberta, Canada.

Hobbes, T.
1985   [1651] *Leviathan,* edited by C. B. MacPherson. Penguin Books, London.

Hodder, I.
1982a *Symbols in Action.* Cambridge University Press, Cambridge.
1982b Theoretical Archaeology: A Reactionary View. In *Symbolic and Structural Archaeology,* edited by I. Hodder, pp. 1–16. Cambridge University Press, Cambridge.
1983   *The Present Past: An Introduction to Anthropology for Archaeologists.* Pica Press, New York.
1984   Burials, Houses, Women and Men in the European Neolithic. In *Ideology, Power and Prehistory,* edited by D. Miller and C. Tilley, pp. 51–68. Cambridge University Press, Cambridge.
1985   Postprocessual Archaeology. In *Advances in Archaeological Method and Theory,* vol. 8, edited by M. B. Schiffer, pp. 1–26. Academic Press, New York.
1986   *Reading the Past: Current Approaches to Interpretation in Archaeology.* Cambridge University Press, Cambridge.
1987a The Meaning of Discard: Ash and Domestic Space in Baringo. In *Method and Theory for Activity Area Research: An Ethnoarchaeological Press,* edited by S. Kent, pp. 424–448. Columbia University Press, New York.
1987b Preface. In *Archaeology as Long-Term History,* edited by I. Hodder, pp. iv–vii. Cambridge University Press, Cambridge.
1989   (ed.) *The Meaning of Things: Material Culture and Symbolic Expression.* Unwin Hyman, London.
1990a *The Domestication of Europe.* Blackwell Publishers, Oxford.
1990b Style as Historic Quality. In *The Uses of Style in Archaeology,* edited by M. W. Conkey and C. A. Hastorf, pp. 44–51. Cambridge University Press, Cambridge.
1991a *Reading the Past: Current Ap-*

proaches to Interpretation in Archaeology, 2nd ed. Cambridge University Press, Cambridge.

1991b Post Processual Archaeology and the Current Debate. In *Processual and Postprocessual Archaeologies,* edited by R. W. Preucel, pp. 30–42. Center for Archaeological Investigation. Southern Illinois University, Carbondale.

1991c Interpretive Archaeology and its Role. *American Antiquity* 56:7–18.

Hodder, I., and C. Orton
1976 *Spatial Analysis in Archaeology.* Cambridge University Press, Cambridge.

Hubbs, C. L.
1945 Review of "Tempo and Mode in Evolution" by G. G. Simpson. *American Naturalist* 79:271–275.

Hughes, N. C., and C. C. Labandeira
1995 The Stability of Species in Taxonomy. *Paleobiology* 21:401–403.

Hughes, S. S.
1998 Getting to the Point: Evolutionary Change in Prehistoric Weaponry. *Journal of Archaeological Method and Theory* 5:345–408.

Hull, D.
1970 Contemporary Systematic Philosophies. *Annual Review of Ecology and Systematics* 1:19–54.

1988a Interactors versus Vehicles. In *The Role of Behavior in Evolution,* edited by H. C. Plotkin, pp. 19–50. MIT Press, Cambridge, Massachusetts.

1988b *Science as a Process: An Evolutionary Account of the Social and Conceptual Development of Science.* University of Chicago Press, Chicago.

Hunt, T. L., C. P. Lipo, and S. L. Sterling
2001 (eds.) *Posing Questions for a Scientific Archaeology.* Bergin and Garvey, Westport, Connecticut.

Hurt, T. D., and G.F.M. Rakita
2001 (eds.) *Style and Function: Conceptual Issues in Evolutionary Archaeology.* Bergin and Garvey, Westport, Connecticut.

Hurt, T. D., T. L. VanPool, G.F.M. Rakita, and R. D. Leonard
2001 Explaining the Co-occurrence of Traits in the Archaeological Record: A Further Consideration of Replicative Success. In *Style and Function: Conceptual Issues in Evolutionary Archaeology,* edited by T. D. Hurt and G.F.M. Rakita, pp. 51–68. Bergin and Garvey, Westport, Connecticut.

Hutson, S. R.
2001 Synergy Through Disunity, Science as Social Practice: Comments on VanPool and VanPool. *American Antiquity* 66:349–360.

Huxley, J. S.
1945 Genetics and Major Evolutionary Change. *Nature* 156:3–4.

Ingersoll, D., J. E. Yellen, and W. Macdonald
1977 (eds.) *Experimental Archaeology.* Columbia University Press, New York.

Jackson, H. E.
1991 The Trade Fair in Hunter-Gatherer Interaction: The Role of Inter-Societal Trade in the Evolution of Poverty Point Culture. In *Between Bands and States: Sedentism, Subsistence, and Interaction in Small Scale Societies,* edited by S. A. Gregg, pp. 265–286. Center for Archaeological Investigation, Occasional Paper 9. Southern Illinois University, Carbondale.

Jefferies, R. W.
1996 The Emergence of Long-Distance Exchange Networks in the Southeastern United States. In *Archaeology of the Mid-Holocene Southeast,* edited by K. E. Sassaman and D. G. Anderson, pp. 222–234. University Press of Florida, Gainesville.

Jeter, M. D., and H. E. Jackson
1990 Poverty Point Extraction and Exchange: The Arkansas Lithic Connections. In *Exchange in the Lower Mississippi Valley and Contiguous Areas at 1100 B.C.,* edited by J. L. Gibson. *Louisiana Archaeology* 17:133–206.

Jochim, M.
1983 Optimization Models in Context. In *Archaeological Hammers and Theories,* edited by J. A. Moore and A. S. Keene, pp. 157–172. Academic Press, New York.

Johnson, G. A.

1982　Organizational Structure and Scalar Stress. In *Theory and Explanation in Archaeology*, edited by A. C. Renfrew, M. J. Rowlands, and B. A. Segraves, pp. 389–420. Academic Press, New York.

Johnson, J. K.

1993　Poverty Point Period Crystal Drill Bits, Microliths, and Social Organization in the Yazoo Basin, Mississippi. *Southeastern Archaeology* 12:59–64.

1994　Prehistoric Exchange in the Southeast. In *Prehistoric Exchange Systems in North America*, edited by T. G. Baugh and J. E. Ericson, pp. 99–125. Plenum Press, New York.

Johnson, M.

1996　*An Archaeology of Capitalism*. Blackwell Publishers, Oxford.

2000　Self-Made Men and the Staging of Agency. In *Agency in Archaeology*, edited by M.-A. Dobres and J. Robb, pp. 213–231. Routledge, New York.

Jones, A.

1998　Where Eagles Dare: Landscape, Animals and the Neolithic of Orkney. *Journal of Material Culture* 3:301–324.

Jones, G. T., R. D. Leonard, and A. L. Abbott

1995　The Structure of Selectionist Explanations in Archaeology. In *Evolutionary Archaeology: Methodological Issues*, edited by P. A. Teltser, pp. 13–32. University of Arizona Press, Tucson.

Jones, S.

1997　*The Archaeology of Ethnicity: Constructing Identities in the Past and Present*. Routledge, London.

Joyce, R. A.

1993　Women's Work: Images of Production and Reproduction in Pre-Hispanic Southern Central America. *Current Anthropology* 34(3):255–266.

1996　The Construction of Gender in Classic Maya Monuments. In *Gender and Archaeology*, edited by R. P. Wright, pp. 167–195. University of Pennsylvania Press, Philadelphia.

2000　Heirlooms and Houses: Materiality and Social Memory. In *Beyond Kinship: Social and Material Reproduction in House Societies*, edited by R. A. Joyce and S. D. Gillespie, pp. 189–212. University of Pennsylvania Press, Philadelphia.

Joyce, R. A., and J. A. Hendon

2000　Heterarchy, History, and Material Reality: "Communities" in Late Classic Honduras. In *The Archaeology of Communities: A New World Perspective*, edited by M. A. Canuto and J. Yaeger, pp. 143–160. Routledge Press, London.

Kantner, J.

1996　Political Competition among the Chaco Anasazi of the American Southwest. *Journal of Anthropological Archaeology* 15:41–105.

1999　The Influence of Self-Interested Behavior on Sociopolitical Change: The Evolution of the Chaco Anasazi in the Prehistoric American Southwest. Ph.D. diss., University of California at Santa Barbara.

Kantner, J., and N. M. Mahoney

2000　(eds.) *Great House Communities across the Chacoan Landscape*. University of Arizona Press, Tucson.

Kaplan, A.

1964　*The Conduct of Inquiry: Methodology for Behavioral Science*. Chandler Publishing, San Francisco.

Karlsson, H.

1998　*Re-Thinking Archaeology*. Gotarc Series B, Gothenburg Archaeological Theses 8, Göteborg University Department of Archaeology, Göteborg.

Kelley, J. H., J. D. Stewart, A. C. MacWilliams, and L. C. Neff

1999　A West Central Chihuahuan Perspective on Chihuahua Culture. In *The Casas Grandes World*, edited by C. F. Schaafsma and C. L. Riley, pp. 63–77. University of Utah Press, Salt Lake City.

Kelley, L. C.

1986　The Mobile Merchants of Molino. In *Ripples in the Chichimec Sea: New Considerations of Southwestern-Mesoamerican Interactions*, edited by F. J. Mathien and R. H. McGuire, pp. 81–104. Southern Illinois University Press, Carbondale and Edwardsville.

Kelly, R.

2000 Elements of a Behavioral Ecological Paradigm for the Study of Prehistoric Hunter-Gatherers. In *Social Theory in Archaeology*, edited by M. B. Schiffer, pp. 63–78. University of Utah Press, Salt Lake City.

2002 American Archaeology in 30 Years. *Anthropology News* 43(1):4.

Kent, S.

1987 Understanding the Use of Space: An Ethnoarchaeological Approach. In *Method and Theory for Activity Area Research: An Ethnoarchaeological Approach*, edited by S. Kent, pp. 1–60. Columbia University Press, New York.

Kertzer, D. I.

1988 *Ritual, Politics and Power.* Yale University Press, New Haven, Connecticut.

Kidder, A. V.

1915 Pottery of the Pajarito Plateau and of Some Adjacent Regions in New Mexico. *American Anthropological Association, Memoir* 2:407–462.

1916 Pottery of the Casas Grandes District, Chihuahua. In *Holmes Anniversary Volume, Anthropological Essays,* pp. 253–268. Peabody Museum, Washington, D.C.

1924 *An Introduction to the Study of Southwestern Archaeology, with a Preliminary Account of the Excavations at Pecos.* Papers of the Southwest Expedition 1. Yale University Press, New Haven, Connecticut.

1932 *The Artifacts of Pecos.* Papers, no. 6, Southwestern Expedition, Phillips Academy. Yale University Press, New Haven, Connecticut.

Kidder, T. R.

1991 New Directions in Poverty Point Settlement Archaeology: An Example from Northeast Louisiana. In *The Poverty Point Culture: Local Manifestations, Subsistence Practices, and Trade Networks*, edited by K. M. Byrd, pp. 27–53. *Geoscience and Man* 29. Louisiana State University, Baton Rouge.

Kloppenberg, J.

1996 Pragmatism: An Old Name for Some New Ways of Thinking? *The Journal of American History* 83:100–138.

Knapp, A. B.

1992 (ed.) *Archaeology, Annales, and Ethnohistory.* Cambridge University Press, Cambridge.

Knapp, A. B., and W. Ashmore

1999 Archaeological Landscapes: Constructed, Conceptualized, Ideational. In *Archaeologies of Landscape: Contemporary Perspectives*, edited by W. Ashmore and A. B. Knapp, pp. 1–30. Blackwell, Oxford.

Knight, V. J.

1997 Some Developmental Parallels between Cahokia and Moundville. In *Cahokia: Domination and Ideology in the Mississippian World*, edited by T. R. Pauketat and T. E. Emerson, pp. 229–247. University of Nebraska Press, Lincoln.

Kohl, P. L.

1993 Limits to a Post-Processual Archaeology (or, The Dangers of a New Scholasticism). In *Archaeological Theory: Who Sets the Agenda?*, edited by N. Yoffee and A. Sherratt, pp. 13–19. Cambridge University Press, Cambridge.

Kolb, M. J., and J. E. Snead

1997 It's a Small World After All: Comparative Analyses of Community Organization in Archaeology. *American Antiquity* 62:609–628.

Kopytoff, I.

1986 The Cultural Biography of Things: Commodization as a Process. In *The Social Life of Things*, edited by A. Appadurai, pp. 64–91. Cambridge University Press, Cambridge.

Kosso, P.

1991 Method in Archaeology: Middle-Range Theory as Hermeneutics. *American Antiquity* 56:621–627.

Kramer, C.

1979 (ed.) *Ethnoarchaeology: Implications of Ethnography for Archaeology.* Columbia University Press, New York.

Kristiansen, K.

1991 Chiefdoms, States, and Systems of

Social Evolution. In *Chiefdoms: Power, Economy, and Ideology*, edited by T. Earle, pp. 16–43. Cambridge University Press, Cambridge.

Kroeber, A. L.

1916   Zuñi Potsherds. *American Museum of Natural History, Anthropological Papers* 18(1):1–37.

1931   Historical Reconstruction of Culture Growths and Organic Evolution. *American Anthropologist* 33:149–156.

1939   *Cultural and Natural Areas of Native North America.* University of California Publications in American Archaeology and Ethnology, vol. 38. Berkeley.

1948   *Anthropology.* Revised ed. Harcourt Brace, New York.

Kuhn, T. S.

1970   *The Structure of Scientific Revolutions.* University of Chicago Press, Chicago.

1977   *The Essential Tension: Selected Studies in Scientific Tradition and Change.* University of Chicago Press, Chicago.

1986   Objectivity, Value Judgment and Theory Choice. In *Critical Theory Since 1965*, edited by H. Adams and L. Searle, pp. 381–393. University of Florida Press, Tallahassee.

Kus, S. M., and V. Raharijaona

1990   Domestic Space and the Tenacity of Tradition among Some Betsileo of Madagascar. In *Domestic Architecture and the Use of Space: A Multidisciplinary Approach*, edited by S. Kent, pp. 21–33. Cambridge University Press, Cambridge.

Kuznar, L. A.

1995   *Reclaiming a Scientific Anthropology.* Altamira Press, Walnut Creek, California.

Laporte, L. F.

2000   *George Gaylord Simpson.* Columbia University Press, New York.

Larson, D.

2000   On the Extrapolationist Bias of Evolutionary Archaeology. *Current Anthropology* 41:840–841.

Latour, B.

1987   *Science in Action: How to Follow Scientists and Engineers Through Society.* Harvard University Press, Cambridge, Massachusetts.

Layton, R.

1989   (ed.) *Conflict in the Archaeology of Living Traditions.* Unwin Hyman, London.

Lears, T.J.J.

1985   The Concept of Cultural Hegemony: Problems and Possibilities. *American Historical Review* 90:567–593.

Lechtman, H.

1977   Style in Technology: Some Early Thoughts. In *Material Culture: Styles, Organization and Dynamics of Technology*, edited by H. Lechtman and R. Merril, pp. 3–20. West Publishers, St. Paul, Minnesota.

1984   Andean Value Systems and the Development of Prehistoric Metallurgy. *Technology and Culture* 25:1–36.

Lehmann, G. R.

1982   *The Jaketown Site: Surface Collections from a Poverty Point Regional Center in the Yazoo Basin, Mississippi.* Archaeological Report No. 9. Mississippi Department of Archives and History, Jackson.

Lekson, S. H.

1988   The Idea of the Kiva in Anasazi Archaeology. *The Kiva* 53:213–234.

1999   *The Chaco Meridian: Centers of Political Power in the Ancient Southwest.* Altamira, Walnut Creek, California.

Lekson, S. H., T. C. Windes, J. R. Stein, and W. J. Judge

1988   The Chaco Canyon Community. *Scientific American* 259:100–109.

Lemonnier, P.

1986   A Study of Material Culture Today: Toward an Anthropology of Technical Systems. *Journal of Anthropological Archaeology* 5:147–168.

1989   Bark Capes, Arrowheads and Concorde: On Social Representations of Technology. In *The Meanings of Things: Material Culture and Symbolic Expression*, edited by I. Hodder, pp. 156–171. Unwin Hyman, London.

Leonard, R. D.

1989   Resource Specialization, Population

Growth, and Agricultural Production in the American Southwest. *American Antiquity* 54:491–503.

1993   The Persistence of an Explanatory Dilemma in Contact Period Studies. In *Perspectives on Change: Ethnohistorical and Archaeological Approaches to Culture Contact,* edited by J. D. Rogers and S. M. Wilson, pp. 31–43. Plenum Press, New York.

2001   Evolutionary Archaeology. In *Archaeological Theory Today: Breaking the Boundaries,* edited by I. Hodder, pp. 65–97. Polity Press, Cambridge.

Leonard, R. D., and G. T. Jones

1987   Elements of an Inclusive Evolutionary Model for Archaeology. *Journal of Anthropological Archaeology* 6:199–219.

Leonard, R. D., and H. E. Reed

1993   Population Aggregation in the Prehistoric American Southwest: A Selectionist Model. *American Antiquity* 58:648–661.

1996   Theory, Models, Explanation, and the Record: Response to Kohler and Sebastian. *American Antiquity* 61:603–608.

Leone, M., and G.-M. Fry

1999   Conjuring in the Big House Kitchen: An Interpretation of African American Belief Systems, Based on the Uses of Archaeology and Folklore Sources. *Journal of American Folklore* 112:445:372–403.

Leone, M., G.-M. Fry, and T. Ruppel

2001   Spirit Management among Americans of African Descent. In *Race and the Archaeology of Identity,* edited by C. Orser, pp. 143–157. University of Utah Press, Salt Lake City.

Lévi-Strauss, C.

1968   *Structural Anthropology.* Allen Lane, London.

Levy, T. E.

1993   Production, Space, and Social Change in Protohistoric Palestine. In *Spatial Boundaries and Social Dynamics: Case Studies from Food-Producing Societies,* edited by A. Holl and T. E. Levy, pp. 63–81. Ethnoarchaeological Series No. 2. International Monographs in Prehistory, Ann Arbor.

Lewontin, R. C.

1970   The Units of Selection. *Annual Review of Ecology and Systematics* 11:1–18.

1974   *The Genetic Basis of Evolutionary Change.* Columbia University Press, New York.

1977   *Sociobiology: A Caricature of Darwinism.* Proceedings of the 1976 Biennial Meeting of the Philosophy of Science Association, vol. 2, edited by F. Suppe and P. D. Asquith, pp. 22–31. Philosophy of Science Association, East Lansing, Michigan.

Lightfoot, K. G., A. Martinez, and A. M. Schiff

1998   Daily Practice and Material Culture in Pluralistic Social Settings: An Archaeological Study of Culture Change and Persistence from Fort Ross, California. *American Antiquity* 63:199–222.

Lindenbaum, S.

1979   *Kuru Socery: Disease and Danger in the New Guinea Highlands.* Mayfield Publishing Company.

Lipo, C. P.

2001   *Science, Style and the Study of Community Structure: An Example from the Central Mississippi River Valley.* British Archaeological Reports, International Series, no 918. Oxford.

Lipo, C. P., and M. E. Madsen

1999   Neutrality. Paper presented at the 64th annual meeting of the Society for American Archaeology, Chicago.

2001   Neutrality, "Style," and Drift: Building Methods for Studying Cultural Transmission in the Archaeological Record. In *Style and Function in Archaeology,* edited by T. D. Hurt and G.F.M. Rakita, pp. 91–118. Bergin and Garvey, Westport, Connecticut.

Lipo, C. P., M. E. Madsen, R. C. Dunnell, and T. Hunt

1997   Population Structure, Cultural Transmission, and Frequency Seriation. *Journal of Anthropological Archaeology* 16:301–334.

Lomaomvaya, M., and T. J. Ferguson

1999   Hisatqatsit Aw Maamatslalwa— Comprehending Our Past Lifeways:

Thoughts About a Hopi Archaeology. Paper presented at the 1999 Chacmool Conference, Indigenous People and Archaeology, Calgary.

Lomnitz-Adler, C.
1991   Concepts for the Study of Regional Culture. *American Ethnologist* 18: 195–233.

Longacre, W. A.
1964   Archaeology as Anthropology: A Case Study. *Science* 144:1454–1455.

1970   *Archaeology as Anthropology: A Case Study.* University of Arizona Anthropological Papers 17. University of Arizona Press, Tucson.

1999   Review of "The Rise and Fall of Culture History" and "Americanist Culture History: Fundamentals of Time, Space, and Form" by R. L. Lyman, M. J. O'Brien, and R. C. Dunnell. *American Anthropologist* 100:794–795.

Longacre, W. A., and J. Ayres
1968   Archaeological Lessons from an Apache Wickiup. In *New Perspectives in Archaeology,* edited by S. R. Binford and L. R. Binford, pp. 151–159. Aldine, Chicago.

Longacre, W. A., and J. M. Skibo
1994a   Preface. In *Kalinga Ethnoarchaeology: Expanding Archaeological Method and Theory,* edited by W. A. Longacre and J. M. Skibo, pp. xiii–xvi. Smithsonian Institution, Washington, D.C.

Longacre, W. A., and J. M. Skibo
1994b   (eds.) *Kalinga Ethnoarchaeology: Expanding Archaeological Method and Theory.* Smithsonian Institution, Washington, D.C.

Longino, H. E.
2002   *The Fate of Knowledge.* Princeton University Press, Oxford.

Lorde, A.
1984   The Master's Tools Will Never Dismantle the Master's House. In *Sister Outsider,* by A. Lorde, pp. 110–113. Crossing Press, Freedom, California.

Loren, D. D.
2001   Manipulating Bodies and Emerging Traditions at the Los Adaes Presidio. In *The Archaeology of Traditions: History and Agency before and after*

Columbus, edited by T. R. Pauketat, pp. 58–76. University Press of Florida, Gainesville.

Ludlow Collective
2001   Archaeology of the Colorado Coal Field War, 1913–1914. In *Archaeologies of the Contemporary Past,* edited by V. Buchli and G. Lucas, pp. 94–107. Routledge Press, London.

Lyman, R. L.
2001   Culture Historical and Biological Approaches to Identifying Homologous Traits. In *Style and Function in Archaeology,* edited by T. D. Hurt and G.F.M. Rakita, pp. 69–89. Bergin and Garvey, Westport, Connecticut.

Lyman, R. L., and M. J. O'Brien
1997   The Concept of Evolution in Early Twentieth-Century Americanist Archaeology. In *Rediscovering Darwin: Evolutionary Theory in Archeological Explanation,* edited by C. M. Barton and G. A. Clark, pp. 21–48. Archeological Papers, no. 7, American Anthropological Association, Washington, D.C.

1998   The Goals of Evolutionary Archaeology: History and Explanation. *Current Anthropology* 39:615–652.

1999   Classification, Systematics, Typology: The Critical Step in Evolutionary Archaeology. Paper presented at the 64th annual meeting of the Society for American Archaeology, Chicago.

2000a   Chronometers and Units in Early Archaeology and Paleontology. *American Antiquity* 65:691–707.

2000b   Measuring and Explaining Change in Artifact Variation with Clade-Diversity Diagrams. *Journal of Anthropological Archaeology* 19: 39–74.

2001a   On Misconceptions of Evolutionary Archaeology: Confusing Macroevolution and Microevolution. *Current Anthropology* 42:408–409.

2001b   The Direct Historical Approach, Analogical Reasoning and Theory in Americanist Archaeology. *Journal of Archaeological Method and Theory* 8:303–342.

2002   *W. C. McKern and the Midwestern*

Taxonomic Method. University of Alabama Press, Tuscaloosa.

Lyman, R. L., M. J. O'Brien, and R. C. Dunnell
1997   *The Rise and Fall of Culture History.* Plenum Press, New York.

Lyman, R. L., S. Wolverton, and M. J. O'Brien
1998   Seriation, Superposition, and Interdigitation: A History of Americanist Graphic Depictions of Culture Change. *American Antiquity* 63: 239–261.

Mace, R., and M. Pagel
1994   The Comparative Method in Anthropology. *Current Anthropology* 35:549–564.

Mach, Z.
1993   *Symbols, Conflict, and Identity: Essays in Political Anthropology.* State University of New York Press, Albany.

MacWilliams, A. C.
2001   Beyond the Reach of Casas Grandes: Archaeology in Central Chihuahua. In *From Paquimé to Mata Ortiz: The Legacy of Ancient Casas Grandes,* edited by G. Johnson, pp. 55–64. San Diego Museum of Man, San Diego, California.

Madison, J., A. Hamilton, and J. Jay
1987   *The Federalist Papers.* Penguin edition, edited by Isaac Kramnick. Harmondsworth, Middlesex, England.

Madsen, M., C. Lipo, and M. Cannon
1999   Fitness and Reproductive Trade-offs in Uncertain Environments: Explaining the Evolution of Cultural Elaboration. *Journal of Anthropological Archaeology* 18:251–281.

Mahoney, N. M.
2000   Redefining the Scale of Chacoan Communities. In *Great House Communities across the Chacoan Landscape,* edited by J. Kantner and N. Mahoney, pp. 19–27. Anthropological Series, University of Arizona Press, Tucson.

Malinowski, B.
1944   *A Scientific Theory of Culture.* University of North Carolina Press, Chapel Hill.

Marcus, G. E., and M.M.J. Fisher
1986   *Anthropology as Cultural Critique: An Experimental Moment in the Human Sciences.* University of Chicago Press, Chicago.

Martin, P. S.
1971   The Revolution in Archaeology. *American Antiquity* 36:1–8.

Marx, K., and F. Engels
1989   *The German Ideology,* Part I. International Publishers, New York.

Maschner, H.D.G.
1998   Review of "Evolutionary Archaeology: Theory and Application" edited by M. J. O'Brien. *Journal of the Royal Anthropological Institute* 4:354–355.

Maschner, H.D.G., and S. Mithen
1996   Darwinian Archaeologies: An Introductory Essay. In *Darwinian Archaeologies,* edited by H.D.G. Maschner, pp. 3–16. Plenum Press, New York.

Mascie-Taylor, C.G.N., and A. J. Boyce
1988   (eds.) *Human Mating Patterns.* Society for the Study of Human Biology Symposium Series 28. Cambridge University Press, Cambridge.

Mason, R.
2000   Archaeology and Native North American Oral Traditions. *American Antiquity* 65:239–266.

Mathien, F. J.
2001   The Organization of Turquoise Production and Consumption by the Prehistoric Chacoans. *American Antiquity* 66:103–118.

Matthews, W., C. French, T. Lawrence, and D. Cutler
1996   Multiple Surfaces: the Micromorphology. In *On the Surface: Catalhoyuk 1993–95,* edited by I. Hodder. McDonald Institute for Archaeological Research, Cambridge, England, and British Institute of Archaeology in Turkey, Ankara.

Maxwell, T. D.
1995   The Use of Comparative and Engineering Analyses in the Study of Prehistoric Agriculture. In *Evolutionary Archaeology: Methodological Issues,* edited by P. A. Teltser, pp. 113–128.

2000   Looking for Adaptation: A Comparative and Engineering Analysis of Prehistoric Agricultural

Technologies in the Southwest. Ph.D. dissertation, Department of Anthropology, University of New Mexico, Albuquerque.

Mayer, E.
1988   *Towards a New Philosophy of Biology: Observations of an Evolutionist.* Harvard University Press, Cambridge, Massachusetts.
1996   The Modern Evolutionary Theory. *Journal of Mammalogy* 77:1–7.
1997   *This is Biology: The Science of the Living World.* Harvard University Press, Cambridge.

Maynard Smith, J.
1988   *Games, Sex and Evolution.* Harvester-Wheatsheaf, New York.

Mayr, E.
1942   *Systematics and the Origin of Species.* Columbia University Press, New York.

Mayr, E., and W. B. Provine
1980   (eds.) *The Evolutionary Synthesis: Perspectives on the Unification of Biology.* Harvard University Press, Cambridge, Massachusetts.

McCall, J.
1999   Structure, Agency, and the Locus of the Social: Why Post-Structural Theory is Good for Archaeology. In *Material Symbols: Culture and Economy in Prehistory,* edited by J. E. Robb, pp. 16–21. Center for Archaeological Investigations, Southern Illinois University, Carbondale, Illinois.

McGimsey, C. R.
1995   Lamellar Flakes and the Illinois Middle Woodland: Diversity, Evolution, and Inheritance. Ph.D. dissertation, Department of Anthropology, Southern Illinois University, Carbondale.

McGuire, R.
1992a   *A Marxist Archaeology.* Academic Press, New York.
1992b   *Death, Society, and Ideology in Hohokam Community.* Westview Press, Boulder, Colorado.
1993   Archaeology and Marxism. In *Archaeological Method and Theory,* vol. 5, edited by M. B. Schiffer, pp. 101–157. University of Arizona Press, Tucson.

McGuire, R., and M. Walker
1999   Class Confrontations in Archaeology. *Historical Archaeology* 33:159–183.

McIntosh, R. J.
1992   From Traditional African Art to the Archaeology of Form in the Middle Niger. In *Dall' Archeologia all'Arte Traditinale Africana,* edited by G. Pezzoli, pp. 145–151. Centro Studi Archeologia Africana, Milan.

Melton, J. G.
1996   *Encyclopedia of American Religions.* 5th ed. Gale, Detroit.

Meltzer, D. J.
1979   Paradigms and the Nature of Change in American Archaeology. *American Antiquity* 44:644–657.
1981   A Study of Style and Function in a Class of Tools. *Journal of Field Archaeology* 8:313–326.

Meltzer, D. J., D. Fowler, and J. Sabloff
1986   (eds.) *American Archaeology: Past and Future.* Smithsonian Institution Press, Washington, D.C.

Menand, L.
1997   An Introduction to Pragmatism. In *Pragmatism,* edited by L. Menand, pp. xi–xxxiv. Vintage, New York.

Merbs, C. F., and R. J. Miller
1985   (eds.) *Health and Disease in the Prehistoric Southwest.* Anthropological Research Papers No. 34. Arizona State University, Tempe.

Miller, D.
1985   *Artifacts as Categories: A Study of Ceramic Variability in Central India.* Cambridge University Press, Cambridge.

Miller, D., M. Rowlands, and C. Tilley
1989   (eds.) *Domination and Resistance.* Unwin Hyman, London.

Milner, G. R.
1998   *The Cahokia Chiefdom: The Archaeology of a Mississippian Society.* Smithsonian Institution Press, Washington, D.C.

Minnegal, M.
1996   A Necessary Unity: The Articulation of Ecological and Social Explanations of Behaviour. *Journal of the Royal Anthropological Institute* (n.s.) 2:141–158.

Minnis, P.

1988   Four Examples of Specialized Pro-
        duction at Casas Grandes, North-
        western Chihuahua. *The Kiva* 53:
        181–193.

Mithen, S.

1989   Evolutionary Theory and Post-
        Processual Archaeology. *Antiquity*
        63:483–494.

1996   *The Prehistory of the Mind: The
        Cognitive Origins of Art and
        Science.* Thames and Hudson,
        London.

Modjeska, N.

1982   Production and Inequality: Perspec-
        tives from Central New Guinea. In
        *Inequality in New Guinea High-
        lands Societies,* edited by A. Strath-
        ern, pp. 50–108. Cambridge Univer-
        sity Press, Cambridge.

1991   Post-Ipomoean Modernism: The
        Duna Example. In *Big Men and
        Great Men: Personification of
        Power in Melanesia,* edited by
        M. Godelier and M. Strathern,
        pp. 234–255. Cambridge University
        Press, Cambridge.

Moore, H. L.

1982   The Interpretation of Spatial Pat-
        terning in Settlement Residues. In
        *Symbolic and Structural Archaeol-
        ogy,* edited by I. Hodder, pp. 74–49.
        Cambridge University Press, Cam-
        bridge.

Moore, J. A.

1983   The Trouble with Know-It-Alls: In-
        formation as a Social and Ecological
        Resource. In *Archaeological Ham-
        mers and Theories,* edited by J. A.
        Moore and A. Keene, pp. 173–191.
        Academic Press, New York.

Moore, J. H.

1994a   Ethnogenetic Theories of Human
        Evolution. *Research and Explo-
        ration* 10:10–23.

1994b   Putting Anthropology Back To-
        gether Again: The Ethnogenetic Cri-
        tique of Cladistic Theory. *American
        Anthropologist* 96:925–948.

Morris, C.

1995   Symbols to Power: Style and Media
        in the Inka State. In *Style, Society
        and Person: Archaeological and
        Ethnological Perspectives,* edited

by C. Carr and J. E. Neitzel, pp.
419–433. Plenum, New York.

Murdock, G. P.

1967   Ethnographic Atlas: A Summary.
        Ethnology 6:108–236.

Murdock, G. P., and C. Provost

1973   Factors in the Division of Labor
        by Sex: A Cross-Cultural Analysis.
        Ethnology 12:202–225.

Murphy, C., and N. Ferris

1990   The Late Woodland Western Basin
        Tradition in Southwestern Ontario.
        In *The Archaeology of Southern
        Ontario to A.D. 1650,* edited by
        C. J. Ellis and N. Ferris, pp. 189–
        290. Occasional Publications of the
        London Chapter, Ontario Archaeo-
        logical Society No. 5.

Myerhoff, B. G.

1976   Shamanic Equilibrium: Balance and
        Mediation in Known and Unknown
        Worlds. In *American Folk Medicine,
        a Symposium,* edited by W. D.
        Hand, pp. 99–108. University of
        California Press, Berkeley.

Nag, Moni

1968   *Factors Affecting Human Fertility in
        Nonindustrial Societies: A Cross-
        Cultural Study.* Human Relations
        Area Files Press, New Haven, Con-
        necticut.

Narancic, N. S., and I. Rudan

2001   Endogamy and Blood Pressure Lev-
        els in Croatian Island Isolates. *Jour-
        nal of Physiological Anthropology
        and Applied Human Science* 20(2):
        85–94.

Naranjo, T.

1996   Thoughts on Migration by Santa
        Clara Pueblo. *Journal of Anthropo-
        logical Archaeology* 14:247–250.

Neff, H.

1992   Ceramics and Evolution. *Archaeo-
        logical Method and Theory* 4:141–
        193.

1999   Populations. Paper presented at the
        64th annual meeting of the Society
        for American Archaeology, Chicago.

2000   On Evolutionary Ecology and Evo-
        lutionary Archaeology: Some Com-
        mon Ground? *Current Anthropol-
        ogy* 41:427–429.

2001   Differential Persistence of What?
        The Scale of Selection Issue in

Evolutionary Archaeology. In *Style and Function in Archaeology*, edited by T. D. Hurt and G.F.M. Rakita, pp. 25–40. Bergin and Garvey, Westport, Connecticut.

Neff, H., and D. O. Larson
1997   Methodology of Comparison in Evolutionary Archaeology. In *Rediscovering Darwin: Evolutionary Theory and Archeological Explanation*, edited by C. M. Barton and G. A. Clark, pp. 75–94. Archeological Papers, no. 7, American Anthropological Association, Washington, D.C.

Neff, H., D. O. Larson, and M. D. Glascock
1997   The Evolution of Anasazi Ceramic Production and Distribution: Compositional Evidence from a Pueblo III Site in South-Central Utah. *Journal of Field Archaeology* 24:473–492.

Neiman, F. D.
1995   Stylistic Variation in Evolutionary Perspective: Implications for Middle Woodland Ceramic Diversity. *American Antiquity* 60:7–36.

Neitzel, J. E.
1989   Regional Exchange Networks in the American Southwest: A Comparative Analysis of Long-Distance Trade. In *The Sociopolitical Structure of Prehistoric Southwestern Societies*, edited by S. Upham, K. G. Lightfoot, and R. A. Jewett, pp. 509–556. Westview Press, Boulder, Colorado.
1995   Elite Styles in Hierarchically Organized Societies: The Chacoan Regional System. In *Style, Society and Person: Archaeological and Ethnological Perspectives*, edited by C. Carr and J. E. Neitzel, pp. 393–417. Plenum, New York.

Nelsen, K., N. Tayles, and K. Domett
2001   Missing Lateral Incisors in Iron Age South-East Asians as Possible Indicators of Dental Agenesis. *Archives of Oral Biology* 46(10):963–971.

Nettle, D.
1997   On the Status of Methodological Individualism. *Current Anthropology* 38:283–286.

Nichols, J.
1996   The Comparative Method as Heuristic. In *The Comparative Method Reviewed: Regularity and Irregularity in Language Change*, edited by M. Durie and M. Ross, pp. 39–71. Oxford University Press, New York.

O'Brien, M. J.
1987   Sedentism, Population Growth, and Resource Selection in the Woodland Midwest: A Review of Coevolutionary Developments. *Current Anthropology* 28:177–197.
1996a   (ed.) *Evolutionary Archaeology: Theory and Application*. University of Utah Press, Salt Lake City.
1996b   The Historical Development of an Evolutionary Archaeology. In *Darwinian Archaeologies*, edited by H.D.G. Maschner, pp. 17–32. Plenum, New York.

O'Brien, M. J., J. Darwent, and R. L. Lyman
2001   Cladistics Is Useful for Reconstructing Archaeological Phylogenies: Paleoindian Points from the Southeastern United States. *Journal of Archaeological Science* 28:1115–1136.

O'Brien, M. J., and T. D. Holland
1990   Variation, Selection, and the Archaeological Record. In *Archaeological Method and Theory*, vol. 2, edited by M. B. Schiffer, pp. 31–79. University of Arizona Press, Tucson.
1992   The Role of Adaptation in Archaeological Explanation. *American Antiquity* 57:3–59.
1995a   The Nature and Premise of a Selection-based Archaeology. In *Evolutionary Archaeology: Methodological Issues*, edited by P. A. Teltser, pp. 175–200. University of Arizona Press, Tucson.
1995b   Behavioral Archaeology and the Extended Phenotype. In *Expanding Archaeology*, edited by J. M. Skibo, W. H. Walker, and A. E. Nielsen, pp. 143–161. University of Utah Press, Salt Lake City.

O'Brien, M. J., T. D. Holland, R. J. Hoard, and G. L. Fox
1994   Evolutionary Implications of Design

and Performance Characteristics of
Prehistoric Pottery. *Journal of Archaeological Method and Theory*
1:259–304.

O'Brien, M. J., and R. D. Leonard
2001   Style and Function: An Introduction.
        In *Style and Function in Archaeol-
        ogy*, edited by T. D. Hurt and G.F.M.
        Rakita, pp. 1–23. Bergin and Gar-
        vey, Westport, Connecticut.

O'Brien, M. J., and R. L. Lyman
1998   *James A. Ford and the Growth of
        Americanist Archaeology.* University
        of Missouri Press, Columbia.
1999a   Meeting Theoretical and Method-
        ological Challenges to the Future of
        Evolutionary Archaeology. *Review
        of Archaeology* 20(2):14–22.
1999b   *Seriation, Stratigraphy, and Index
        Fossils: The Backbone of Archaeo-
        logical Dating.* Kluwer
        Academic/Plenum, New York.
2000a   Evolutionary Archaeology: Recon-
        structing and Explaining Historical
        Lineages. In *Social Theory in Ar-
        chaeology*, edited by M. B. Schiffer,
        pp. 126–142. University of Utah
        Press, Salt Lake City.
2000b   *Applying Evolutionary Archaeol-
        ogy: A Systematic Approach.*
        Kluwer/Plenum, New York.
2002a   The Epistemological Nature of Ar-
        chaeological Units. *Anthropological
        Theory* 2:37–57.
2002b   Evolutionary Archaeology: Current
        Status and Future Prospects. *Evolu-
        tionary Anthropology* 11:26–36.

O'Brien, M. J., R. L. Lyman, and
R. D. Leonard
1998   Basic Incompatibilities between Evo-
        lutionary and Behavioral Archaeol-
        ogy. *American Antiquity* 63:485–
        498.

O'Brien, M. B., and H. C. Wilson
1988   A Paradigmatic Shift in the Search
        for the Origin of Agriculture. *Ameri-
        can Anthropologist* 90:958–965.

Palkovich, A. M.
1984   Agriculture, Marginal Environ-
        ments, and Nutritional Stress in the
        Prehistoric Southwest. In *Paleo-
        pathology at the Origins of Agricul-
        ture*, edited by M. N. Cohen and
G. J. Armelagos, pp. 425–438.
Academic Press, Orlando.

Palmer, C. T., B. E. Fredrickson, and C. F. Tilley
1995   On Cultural Group Selection. *Cur-
        rent Anthropology* 36(4):657–658.

Pauketat, T. R.
1993   *Temples for Cahokia Lords: Preston
        Holder's 1955–1956 Excavations of
        Kunnemann Mound.* University of
        Michigan, Museum of Anthropol-
        ogy Memoir 26. Ann Arbor.
1994   *The Ascent of Chiefs: Cahokia and
        Mississippian Politics in Native
        North America.* University of Al-
        abama Press, Tuscaloosa.
1996   The Place of Post-Circle Monuments
        in Cahokian Political History. *The
        Wisconsin Archeologist* 77:72–82.
1997a   Cahokian Political Economy. In *Ca-
        hokia: Domination and Ideology in
        the Mississippian World*, edited by
        T. R. Pauketat and T. E. Emerson,
        pp. 30–51. University of Nebraska
        Press, Lincoln.
1997b   Specialization, Political Symbols,
        and the Crafty Elite of Cahokia.
        Southeastern Archaeology 16:1–15.
1998   Refiguring the Archaeology of
        Greater Cahokia. *Journal of Archae-
        ological Research* 6:45–89.
2000a   Practice and History in Archaeol-
        ogy: An Emerging Paradigm. *An-
        thropological Theory* 1:73–98.
2000b   The Tragedy of the Commoners. In
        Agency in Archaeology, edited by
        M.-A. Dobres and J. Robb, pp. 130–
        147. Routledge, New York.
2001a   A New Tradition in Archaeology.
        In *The Archaeology of Traditions:
        Agency and History before and after
        Columbus*, edited by T. R. Pauketat,
        pp. 1–16. University Press of
        Florida, Gainesville.
2001b   Practice and History in Archaeol-
        ogy: An Emerging Paradigm. *An-
        thropological Theory* 1:73–98.
2001c   (ed.) *The Archaeology of Traditions:
        Agency and History before and after
        Columbus.* University Press of
        Florida, Gainesville.
2003   Resettled Farmers and the Making
        of a Mississippian Polity. *American
        Antiquity* 68:39–66.

Pauketat, T. R., and T. E. Emerson
1997   Introduction: Domination and Ideology in the Mississippian World. In *Cahokia: Domination and Ideology in the Mississippian World,* edited by T. R. Pauketat and T. E. Emerson, pp. 30–51. University of Nebraska Press, Lincoln.

1999   The Representation of Hegemony as Community at Cahokia. In *Material Symbols: Culture and Economy in Prehistory,* edited by J. Robb, pp. 302–317. Occasional Paper No. 26. Southern Illinois University, Carbondale.

Pauketat, T. R., L. S. Kelly, G. Fritz, N. H. Lopinot, S. Elias, and E. Hargrave
2002   The Residues of Feasting and Public Ritual at Early Cahokia. *American Antiquity* 67:257–279.

Paynter, R., and R. H. McGuire
1991   The Archaeology of Inequality: Material Culture, Domination, and Resistance. In *The Archaeology of Inequality,* edited by R. H. McGuire and R. Paynter, pp. 1–27. Blackwell, Oxford.

Pepper, J. W., and B. B. Smuts
2000   The Evolution of Cooperation in an Ecological Context: An Agent-Based Model. In *Dynamics in Human and Primate Societies,* edited by T. Kohler and G. Gumerman, pp. 45–76. Oxford University Press, New York.

Perino, G.
1973   The Damiansville Site, Clinton County, Illinois. *Central States Archaeological Journal,* October: 164–165.

Pfaffenberger, B.
1992   Social Anthropology of Technology. *Annual Review of Anthropology* 21:491–516.

Pfeffer, M. T.
2001   Implications of New Studies of Hawaiian Fishhook Variability for Our Understanding of Polynesian Settlement History. In *Style and Function in Archaeology,* edited by T. D. Hurt and G.F.M. Rakita, pp. 165–181. Bergin and Garvey, Westport, Connecticut.

Phillips, D. A., Jr.
1989   Prehistory of Chihuahua and Sonora, Mexico. *Journal of World Prehistory* 3:373–401.

Phillips, P.
1955   American Archaeology and General Anthropological Theory. *Southwestern Journal of Anthropology* 11: 246–250.

Platnick, N. I., and D. Cameron
1977   Cladistic Methods in Textual, Linguistic, and Phylogenetic Analysis. *Systematic Zoology* 26:380–385.

Plog, F. T.
1974   *The Study of Prehistoric Change.* Academic Press, New York.

Plog, S.
1976   Measurement of Prehistoric Interaction between Communities. In *The Early Mesoamerican Village,* edited by K. V. Flannery, pp. 255–272. Academic Press, New York.

1978   Social Interaction and Stylistic Similarity: A Reanalysis. *Advances in Archaeological Method and Theory,* vol. 5, edited by M. B. Schiffer, pp. 143–152. Academic Press, New York.

1980   Village Autonomy in the American Southwest: An Evaluation of the Evidence. In *Models and Methods in Regional Exchange,* edited by R. E. Fry, pp. 135–146. SAA Papers No. 1. Society for American Archaeology, Washington, D.C.

1983   Analysis of Style in Artifacts. *Annual Review of Anthropology* 12:125–142.

1997   *Ancient Peoples of the American Southwest.* Thames and Hudson, London.

Posner, R.
1990   A Pragmatist Manifesto. In *The Problems of Jurisprudence,* by R. Posner, pp. 454–469. Harvard University Press, Cambridge.

Powell, S.
1988   Anasazi Demographic Patterns and Organizational Responses: Assumptions and Interpretive Difficulties. In *The Anasazi in a Changing Environment,* edited by G. J. Gumerman, pp. 168–191. School of American

Research Press, Santa Fe, New Mexico.

Preston, D.
1997   The Lost Man. *The New Yorker,* June 16.

Preucel, R. W.
1995   The Post-Processual Condition. *Journal of Archaeological Research* 3:147–175.
1999   Review of "Evolutionary Archaeology: Theory and Application" by M. J. O'Brien. *Journal of Field Archaeology* 26:93–99.

Preucel, R. W., and I. Hodder
1996   *Contemporary Archaeology in Theory: A Reader.* Blackwell Publishers, Cambridge, Massachusetts.

Price, P. W.
1996   *Biological Evolution.* Sanders College Publishing, Fort Worth, Texas.

Raab, L. M., and A. C. Goodyear
1984   Middle-Range Theory in Archaeology: A Critical Review of Origins and Applications. *American Antiquity* 49:255–268.

Rakita, G.F.M.
2001   Social Complexity, Religious Organization, and Mortuary Ritual in the Casas Grandes Region of Chihuahua, Mexico. Unpublished Ph.D. disseration, Department of Anthropology, University of New Mexico, Albuquerque.

Ramenofsky, A. F.
1987   *Vectors of Death: The Archaeology of European Contact.* University of New Mexico Press, Albuquerque.
1995   Evolutionary Theory and Native American Artifact Change in the Postcontact Period. In *Evolutionary Archaeology: Methodological Issues,* edited by P. A. Teltser, pp. 129–148. University of Arizona Press, Tucson.

Ramenofsky, A. F., and A. Steffen
1998   (eds.) *Unit Issues in Archaeology: Measuring Time, Space, and Material.* University of Utah Press, Salt Lake City.

Rappaport, R. A.
1979   *Ecology, Meaning, and Religion.* North Atlantic Books, Berkeley, California.

Rautman, Alison E.
1996   Risk, Reciprocity, and the Operation of Social Networks. In *Evolving Complexity and Environmental Risk in the Prehistoric Southwest,* edited by J. A. Tainter and B. Bagley Tainter, pp. 197–222. Santa Fe Institute Studies in the Sciences of Complexity Proceedings No. 24. Addison-Wesley Publishing, Reading, Pennsylvania.

Ravesloot, J. C.
1988   *Mortuary Practices and Social Differentiation at Casas Grandes, Chihuahua, Mexico.* Anthropological Papers of the University of Arizona, No. 49, University of Arizona Press, Tucson.

Reed, E. K.
1962   Human Skeletal Material from Site 59, Chaco Canyon National Monument. *El Palacio* winter:240–247.
1967   Variations of the Spine in Human Skeletal Material from Southwestern Archaeological Collections. In *Miscellaneous Papers in Paleopathology,* edited by W. D. Wade, pp. 30–39. Technical Series No. 7. University of Northern Arizona, Flagstaff.

Reid, J., and S. Whittlesey
1999   A Search for the Philosophical Julian: American Pragmatism and Southwestern Archaeology. *Kiva* 64:275–286.

Renfrew, C.
1987   Introduction: Peer Polity Inter action and Socio-Political Change. In *Peer Polity Interaction and Socio-Political Change,* edited by C. Renfrew and J. F. Cherry, pp. 1–18. Cambridge University Press, Cambridge.
1992   Archaeology, Genetics and Linguistic Diversity. *Man* (n.s.) 27:445–478.

Richerson, P. J., and R. Boyd
1992   Cultural Inheritance and Evolutionary Ecology. In *Evolutionary Ecology and Human Behavior,* edited by E. A. Smith and B. Winterhalder, pp. 61–94. Aldine de Gruyter, New York.

Rindos, D.
1989a   Symbiosis, Instability, and the

Origins and Spread of Agriculture: A New Model. *Current Anthropology* 21:751–772.

1989b   Darwinism and its Role in the Explanation of Domestication. In *Foraging and Farming: The Evolution of Plant Exploitation*, edited by D. R. Harris and G. C. Hillman, pp. 27–41. Unwin Hyman, Ltd., London.

1989c   Undirected Variation and the Darwinian Explanation of Cultural Change. In *Archaeological Method and Theory*, vol. 1, edited by M. B. Schiffer, pp. 1–45. University of Arizona Press, Tucson.

Robb, J. E.
1998   The Archaeology of Symbols. *Annual Review of Anthropology* 27:329–346.

1999   Secret Agents: Culture, Economy, and Social Reproduction. In *Material Symbols: Culture and Economy in Prehistory*, edited by J. E. Robb, pp. 3–15. Southern Illinois University, Occasional Paper No. 26, Carbondale.

Roe, D.
1984   Advancing the Study of Early Man in East Africa. *Quarterly Review of Archaeology* 5:3–4.

Rorty, R.
1989   Science as Solidarity. In *Dismantling Truth: Reality in the Postmodern World*, edited by H. Lawson and L. Appignanesi, pp. 6–23. St. Martin's Press, New York.

1998   *Achieving Our Country: Leftist Thought in Twentieth Century America*. Harvard University Press, Cambridge.

Roscoe, P. B.
1993   Practice and Political Centralisation. *Current Anthropology* 34(2):111–140.

Rosenberg, S. M.
2001   Evolving Responsively: Adaptive Mutation. *Nature Reviews Genetics* 2:504–515.

Ross, M.
1997   Comment on "The Dimensions of Social Life in the Pacific: Human Diversity and the Myth of the Primitive Isolate" by J. E. Terrell, T. L. Hunt,

and C. Gosden. *Current Anthropology* 38:182–184.

Sackett, J. R.
1973   Style, Function and Artifact Variability in Palaeolithic Assemblages. In *The Explanation of Culture Change: Models in Prehistory*, edited by Colin Renfrew. pp. 317–325. Duckworth, London.

1977   The Meaning of Style in Archaeology: A General Model. *American Antiquity* 42(3):369–380.

1982   Approaches to Style in Lithic Archaeology. *Journal of Anthropological Archaeology* 1:59–112.

1985a   Style and Ethnicity in the Kalahari: A Reply to Wiessner. *American Antiquity* 50(1):154–159.

1985b   Style, Ethnicity, and Stone Tools. In *Status, Structure and Stratification: Current Archaeological Reconstructions*, edited by M. Thompson, M. T. Marcia, and F. J. Kense, pp. 277–282. Proceedings of the 16th Annual Chacmool Conference. University of Calgary Press, Calgary.

1986a   Isochrestism and Style: A Clarification. *Journal of Anthropological Archaeology* 5:266–277.

1986b   Style, Function and Assemblage Variability: A Reply to Binford. *American Antiquity* 51:628–634.

1990   Style and Ethnicity in Archaeology: The Case for Isochrestism. In *The Uses of Style in Archaeology*, edited by M. W. Conkey and C. A. Hastorf, pp. 32–43. Cambridge University Press, Cambridge.

Saiedi, N.
1993   *The Birth of Social Theory: Social Thought in the Enlightenment and Romanticism*. University Press of America, New York.

Saitta, D. J.
1992   Radical Archaeology and Middle-Range Methodology. *Antiquity* 66:886–897.

1999   Prestige, Agency, and Change in Middle-Range Societies. In *Material Symbols: Culture and Economy in Prehistory*, edited by J. E. Robb, pp. 135–152. Center for Archaeological Investigations, Southern Illinois University, Carbondale.

Santley, R. S., P. J. Arnold III, and C. A. Pool
1989   The Ceramic Production System of Matacapan, Veracruz, Mexico. *Journal of Field Archaeology* 16: 107–132.

Sassaman, K. E.
1995   The Cultural Diversity of Interactions among Mid-Holocene Societies of the American Southeast. In *Native American Interactions: Multiscalar Analyses and Interpretations in the Eastern Woodlands*, edited by M. S. Nassaney and K. E. Sassaman, pp. 174–204. University of Tennessee Press, Knoxville.

1998   Crafting Cultural Identity in Hunter-Gatherer Economies. In *Craft and Social Identity*, edited by C. Costin and R. Wright, pp. 93–107. Archeological Papers of the American Anthropological Association No. 8. Washington, D.C.

Sayles, E. B.
1936   *An Archaeological Survey of Chihuahua, Mexico.* Medallion Papers 22. Gila Pueblo Foundation, Globe, Arizona.

Schaafsma, C. F., and C. L. Riley
1999   The Casas Grandes World: Analysis and Conclusion. In *The Casas Grandes World*, edited by C. F. Schaafsma and C. L. Riley, pp. 237–250. University of Utah Press, Salt Lake City.

Schaafsma, P.
1998   The Paquimé Rock Art Style, Chihuahua, Mexico. *Rock Art of the Chihuahua Desert Borderlands*, edited by S. Smith-Savage and R. J. Mallouf, pp. 33–44. Center for Big Bend Studies, Alpine, Texas.

Schiffer, M. B.
1976   *Behavioral Archaeology.* Academic Press, New York.

1988   The Structure of Archaeological Theory. *American Antiquity* 53: 461–485.

1995   *Behavioral Archaeology: First Principles.* University of Utah Press, Salt Lake City.

1996   Some Relationships between Behavioral and Evolutionary Archaeologies. *American Antiquity* 61:643–662.

1999a   Return to Holism. *Anthropology Newsletter,* March, pp. 62, 64.

1999b   A Behavioral Theory of Meaning. In *Pottery and People: A Dynamic Interaction,* edited by J. M. Skibo and G. M. Feinman, pp. 199–217. University of Utah Press, Salt Lake City.

1999c   Behavioral Archaeology: Some Clarifications. *American Antiquity* 64: 166–168.

2000   Social Theory in Archaeology: Building Bridges. In *Social Theory in Archaeology,* edited by M. B. Schiffer, pp. 1–13. University of Utah Press, Salt Lake City.

Schiffer, M. B., and J. M. Skibo
1987   Theory and Experiment in the Study of Technological Change. *Current Anthropology* 28:595–622.

1997   The Explanation of Artifact Variability. *American Antiquity* 62:27–55.

Schilcher, F. von, and N. Tennant
1984   *Philosophy, Evolution and Human Nature.* Routledge and Kegan Paul, London.

Schmid, M.
1987   Collective Action and the Selection of Rules: Some Notes on the Evolutionary Paradigm in Social Theory. In *Evolutionary Theory in Social Science,* edited by M. Schmid and F. M. Wuketits. D. Reidel Publishing, Boston.

Schmidt, P., and T. Patterson
1995   (eds.) *Making Alternative Histories: The Practice of Archaeology and History in Non-Western Settings.* School of American Research, Santa Fe, New Mexico.

Schrire, C.
1995   *Digging Through Darkness: Chronicles of an Archaeologist.* University of Virginia Press, Charlottesville.

Scott, E.
2002   Interpreting Ethnicity from Archaeological Faunal Remains. Paper presented at the 35th Conference on Historical and Underwater Archaeology, Society for Historical Archaeology, January 8–12, Mobile, Alabama.

Scott, J. C.
1990   *Domination and the Arts of*

Resistance: Hidden Transcripts. Yale University Press, New Haven, Connecticut.

Scott, S. D.
1966   *Dendrochronology in Mexico.* Papers of the Laboratory of Tree-Ring Research No. 2. University of Arizona Press, Tucson.

Sebastian, L.
1991   Sociopolitical Complexity and the Chaco System. In *Chaco and Hohokam: Prehistoric Regional Systems in the American Southwest,* edited by P. L. Crown and W. J. Judge, pp. 111–134. School of American Research Press, Santa Fe, New Mexico.
1992   Chaco Canyon and the Anasazi Southwest: Changing Views of Sociopolitical Organization. In *Anasazi Regional Organization and the Chaco System,* edited by D. E. Doyel, pp. 23–31. Maxwell Museum of Anthropology, Anthropological Papers No. 5, Albuquerque.

Service, E. R.
1964   Archaeological Theory and Ethnological Fact. In *Process and Pattern in Culture: Essays in Honor of Julian H. Steward,* edited by R. A. Manners, pp. 364–375. Aldine, Chicago.

Shanks, M., and I. Hodder
1995   "Processual, Postprocessual and Interpretive Archaeologies." In *Interpreting Archaeology: Finding Meaning in the Past,* edited by I. Hodder, M. Shanks, A. Alexandri, V. Buchli, J. Carman, J. Last, and G. Lucas, pp.3–29. Routledge, New York.

Shanks, M., and R. McGuire
1996   The Craft of Archaeology. *American Antiquity* 61:75–88.

Shanks, M., and C. Tilley
1982   Ideology, Symbolic Power, and Ritual Communication: A Reinterpretation of Neolithic Mortuary Practices. In *Symbolic and Structural Archaeology,* edited by I. Hodder, pp. 129–154. Cambridge University Press, Cambridge.
1987   *Re-Constructing Archaeology: Theory and Practice.* Cambridge University Press, Cambridge.

1988   *Social Theory and Archaeology.* 2nd ed. University of New Mexico Press, Albuquerque.
1992   [1987] *Re-Constructing Archaeology: Theory and Practice.* 2nd ed. Routledge, London.

Sharon, D.
1993   The Metaphysics of Curanderismo and its Cultural Roots. In *Sorcery and Shamanism: Curanderos and Clients in Northern Peru,* edited by D. Joralemon and D. Sharon, pp. 165–187. University of Utah Press, Salt Lake City.

Shaw, A. B.
1969   Adam and Eve, Paleontology, and the Non-Objective Arts. *Journal of Paleontology* 43:1085–1098.

Shennan, S.
1993   After Social Evolution: A New Archaeological Agenda? In *Archaeological Theory: Who Sets the Agenda?,* edited by N. Yoffee and A. Sherratt, pp. 53–59. Cambridge University Press, Cambridge.

Simpson, G. G.
1944   *Tempo and Mode in Evolution.* Columbia University Press, New York.
1961   *Principles of Animal Taxonomy.* Columbia University Press, New York.

Skibo, J. M., W. H. Walker, and A. E. Nielson
1995   (eds.) *Expanding Archaeology.* University of Utah Press, Salt Lake City.

Smith, A. B.
1994   *Systematics and the Fossil Record: Documenting Evolutionary Patterns.* Blackwell, London.

Smith, E. A.
2000   Three Styles in the Evolutionary Analysis of Human Behavior. In *Adaptation and Human Behavior,* edited by L. Cronk. N. Chagnon, and W. Irons, pp. 27–46. Aldine de Gruyter, New York.

Smith, E. A., and R. Boyd
1990   Risk and Reciprocity: Hunter-Gatherer Socioecology and the Problem of Collective Action. In *Risk and Uncertainty in Tribal and Peasant Economies,* edited by E. Cashdan, pp. 167–191. Westview Press, Boulder, Colorado.

Smith, E. A., and B. Winterhalder
1992   Natural Selection and Decision

Making: Some Fundamental Principles. In *Evolutionary Ecology and Human Behavior,* edited by E. A. Smith and B. Winterhalder, pp. 25–60. Aldine de Gruyter, New York.

Smith, J. M., R. Burian, S. Kauffman, P. Alberch, J. Campbell, B. Goodwin, R. Lande, D. Raup, and L. Wolpert
1985   Developmental Constraints and Evolution. *Quarterly Review of Biology* 60(3):265–287.

Smith, M. E.
1992   Braudel's Temporal Rhythms and Chronology Theory in Archaeology. In *Archaeology, Annales and Ethnohistory,* edited by A. B. Knapp, pp. 23–34. Cambridge University Press, Cambridge.

Soltis, J., R. Boyd, and P. J. Richerson
1995   Can Group-Functional Behaviors Evolve by Cultural Group Selection? An Empirical Test. *Current Anthropology* 36(3):473–494.

Spencer, C. S.
1992   Homology, Analogy, and Comparative Research in Archaeology. *Behavior Science Research* 26:1–4.
1997   Evolutionary Approaches in Archaeology. *Journal of Archaeological Research* 5:209–264.

Stanley, S. M.
1975   A Theory of Evolution above the Species Level. *National Academy of Sciences, Proceedings* 72:646–650.

Stark, B. L.
1985   Archaeological Identification of Pottery-Production Locations: Ethnoarchaeological and Archaeological Data in Mesoamerica. In *Decoding Prehistoric Ceramics,* edited by B. A. Nelson, pp. 158–194. Southern Illinois University Press, Carbondale.

Stark, M. T.
1994   Pottery Exchange and the Regional System: A Dalupa Case Study. In *Kalinga Ethnoarchaeology: Expanding Archaeological Method and Theory,* edited by W. A. Longacre and J. M. Skibo, pp. 169–197. Smithsonian Institution Press, Washington, D.C.
1998   Technical Choices and Social Boundaries in Material Culture Patterning: An Introduction. In *The*

Archaeology of Social Boundaries, edited by M. T. Stark, pp. 1–11. Smithsonian Institution Press, Washington, D.C.

Stein, G. J.
1999   Material Culture and Social Identity: The Evidence for a 4th Millennium B.C. Mesopotamian Uruk Colony at Hacinebi, Turkey. *Paléorient* 25:11–22.

Stein, J. R., and S. H. Lekson
1992   Anasazi Ritual Landscapes. In *Anasazi Regional Organization and the Chaco System,* edited by D. E. Doyel, pp. 87–100. Maxwell Museum of Anthropology, Anthropological Papers No. 5, Albuquerque.

Stein, S. J.
1992   *The Shaker Experience in America.* Yale University Press, New Haven, Connecticut.

Stearns, S. C.
1986   Natural Selection and Fitness, Adaptation and Constraint. In *Patterns and Processes in the History of Life,* edited by D. M. Raup and D. Jablonski, pp. 23–44. Dahlem Konferenzen, Berlin.

Steward, J. H.
1929   Diffusion and Independent Invention: A Critique of Logic. *American Anthropologist* 31:491–495.
1942   The Direct Historical Approach to Archaeology. *American Antiquity* 7:337–343.
1944   Re: Archaeological Tools and Jobs. *American Antiquity* 10:99–100.
1955   *Theory of Culture Change: The Methodology of Multilinear Evolution.* University of Illinois Press, Urbana.

Stonich, S.
1999   Comment on Escobar's 'After Nature.' *Current Anthropology* 40:23–24.

Swofford, D.
1998   PAUP*: Phylogenetic Analysis Using Parsimony (*and Other Methods) (version 4). Sinauer, Sunderland, Massachusetts.

Szalay, F. S., and W. J. Bock
1991   Evolutionary Theory and Systematics: Relationships between Process

and Patterns. *Zeitschrift für Zoologische Systematik und Evolutionsforschung* 29:1–39.

Sztompka, P.
1991   *Society in Action: The Theory of Social Becoming.* University of Chicago Press, Chicago.

Tarlow, S., and S. West
1999   (eds.) *Familiar Past? Archaeologies of Later Historical Britain.* Routledge, New York.

Taylor, W. W.
1948   *A Study of Archeology.* Memoir, no. 69, American Anthropological Association, Washington, D.C.

1999   Technology and Archaeology in the Deep Sea: Toward a New Synthesis. A conference sponsored by Massachusetts Institute of Technology, and the Institute for Exploration; organizers D. A. Mindell and R. D. Ballard; January 29–31, 1999, MIT, Cambridge, Massachusetts.

Teltser, P. A.
1995a   (ed.) *Evolutionary Archaeology: Methodological Issues.* University of Arizona Press, Tucson.

1995b   Culture History, Evolutionary Theory, and Frequency Seriation. In *Evolutionary Archaeology: Methodological Issues,* edited by P. A. Teltser, pp. 51–68. University of Arizona Press, Tucson.

1995c   The Methodological Challenge of Evolutionary Theory in Archaeology. In *Evolutionary Archaeology: Methodological Issues,* edited by P. A. Teltser, pp. 1–12. University of Arizona Press, Tucson.

Terrell, J. E.
1988   History as a Family Tree, History as an Entangled Bank: Constructing Images and Interpretations of Prehistory in the South Pacific. *Antiquity* 62:642–657.

2001   Introduction. In *Archaeology, Language, and History: Essays on Culture and Ethnicity,* edited by J. E. Terrell, pp. 1–10. Bergin and Garvey, Westport, Connecticut.

Terrell, J. E., T. L. Hunt, and C. Gosden
1997   The Dimensions of Social Life in the Pacific: Human Diversity and the Myth of the Primitive Isolate. *Current Anthropology* 38:155–195.

Terrell, J. E., and P. J. Stewart
1996   The Paradox of Human Population Genetics at the End of the Twentieth Century. *Reviews in Anthropology* 26:13–33.

Thomas, D. H., and S. L. Bierwirth
1983   Material Culture of Gatecliff Shelter: Projectile Points. In *The Archaeology of Monitor Valley 2: Gatecliff Shelter,* by D. H. Thomas, pp. 177–211. Anthropological Papers, vol. 59, American Museum of Natural History, New York.

Thomas, J.
1996a   Where Are We Now? Archaeological Theory in the 1990s. In *Theory in Archaeology,* edited by P. Ucko, pp. 343–362. Routledge, London.

1996b   *Time, Culture and Identity: An Interpretive Archaeology.* Routledge, London.

Tilley, C.
1990   *Reading Material Culture: Structuralism, Hermeneutics and Post-Structuralism.* Basil Blackwell, Oxford.

1994   *A Phenomenology of Landscape: Places, Paths, and Monuments.* Berg, Oxford.

1999   *Metaphor and Material Culture.* Blackwell Publishers, Oxford.

Timmins, P.
1997   *The Calvert Site: An Interpretive Framework for the Early Iroquoian Village.* Canadian Museum of Civilization, Hull, Quebec.

Toch, H.
1965   *The Social Psychology of Social Movements.* The Bobbs-Merrill Company, Indianapolis.

Toll, H. W.
1991   Material Distributions and Exchange in the Chaco System. In *Chaco and Hohokam: Prehistoric Regional Systems in the American Southwest,* edited by P. L. Crown and W. J. Judge, pp. 77–107. School of American Research Press, Santa Fe, New Mexico.

Trigger, B. G.
1980   Archaeology and the Image of the

American Indian. *American Antiquity* 45:662–676.

1989   *A History of Archaeological Thought.* Cambridge University Press, Cambridge.

1990   Monumental Architecture: A Thermodynamic Explanation of Symbolic Behavior. *World Archaeology* 22(2):119–132.

1991   Distinguished Lecture in Archeology: Constraint and Freedom—A New Synthesis for Archeological Explanation. *American Anthropologist* 93:551–569.

1993   Marxism in Contemporary Western Archaeology. In *Archaeological Method and Theory,* vol. 5, edited by M. B. Schiffer, pp. 159–200. University of Arizona Press, Tucson.

1998   Archaeology and Epistemology: Dialoguing across the Darwinian Chasm. *American Journal of Archaeology* 102:1–34.

Trouillot, M-R.
1995   *Silencing the Past: Power and the Production of History.* Beacon Press, Boston.

Tschauner, H.
1996   Middle-Range Theory, Behavioral Archaeology, and Postempiricist Philosophy of Science in Archaeology. *Journal of Archaeological Method and Theory* 3:1–30.

Turner, J. S.
2000   *The Extended Organism: The Physiology of Animal-Built Structures.* Harvard University Press, Cambridge, Massachusetts.

Uhen, M. D.
1996   An Evaluation of Clade-Shape Statistics Using Simulations and Extinct Families of Mammals. *Paleobiology* 22:8–22.

Van der Leeuw, S. E.
1993   Giving the Potter a Choice: Conceptual Aspects of Pottery Techniques. In *Technological Choices: Transformation in Material Cultures since the Neolithic,* edited by P. Lemmonier, pp. 238–288. Routledge, London.

1994   Cognitive Aspects of "Technique." In *The Ancient Mind: Elements of Cognitive Archaeology,* edited by C. Renfrew and E. Zubrow, pp. 135–142. Cambridge University Press, Cambridge.

VanPool, C. S.
2001   Birds, Burials, and Beliefs at Paquimé, Chihuahua, Mexico. In *From Paquimé to Mata Ortiz: The Legacy of Ancient Casas Grandes,* edited by G. Johnson, pp. 73–88. San Diego Museum Papers 40. San Diego, California.

2002   Flight of the Shaman. *Archaeology* 55(1):40–43.

VanPool, C. S., and T. L. VanPool
1999   The Scientific Nature of Postprocessualism. *American Antiquity* 64:33–53.

2002   Dichotomy and Duality: The Structure of Casas Grandes Art. In *Talking Birds, Plumed Serpents and Painted Women: Ceramics of Casas Grandes,* edited by J. Stuhr, pp. 71–75. Tucson Museum of Art, Tucson, Arizona.

VanPool, C. S., T. L. VanPool, D. A. Phillips, and M. Harmon
2000   The Changing Faces of Horned/Plumed Serpents in the Greater North American Southwest. A paper presented at the 2000 Chacmool Conference, University of Calgary, Canada.

VanPool, T. L.
2001   Style, Function, and Variation: Identifying the Evolutionary Importance of Traits in the Archaeological Record. In *Style and Function in Archaeology,* edited by T. D. Hurt and G. F. M. Rakita, pp. 119–140. Bergin and Garvey, Westport, Connecticut.

VanPool, T. L., and R. D. Leonard
2002   Specialized Ground Stone Production in the Casas Grandes Region of Northern Chihuahua, Mexico. *American Antiquity* 67:710–730.

Vargas, V. D.
1995   *Copper Bell Trade Patterns in the Prehispanic U.S. Southwest and Northwest Mexico.* Arizona State Museum Archaeological Series No. 187. University of Arizona, Tucson.

2001 Mesoamerican Copper Bells in the Pre-Hispanic Southwestern United States and Northwestern Mexico. In *The Road to Aztlan: Art from a Mythic Homeland,* edited by V. M. Fields, and V. Zamudio-Taylor, pp. 196–211. Los Angeles County Museum of Art, Los Angeles.

Varien, M. D.
1999 *Sedentism and Mobility in a Social Landscape: Mesa Verde and Beyond.* University of Arizona Press, Tucson.

Vaughan, C. D.
2001 A Million Years of Style and Function: Regional and Temporal Variation in Acheulean Handaxes. In *Style and Function in Archaeology,* edited by T. D. Hurt and G. F. M. Rakita, pp. 141–163. Bergin and Garvey, Westport, Connecticut.

von Frisch, K., and O. von Frisch
1974 *Animal Architecture.* Harcourt, Brace, Jovanovich, New York.

Vos, J. A., and R. L. Young
1995 Style and the Self. In *Style, Society and Person: Archaeological and Ethnological Perspectives,* edited by C. Carr and J. E. Neitzel, pp. 7–99. Plenum, New York.

Wade, W. D.
1979 *An Osteological Analysis of Human Remains from Kayenta Anasazi Sites in Northern Arizona.* Anthropology Papers No. 25. University of Manitoba, Winnipeg.
1981 Klippel-Feil Syndrome in a Prehistoric Population of Northern Arizona. In *Contributions to Physical Anthropology, 1978–1980,* edited by J. S. Cybulski, pp. 115–126. Archaeological Survey of Canada No. 106. National Museums of Canada, Ottawa.

Walker, W. H., and L. J. Lucero
2000 The Depositional History of Ritual and Power. In *Agency in Archaeology,* edited by M.-A. Dobres and J. Robb, pp. 130–147. Routledge, New York.

Walker, W. H., and G. MaGahee
2001 Animated Waters: The Ritualized Life History of Wells, Reservoirs, and Springs at Casas Grandes, Chi-huahua. Paper presented at the 66th Annual Meetings of the Society for American Archaeology, New Orleans.

Walthall, J. A., C. H. Webb, S. H. Stow, and S. I. Goad
1982 Galena Analysis and Poverty Point Trade. *Midcontinental Journal of Archaeology* 7:133–148.

Warren, M.
1983 Effects of Undernutrition on Reproductive Function in the Human. *Endocrine Reviews* 4:363–377.

Watson, P. J.
1986 Archaeological Interpretation, 1985. In *American Archaeology: Past and Future,* edited by D. Meltzer, D. Fowler, and I. Sabloff, pp. 439–457. Smithsonian Institution Press, Washington, D.C.
1995 Archaeology, Anthropology, and the Culture Concept. *American Anthropologist* 97:683–694.

Watson, P. J., S. A. LeBlanc, and C. L. Redman
1971 *Explanation in Archaeology: An Explicitly Scientific Approach.* Columbia University Press, New York.
1984 *Archaeological Explanation: The Scientific Method in Archeology.* Columbia University Press, New York.

Webb, C. H.
1968 The Extent and Content of Poverty Point Culture. *American Antiquity* 33:297–321.

Webb, C. H., and J. L. Gibson
1981 Studies of the Microflint Industry at Poverty Point Site. *Geoscience and Man* 22:85–101.

Webster, Gary S.
1996 Social Archaeology and the Irrational. *Current Anthropology* 37:609–627.

Welsch, R. L., and J. E. Terrell
1994 Reply to Moore and Romney. *American Anthropologist* 96:392–396.

Welsch, R. L., J. E. Terrell, and J. A. Nadolski
1992 Language and Culture on the North Coast of New Guinea. *American Anthropologist* 94:568–600.

Whalen, M. E., and P. E. Minnis
2001 *Casas Grandes and its Hinterland: Prehistoric Regional Organization in Northwest Mexico.* University of Arizona, Tucson.

Whallon, R.
1968 Investigations of Late Prehistoric Social Organization in New York State. In *New Perspectives in Archaeology*, edited by S. R. Binford and L. R. Binford, pp. 223–244. Aldine, Chicago.

Wheatley, P.
1975 Satyanrta in Suvarnadvipa: From Reciprocity to Redistribution in Ancient Southeast Asia. In *Ancient Civilization and Trade*, edited by J. A. Sabloff and C. C. Lamberg-Karlovsky, pp. 227–283. University of New Mexico Press, Albuquerque.

White, L. A.
1949 *The Science of Culture: A Study of Man and Civilization*. Grove Press, New York.
1959 *The Evolution of Culture: The Development of Civilization to the Fall of Rome*. McGraw-Hill, New York.

Wiessner, P.
1983 Style and Social Information in Kalahari San Projectile Points. *American Antiquity* 49:253–276.
1985 Style or Isochrestic Variation: A Reply to Sackett. *American Antiquity* 50:160–166.
1989 Style and Changing Relations between the Individual and Society. In *The Meanings of Things: Material Culture and Symbolic Expression*, edited by I. Hodder, pp. 56–63. Unwin Hyman, London.
1990 Is There a Unity to Style? In *The Uses of Style in Archaeology*, edited by M. W. Conkey and C. A. Hastorf, pp. 105–112. Cambridge University Press, Cambridge.

Wilcox, D. R.
1999 A Preliminary Graph-Theoretic Analysis of Access Relationships at Casas Grandes. In *The Casas Grandes World*, edited by C. F. Schaafsma and C. L. Riley, pp. 93–104. University of Utah Press, Salt Lake City.

Wilhelmsen, K.
2001 Building the Framework for an Evolutionary Explanation of Projectile Point Variation: An Example from the Central Mississippi River Valley. In *Posing Questions for a Scientific

Archaeology*, edited by T. L. Hunt, C. P. Lipo, and S. L. Sterling, pp. 97–144. Bergin and Garvey, Westport, Connecticut.

Wilkinson, T. J.
1982 The Definition of Ancient Manured Zones by Means of Extensive Sherd-Sampling Techniques. *Journal of Field Archaeology* 9:323–333.

Willey, G. R.
1953 Archaeological Theories and Interpretation: New World. In *Anthropology Today*, edited by A. L. Kroeber, pp. 361–385. University of Chicago Press, Chicago.

Willey, G. R., and P. Phillips
1958 *Method and Theory in American Archaeology*. University of Chicago Press, Chicago.

Williams, R.
1977 *Marxism and Literature*. Oxford University Press, Oxford.

Williamson, T.
1999 The Archaeological Study of Post-Medieval Gardens: Practice and Theory. In *The Familiar Past?*, edited by S. Tarlow and S. Wise, pp. 246–260. Routledge, New York.

Wills, W. H.
2000 Political Leadership and the Construction of Chacoan Great Houses, A.D. 1020–1140. In *Alternative Leadership Strategies in the Prehispanic Southwest*, edited by B. J. Mills, pp. 19–44. University of Arizona Press, Tucson.

Wilmsen, E. N., and F.H.H. Roberts
1978 *Lindenmeier, 1934–1974: Concluding Report on Investigations*. Smithsonian Contributions to Anthropology 24. Smithsonian Institution, Washington D.C.

Wilson, D. S.
1998 Hunting, Sharing, and Multilevel Selection: The Tolerated-Theft Model Revisited. *Current Anthropology* 39:73–97.

Wimsatt, W. C.
1994 The Ontology of Complex Systems: Levels of Organization, Perspectives, and Causal Thickets. In *Biology and Society: Reflections on Methodology*, edited by M. Matthen and R. X. Ware, pp. 207–274. Canadian Jour-

nal of Philosophy Supplementary vol. 20. University of Calgary Press, Calgary.

Winterhalder, B., F. Lu, and B. Tucker
1999 Risk-Sensitive Adaptive Tactics: Models and Evidence from Subsistence Studies in Biology and Anthropology. *Journal of Archaeological Research* 7(4):301–348.

Winterhalder, B., and E. A. Smith
2000 Analyzing Adaptive Strategies: Human Behavioral Ecology at Twenty-Five. *Evolutionary Anthropology* 9:51–72.

Wobst, H. M.
1974 Boundary Conditions for Paleolithic Social Systems: A Simulation Approach. *American Antiquity* 39:147–178.
1975 The Demography of Finite Populations and the Origins of the Incest Taboo. *American Antiquity* 40:75–81.
1977 Stylistic Behavior and Information Exchange. In *Papers for the Director: Research Essays in Honor of James B. Griffin*, edited by C. E. Cleland, pp. 317–342. Academic Press, New York.
1996 Toward an 'Appropriate Mertology' of Human Action in Archaeology. In *Time, Process, and Structured Transformation in Archaeology*, edited by S. E. van der Leeuw and J. McGlade, pp. 426–448. Routledge, New York.
1999 Style in Archaeology or Archaeologists in Style. In *Material Meanings: Critical Approaches to the Interpretation of Material Culture*, edited by E. S. Chilton, pp. 118–132. University of Utah Press, Salt Lake City.
2000 Agency in (Spite of) Material Culture. In *Agency in Archaeology*, edited by M.-A. Dobres and J. Robb, pp. 40–50. Routledge, New York.

Wolf, E.
1982 *Europe and the People Without History*. University of California Press, Berkeley.

Woods, C. A.
1934 A Criticism of Wissler's North American Culture Areas. *American Anthropologist* 36:517–523.

Woosley, A. I.
2001 Shadows on a Silent Landscape: Art and Symbol at Prehistoric Casas Grandes. In *The Road to Aztlan: Art from a Mythic Homeland*, edited by V. M. Fields, and V. Zamudio-Taylor, pp. 164–183. Los Angeles County Museum of Art, Los Angeles.

Wright, S.
1945 Tempo and Mode in Evolution: A Critical Review. *Ecology* 26:415–419.

Wylie, A.
1985 The Reaction Against Analogy. In *Advances in Archaeological Method and Theory*, vol. 8, edited by M. B. Schiffer, pp. 63–111. Academic Press, New York.
1989a The Interpretive Dilemma. In *Critical Traditions in Contemporary Archaeology: Essays in the Philosophy, History, and Socio-Politics of Archaeology*, edited by V. Pinsky and A. Wylie, pp. 18–27. Cambridge University Press, Cambridge.
1989b Matters of Fact and Matters of Interest. In *Archaeological Approaches to Cultural Identity*, edited by S. Shennan, pp. 94–109. Unwin Hyman, London.
1992 The Interplay of Evidential Constraints and Political Interests: Recent Archaeological Research on Gender. *American Antiquity* 57:15–35.
1993 A Proliferation of New Archaeologies: "Beyond Objectivism and Relativism." In *Archaeological Theory: Who Sets the Agenda?* edited by N. Yoffee and A. Sherrat, pp. 60–78. Cambridge University Press, Cambridge.
1995 Epistemic Disunity and Political Integrity. In *Making Alternative Histories: The Practice of Archaeology and History in Non-Western Settings*, edited by P. Schmidt and T. Patterson, pp. 255–272. School of American Research, Santa Fe, New Mexico.
1999 Why Should Historical Archaeologists Study Capitalists? *Historical*

Archaeology of Capitalism, edited by M. P. Leone and P. B. Potter Jr., pp. 23–50. Kluwer, New York.

2000 Questions of Evidence, Legitimacy, and the (Dis)Unity of Science. *American Antiquity* 65:227–238.

Yates, T.

1989 Habitus and Social Space: Some Suggestions about Meaning in the Saami (Lapp) Tent ca. 1700–1900. In *The Meanings of Things: Material Culture and Symbolic Expression*, edited by I. Hodder, pp. 249–262. Unwin Hyman, London.

Yoffee, Norman

1993 Too Many Chiefs? (or, Safe Texts for the '90s). In *Archaeological Theory: Who Sets the Agenda?*, edited by N. Yoffee and A. Sherratt, pp. 60–78. Cambridge University Press, Cambridge.

Zeder, Melinda A.

1997 *The American Archaeologist: A Profile*. Altamira Press, Sage Publications, Walnut Creek, California, in cooperation with the Society for American Archaeology.l

Contributors

Philip J. Arnold III
Department of Sociology and Anthropology
Loyola University Chicago

Jerimy J. Cunningham
Department of Anthropology
McGill University

Ian Hodder
Department of Cultural and
Social Anthropology
Stanford University

John Kantner
Department of Anthropology and
Geography
Georgia State University

Robert D. Leonard
Department of Anthropology
University of New Mexico

Mark P. Leone
Department of Anthropology
University of Maryland
College Park

R. Lee Lyman
Department of Anthropology
University of Missouri
Columbia

Michael J. O'Brien
Department of Anthropology
University of Missouri
Columbia

Timothy R. Pauketat
Department of Anthropology
University of Illinois
Urbana

Dean J. Saitta
Department of Anthropology
University of Denver

Christine S. VanPool
Department of Anthropology
University of New Mexico

Todd L. VanPool
Office of Contract Archeology
University of New Mexico

Patty Jo Watson
Department of Anthropology
Washington University

Index

adaptation, and adaptability, 71. *See also* group adaptationism; natural selection

affinity, and archaeological phylogenies, 120

African Americans, and historical archaeology, 20, 21, 22

Agency in Archaeology (Dobres & Robb, 2000), 90

agency-based approaches: and evolutionary archaeology, 89–113; and human behavioral ecology, 75–76

agriculture: and agency-based approaches to decision-making, 96–97; and climate change in Casas Grandes region, 109–10

analogy, and archaeological phylogenies, 126–34

Anderson, Benedict, 18–21

Annales history, and concepts of style and function, 26, 30

Annapolis (Maryland), and historical archaeology, 20, 21, 22

anthropology: antiessentialism and ecological, 34; colonialism and concept of culture, 19, 20, 21; and subcultures in archaeology, 9

antifoundationalism, and pragmatism, 12, 15

Appleby, J., 12

Archaeological Conservancy, 140

Archaeological Conservation Act (1974), 138

Archaeological Explanation: The Scientific Method in Archaeology (Watson, LeBlanc, & Redman, 1984), 152

archaeology: and agency-based approaches in evolutionary theory, 89–113; behavioral ecology and analysis of decision-making, 67–87; future of Americanist, 137–41; and historical processualism, 41–52; materialism versus idealism and concepts of style and function, 23–39; and middle-range program, 55–66; phylogeny and evolutionary theory, 115–35; and pragmatism, 11–15; recent debates on theory and method, 1–4, 143–52; and reconceptualization of historical archaeology, 17–22; and renegotiation of disciplinary boundaries, 5–9. *See also* behavioral archaeology; biological evolutionary archaeology; evolutionary archaeology; postprocessual archaeology; processualist archaeology

Arizona, osteological analyses at sites in, 79

Arnold, Phillip J., III, 150

Barnes, E., 79

behavioral archaeology: and historical processualism, 42–43; materialism and concepts of style and function in, 32

behavioral ecology: and individual decision-making, 74–77, 86–87; examples of individual decision-making from Southwest, 77–86; and group adaptationism, 70–72; and Neo-Darwinian evolution, 68–70; and selectionism, 72–74. *See also* evolutionary archaeology

Bernstein, Richard, 12

Binford, L. R., 24, 27–28, 31, 39n1, 55, 57, 58, 59, 60, 61, 62, 63, 138

Blackmore, S., 98, 99

Blintoff, J., 61

Boas, Franz, 151

Bodnar, J., 13

Bohman, J., 40n6

Boone, J. L., 74, 95–96

Bourdieu, Pierre, 30, 39n3, 41, 145

Boyd, R., 30, 39n2

Brandon, R. N., 68, 69

Brathwaite, M., 61

Braun, David, 30

Brew, J. O., 116, 134

Brumfiel, Elizabeth, 67

Buikstra, J. E., 94, 101

Butterfield, Herbert, 150

Cahokia (Missouri), 47–48, 49–50, 51

cannibalism, and kuru in New Guinea, 99

Carr, C., 35

Casas Grandes region, and agency-based approach to evolutionary archaeology, 104–13

Castañeda, Quetzil, 18–21

causal relationships, and middle-range program, 57

Cavalli-Sforza, L. L., 99

ceramics: agency-based approach to analysis in Casas Grandes region, 104–107, 111–13; fertility in Late Woodland and Mississippian Illinois and